D0036095

Led Zeppelin
and Philosophy

Popular Culture and Philosophy®
Series Editor: George A. Reisch

For full details of all Popular Culture and Philosophy® books, visit www.opencourtbooks.com.

Led Zeppelin and Philosophy

All Will Be Revealed

Edited by
SCOTT CALEF

With a Foreword by
DAVE LEWIS

OPEN COURT
Chicago and La Salle, Illinois

Volume 44 in the series, Popular Culture and Philosophy™, edited by George A. Reisch

To order books from Open Court, call toll-free 1-800-815-2280, or visit our website at www.opencourtbooks.com.

Open Court Publishing Company is a division of Carus Publishing Company.

Library of Congress Cataloging-in-Publication Data

Led Zeppelin and philosophy : all will be revealed / edited by Scott Calef.
       p. cm. —(Popular culture and philosophy ; v. 44)
    Includes bibliographical references and index.
    ISBN 978-0-8126-9672-1 (trade paper : alk. paper)
    1. Led Zeppelin (Musical group) 2. Music and philosophy.
  I. Calef, Scott, 1959-
    ML421.L4L388 2009
    782.42166092'2—dc22

                                  2009032400

Contents

Foreword

For a band that was together for only twelve years, the lasting fascination for all things Led Zeppelin goes on undimmed.

Though their last studio album was issued some thirty years ago, the effect of the extraordinary catalogue of music they recorded between 1968 and 1980 continues to resonate with fans old and new. It's an unparalleled body of work that charts a pioneering journey encompassing blues, rock, folk, funk, and eastern influences.

The chemistry was of course perfect. Jimmy Page—the relentless riff architect and sonic producer, Robert Plant—silver throated vocalist with the golden god front man appeal, John Paul Jones—immensely talented bassist and keyboard player, the man for all seasons and all instruments, and John 'Bonzo' Bonham—thunderous but incisive percussionist who knew exactly when to lay on and off the beat.

Under the maverick management of Peter Grant, they flaunted regular rock business convention to carve a unique niche that allowed them total artistic freedom, and a hedonistic on-the-road lifestyle that is almost as legendary as the music they created.

Led Zeppelin and Philosophy dissects the band in minute detail. The albums, personalities, live performances, art work, myths, influences, and more, all come under the microscope. Compelling insights and observations add more depth to a subject that continues to thrill and inspire. Each chapter is driven by an unquenchable thirst for Zeppelin knowledge and pulls the reader deeper into the world of Led Zeppelin, where the fascination continues. . . .

DAVE LEWIS
August 2009

Acknowledgments

Thanks to everyone who helped to see this book through to completion, and especially to my beautiful, gracious, and loving wife, Hannah. Zachary, Hannah Grace, Hillary, Lucy and Sophie: "All My Love." Thank you, Lisa and Michael, John and Patricia, for your generous hospitality through the years. I owe a heavy debt of gratitude to George Reisch and David Ramsay Steele at Open Court for their editorial assistance, patience, and invaluable advice. Thanks to John Stone-Mediatore and Emma Rees for their help with the first appendix. Thanks to the staff and volunteers at the Meher Spiritual Center in South Carolina, a special place for renewal, inspiration and philosophical contemplation. Finally, I am pleased to acknowledge generous financial support from the Office of the Provost at Ohio Wesleyan University for preparation of the index, and Alfred Publishing for their kind permission to use the lyrics.

And If You Listen Very Hard . . .

I think I will go to Kashmir one day, when some great change hits me and I have to . . . think about my future as a man rather than a prancing boy.

—ROBERT PLANT

On *Physical Graffiti* Robert Plant penned the words to the haunting and lovely "Ten Years Gone." As I write this in July 2009, it's forty years gone since the first Led Zeppelin albums and nearly thirty years gone since the band's demise. Called the last band of the Sixties and the first band of the Seventies, in all that time their influence and importance in the lives of millions has only grown.

Communication Breakdown

Much to the chagrin of some. Led Zeppelin's animosity towards rock journalists was legendary, and perhaps rivaled only by the rock press's animosity towards them. Despite making a huge splash with the fans, the band was slagged from the start, to the extent that early reviews of Plant had to be hidden to prevent shattering his confidence. All this negativity was understandably bewildering to the group, for whom the only plausible explanation was that the critics didn't know shit about music.

That seems a little extreme too, but what else could it be? Maybe the media were just jealous because Zep happened to have a manager in Peter Grant who—unlike the famously inept Brian Epstein—actually secured them a lucrative advance and favorable contract terms. To the press, it seemed like Led Zeppelin arrived out of nowhere and made it big without effort. So, they were immediately dismissed as pure hype—Superhype, in fact. How else could a new band comprised mostly of complete unknowns and with only the most tenuous association with the Yardbirds—a group long in decline, irrelevant in the UK, and frequently a disaster on the road—become rich and successful without paying their dues?

Of course, these accusations were absurd.[1] Led Zeppelin had already produced a killer album at their own expense prior to being signed, and at least part of the reason Atlantic ponied up the money[2] was because when they heard it, they were rightly blown away. That's not to deny the group benefitted from a combination of luck and good timing. Other reasons for Atlantic's eagerness to attract Zep to the label included the eminent demise of Cream, the enthusiastic endorsement of John Paul Jones by Dusty Springfield, the commercial success of the Experience and Jeff Beck Group in the US, and the fact that Atlantic would incur very little studio expense in signing Zep since the recording costs of the first LP had already been absorbed by Page.

Luck notwithstanding, so far from coasting to fame and fortune without paying their dues, Jones and Page had been making hits for other bands for years. The sonic impact of *Led Zeppelin I* was light-years ahead of just about anything else at the time, and that was made possible because of production techniques absorbed by Page over the course of his long apprenticeship in the studio. Plant and Bonham meanwhile had been struggling to put food on the

---

[1] It also irked rock journalists in the 1960s and early 1970s that the band wasn't fashionably aligned with leftist political causes (an accusation that found new life when the punk movement gathered momentum). While less absurd than the claim that Zep were all hype (since there's at least some truth to the allegations—Plant's frequent rants against Britain's progressive tax structure hardly endeared the band to social liberals) such attacks were equally unfair. After all, the Rolling Stones were a highly successful and relatively apolitical group, and yet the press adored them. Although Zeppelin's band members did speak out in interviews against police brutality, racism, and intolerance in America, for the most part, politically as musically, they maintained their independence. It served them well. "Protest" songs from groups like the Buffalo Springfield, Jefferson Airplane, Country Joe, and Steppenwolf now sound dated, whereas Led Zeppelin's music has a freshness, a timeless quality and enduring appeal.

[2] Atlantic's signing advance to Led Zeppelin was reportedly in the neighborhood of $200,000, a fortune at the time.

table rather than abandon playing the music they loved: Plant spread asphalt to make ends meet (kind of a Black Country version of workin' on the railroad) and Bonham worried he couldn't afford to join the band unless they also hired him to drive the van. The fact is, Led Zeppelin were probably the most determined and hard-working group in the biz, producing four albums in their first two years while touring virtually non-stop. In 1969 alone they released two albums, toured the US four times, toured the UK once, and played numerous additional concerts in Europe and elsewhere! But of course, that only meant Zep were sell-outs, neglecting their native Isle for the more lucrative shores of America.

Although the reports of bad press have been exaggerated—Zep certainly had their champions, too—the comments of some journalists were so negative and over-the-top you have to wonder, "Were these guys really listening to the albums they were writing about?" All questions of dues paying aside, Zep's detractors seemed positively eager to attack the music itself. Rather than write original material and perform it with sincerity and restraint, the group was initially dismissed as just another band of white boys ripping off African American bluesmen. After all, how authentic could a London dandy (or, as Lester Bangs put it, an "emaciated fop") like Jimmy Page covering Willie Dixon really be? The first two albums, critics complained, were loud, overblown, obvious and totally undisciplined. Without doubt, the group had legions of fans, but the masses easily mistake musical *excess* for musical *success*. Thankfully, the press were there to make damn sure they knew the difference.

When the group decided to incorporate a more acoustic vibe into *III*—which, given the broad acceptance of The Band, Fairport Convention, Bob Dylan, Joni Mitchell and CSN might have been thought a welcome change of pace—they were condemned for departing from their previously successful formula. (*Disc & Music Echo,* for example, greeted the album with the headline "Zepp Weaken!") But if Led Zeppelin were anything, they were most definitely *not* a band who stuck to prescribed formulas and that was part of their magic, their mystery. This really became apparent with the fourth album.

IV summarized, synthesized and transcended everything the band had accomplished to that point. A masterpiece by any reasonable standard, it was nevertheless dismissed by critics as a boring, airy-fairy departure from the blues-based rock that the band did best. Even when granted a certain grudging admiration, it was damned with faint praise.[3] *Houses of the Holy*—one of the group's most underrated efforts—received some of the worst reviews of all and it seemingly wasn't until *Physical Graffiti* that mainstay rags like *Rolling Stone* had a kind word. But thereafter the band began to slip. The remainder of its catalogue—*Presence*, the *Soundtrack*, *In Through the Out Door*, and the posthumous collection of outtakes, *Coda*, proved somewhat uneven, frequently failing to capture the excitement of the band in its prime. By then the Punks had arrived and Zep had become lumbering dinosaurs knee-deep in the tar pits, representatives of an elite and outmoded Rock aristocracy whose primary, anti-democratic sin was actually being able to play their instruments. In other words, the musical antithesis of anarchy.

The Philosopher's Stone

And yet! With all due respect to anarchy, Zep attracts new fans in each generation because genuine musicianship never goes out of fashion or ceases to inspire admiration and respect. Plus, they totally rock! Like Page, the time-defying wizard in his filmed fantasy sequence, the band has retained its aura and magic through the decades because "the four musical elements of Led Zeppelin making a fifth is magick itself. That's the alchemical process."[4]

Alchemy seeks to transmute base metals like lead into precious ones,[5] and there can be little doubt Jimmy Page—the consummate heavy-metal Merlin—accomplished the feat in record time. By the second LP the first album's earthbound black and white balloon had been transformed into pure gold—the gleaming, yellow, spotlit zeppelin of *II*'s inner gatefold. Having gone gold, it went platinum. Then diamond. The flaming dirigible crashing to the tarmac had

---

[3] Lenny Kaye (later guitarist of the Patti Smith Group) wrote in his review for *Rolling Stone*: "If this thing with the semi-metaphysical title isn't quite their best to date, . . . it certainly comes off as their most consistently good."

[4] Jimmy Page, quoted in *Guitar World*, January 2008.

[5] The Wikipedia page avers that alchemy "is both a *philosophy* and a practice with an aim of achieving ultimate *wisdom*:" http://en.wikipedia.org/wiki/Alchemy (accessed July 3rd, 2009). "Philosophy" means "the love of wisdom." Since Page repeatedly asserted that Zep were a fifth element resulting from an alchemical fusion of its individual elements, this ought to tell us something about the possibility that Zep can be approached philosophically.

become a blazing Mothership blasting into the stratosphere.[6] (Unfortunately, what goes up must come down, whether the space shuttle Columbia, the agonized Icarus figure of the Swan Song logo, a randy rock-star erection, or the TVs in the upper-floor suites of Bonzo's hotel accommodation!)

That Zep were to be a dynamic, evolving, transformative band was all according to plan. Page wanted Zeppelin to implement his original vision for a new kind of rock, one both light and heavy, soft and hard, light and dark. So far from being a formula, though, this was the rejection of all genres, of everything formulaic. The band's music defies easy classification, and attempts to pigeon-hole them as "hard rock," "heavy metal," or "psychedelic blues" invariably over-simplify their creative legacy. And just as the richness and complexity of Zep's musical output challenge and stubbornly resist our tidy musical categories, philosophy challenges and clarifies the customary and everyday categories we use to think about creativity, experience, recognition, consciousness, reality, ethics, knowledge, religion, art, beauty, meaning, identity, love, and yes, sex, drugs, and rock'n'roll.

These Things Are Clear to All from Time to Time

When friends and colleagues found out that I was editing a philosophy book on Led Zeppelin, their reaction quickly became predictable: "What does Led Zeppelin have to do with philosophy?" Apparently, because Zep can bump, pound, pump, grind, and drink, lots of people assume they've got nothing very profound to say (and, more to the point, that nothing very profound can be said about them). This is a book on Led Zeppelin *and* philosophy, not the philosophy *of* Led Zeppelin (though some of the contributions within do argue that there's a philosophy of the group and set out to explore that philosophy). But Jimmy Page and Robert Plant were not shallow people. Page was an ardent student of esoteric thought, and Plant was very well read in mythology and British history. They were keenly aware of non-western philosophic and spiritual traditions through their travels in the Orient, India, and Arabic North Africa, and both "yearned for wider recognition, not only of their talent but of

---

[6] No wonder the band members are depicted as astronauts on the *Early Days* and *Latter Days* compilations!

their increasing sophistication and worldliness."[7] They were, in their own ways, travelers of both time and space, spiritual aspirants seeking the truth (a point emphasized by Page's ascent and transformation in *The Song Remains the Same*).

For many this first became obvious when Zep firmly asserted their artistic prerogatives over the packaging of their fourth album.[8] The hermit that graces the inner gatefold of *IV* is a figure from the Tarot signifying wisdom, the inner search, philosophy, self-reliance and truth. Plant's feather symbol on the inner bag of *IV* connotes truth also. Robert sings on "Stairway"—the first lyrics ever printed on a Zeppelin album and the only lyrics printed from *IV*—that "if you listen very hard, the tune will come to you at last." The piper will lead us to reason.

He also, at the end of three verses, expresses childlike wonder—at our words, meanings, thoughts, voices and choices. Aristotle claimed that philosophy begins in just such wonder. If you've ever wondered how much there is to know, the contributors to this volume offer some signposts to the confounded bridge.

SCOTT CALEF

---

[7] The cover art for the follow-up, *Houses of the Holy*, is similarly evocative and amusingly tied to Socrates. Bill and Ted—hardly model students, though they really came up with the goods at crunch time—traveled back in time to fetch Socrates for their history project and had this to say about his homeland: "In 470 B.C. . . . much of the world looked like the cover of the Led Zeppelin album *Houses of the Holy*." I argue in Chapter 9 that the cover art for *Presence* is almost as philosophically heavy as the songs are musically heavy. And the winged male nude of the Swan Song logo, though ambiguous, has definite philosophical associations. If the winged figure is Apollo, as is usually supposed, we have not only the lyre-toting god of music and poetry, but the god of light and truth and wisdom and prophecy. Through his oracle at Delphi, Apollo famously declared that no one was wiser than Socrates, a pronouncement that set Socrates on the path of philosophy and changed the course of Western thought. If the figure is Icarus, the wings were made by his father Daedalus, who was a reputed ancestor of Socrates. And if the figure is Lucifer, his irresistible offer to Eve was the promise of wisdom: If she would but taste of the fruit from the forbidden tree, her eyes would be opened and she would "be like God, knowing good and evil." Clearly, Satan wanted humans to know something about ethics, and the original couple must have thought this wasn't such a bad idea.

[8] Keith Shadwick, *Led Zeppelin: The Story of the Band and Their Music: 1968–1980* (Backbeat Books, 2005), p. 184.

1
The Ocean's Roar

JOHN STONE-MEDIATORE

Suddenly the lights go down and the immense, cavernous space is dark. Point by point out of the blackness a constellation of tiny flames appears, accompanied by an overwhelming roar, as thirty thousand people rise to their feet. This is the moment you've awaited: to see if, in real life, these musicians live up to their status in your mind as the demigods of hard rock.

Now the sound of drums explodes from the PA—the sizzle of a high hat and the punch of a snare that lands like a round of blows to your chest. Four bars later, electric guitar and bass join the assault, the stage lights burst on, and there they are. In a black, open-chested suit, spangled with stars, moons, and "666," Jimmy Page leans back and conjures the song's signature riff from his Les Paul, looking like some rock'n'roll warlock. John Bonham, half hippie, half barbarian, continues the onslaught on drums, locking into a hard, driving groove with Jonesy's bass. Finally, Robert Plant, the consummate rock front man, turns to the crowd, strikes a pose, and raises his mike, as from a massive wall of speakers and Marshall amps comes the best and loudest sound you've ever heard: "Been a long time since I rock and rolled . . ."

Yet this is more than the opening of a classic Led Zeppelin concert: it's a quintessential experience of what philosophers call "the sublime." Therefore, in order to understand more deeply the magic and power of moments like this, we need to go beyond the descriptions and pronouncements of music critics and turn to the philosophers who, for nearly two millennia, have sought out the essence of the sublime in art and nature. By better understanding the sublime we can attain new insight into the enduring power of

1

Led Zeppelin, and, more broadly, into a primary source of rock music's appeal as a genre. Moreover, since critics have long used sublimity as a criterion for defining "great art," understanding the sublimity of Led Zeppelin helps justify a new critical assessment of the music, elevating it above its pedestrian status as "low-brow" or "popular culture" to a loftier position among the other time-honored art-works of the Western tradition.

What Is the Sublime?

In 1757, Edmund Burke published one of the first major treatises on the sublime, *A Philosophical Enquiry into the Origin of our Ideas of the Sublime and the Beautiful*. Like the yin and yang of aesthetic experience, the sublime and the beautiful oppose and complement each other in our perception of the world and the arts. According to Burke, the beautiful is rooted in human instincts and emotions relating to "society." The most important of these is "love" and the pleasures associated with it. In a way, this makes perfect sense: sex appeal and beauty are often closely associated in our minds (although, according to Burke, in the properly *aesthetic* experience, the beautiful must be dissociated from the baser feeling of lust). Beautiful objects typically evoke feelings of melting, languor, sympathy, love, and sometimes melancholy,[1] and Burke catalogs the characteristic qualities of the beautiful as follows: *smoothness, gradual variation, delicacy, grace, elegance, softness, unbroken continuance, smallness, weakness, clarity*, and *evenness*.

In contrast to the beautiful, Burke contends, the sublime is rooted in the basic human instinct of *self-preservation*. It therefore concerns emotions related to life-threatening situations, including pain, isolation, privation, death, terror, danger, suffering, anguish, and torment (pp. 38–39, 86). At first, this may seem counter-intuitive: if the sublime derives from feelings of pain and fear, why do we find sublime experiences such as a Led Zeppelin concert pleasurable? Burke's answer is that pain, death, and terror are obviously *not* pleasurable in themselves, but "at certain distances, and with certain modifications," when we ourselves are not in immediate danger or pain, we experience them as pleasing. This kind of distancing takes place when we observe life-threatening or painful

---

[1] *A Philosophical Enquiry into the Origin of our Ideas of the Sublime and the Beautiful* (University of Notre Dame Press, 1958), p. 123.

objects like tornados, battles, or volcanic eruptions from a safe remove, or (more germane to the present context) when such things are *imitated* or represented artistically in pictures, poems, or rock songs (p. 49).

The beautiful is undoubtedly a major dimension of Led Zeppelin's oeuvre—particularly in gentler songs like "Bron Yr Aur," "Going to California," "Thank You," "Babe, I'm Gonna Leave You," and the early parts of "Stairway to Heaven"; however, notwithstanding these moments of true beauty, the predominant quality of Zeppelin's music is its sublimity. This can be seen on many levels in Zeppelin's songs, including the thematic: the sublime themes of pain, loss, solitude, violence, fear and death pervade their music.

One classic example is "Gallows Pole," in which a condemned man implores his friends to bring the hangman silver and gold to save him from the noose. When that fails, he begs his sister to offer the hangman her body as a sexual bribe. But the song ends with horrific black humor when, despite the desperate gifts rendered, the hangman executes his victim and laughs to see him "swinging on the gallows pole." Other songs with similar sublime themes include "Immigrant Song" (in which a warrior anticipates entering Valhalla); "No Quarter" (about a lonely messenger who trudges by Death's side, accompanied by the howling "dogs of doom"); and "The Battle of Evermore." Songs like these represent the sublime on its most basic level, engaging primal themes of physical pain and death.

One of the subtler expressions of the sublime in rock music is its ubiquitous focus on the pain caused by love. Zeppelin's first album is a classic example, with its pervasive themes of separation, loss, isolation, and the painful and destructive qualities of desire. One thinks of "Good Times Bad Times" ("I know what it means to be alone"), the imminent pain of separation in the melancholy "Babe I'm Gonna Leave You," the obsessive desire and sexual frustration of "Communication Breakdown" ("Having a nervous breakdown / Drivin' me insane"), and the tortured ambivalence of self-destructive love in "I Can't Quit You Babe." In later albums, songs on similar themes include "The Lemon Song," "Tangerine," "Heartbreaker," "Since I've Been Loving You," and "In the Evening." Yet the most powerful expression of obsessive, destructive desire on *Led Zeppelin I* is in "Dazed and Confused," where Robert Plant laments a demonic woman who "hurts," "abuse[s]," and cheats on him, but whom he nonetheless continues to want obsessively. The pain in these songs is intensified and given visceral immediacy by Plant's anguished cries; indeed, Plant's musical howls, moans, and screams are among the most sublime elements of Zeppelin's music. Clearly, Burke would agree: "Such sounds as imitate the natural inarticulate voices of men, or any animals in pain and danger, are capable of conveying great ideas. . . . The modifications of sound, which may be productive of the sublime, are almost infinite" (pp. 84–85).

Sublime Subtleties

Yet the sublime is a more complex category of aesthetic experience than suggested by the experiences of death and suffering described above. In *A Philosophical Enquiry*, Burke describes in detail the characteristics of sublime objects and the emotions they evoke. His extensive list includes *astonishment, obscurity, power, privation, vastness, infinity, succession, uniformity, magnitude, difficulty, magnificence, darkness, gloom, confusion, violence, overpowering light, loudness, suddenness,* and *intermitting sounds.* Burke's discussion of the sublime in sound is particularly illuminating:

> The eye is not the only organ of sensation, by which a sublime passion may be produced. Sounds have a great power in these as in most other passions. . . . Excessive loudness alone is sufficient to overpower the soul, to suspend its action, and to fill it with terror. The noise of vast cataracts, raging storms, thunder, or artillery, awakes a great and aweful [sic] sensation in the mind. . . . The shouting of multitudes has a similar effect; and by the sole strength of the sound, so amazes and confounds the imagination, that in this staggering, and hurry of the mind, the best established tempers can scarce forbear being borne down, in joining in the common cry, and common resolution of the crowd. (p. 82)

Anyone lucky enough to have attended a Zeppelin show—or for that matter any great rock concert—understands how "excessive loudness" of music can "overpower the soul." (One look at the formidable wall of Marshall stacks at a Zeppelin concert shows how well Jimmy Page understood this!) At the same time, Burke's comment on "the shouting of multitudes," calls to mind a frenzied, sold-out concert crowd and the irresistible power of being part of it, as immortalized in Plant's lyrics, "Singing to the ocean, I can hear the ocean's roar."

Burke's discussion of the effects of loud, powerful sounds also illuminates how the explosive force of John Bonham's drumming contributes to the sublimity of Zeppelin's music. The rock drum kit itself produces a loud, powerful sound, with a short attack and a quick decay. According to Burke, "a sudden beginning, or sudden cessation of sound of any considerable force has the same power. The attention is roused by this; and the faculties driven forward, as it were, on their guard." Burke goes on to cite the drum as an instrument that produces precisely this kind of effect (p. 83). The sublime qualities of Bonham's drum playing are enhanced by Page's innovative recording decisions to use distant microphones and place the kit in vast spaces (such as the stairway in Headley Grange). Coupled with Bonham's explosive style, this use of of natural reverb generated massive, overpowering drum sounds. "When the Levee Breaks," "Four Sticks," and "In the Evening" are outstanding examples. Yet Page's recording techniques only enhance what is already there: tremendous force combined with brilliant musicality and finesse. The matchless power of Bonham's style and sound make him arguably the most sublime drummer in the history of rock'n'roll.

Like Bonham's drumming, Page's electric guitar playing epitomizes sublime power. The timbre of Page's guitar, achieved through overdriving his tube amplifiers or engaging a fuzz pedal, is key. Such techniques thicken the guitars' sound (enhancing "magnitude"), while also increasing sustain, which heightens the guitar's perceived energy and loudness. Page's switch in the early 1970s from a Fender Telecaster as his primary guitar to a Gibson Les Paul equipped with humbucking pickups gave him a bigger, fatter tone, further augmenting the power of his sound. On a more subtle level, "power" also describes the sound of Page's typical chord voicings. Known among musicians as "power chords," these voicings are composed of the first and fifth notes of the diatonic scale and can be heard in many Zeppelin songs, including the main riff of "No Quarter," the last part of "Stairway to Heaven," and in the long, sustained chords Page plays under Plant's lead vocal in "Rock and Roll."

Another factor contributing to the sublimity of Page's playing is the characteristic roughness of his sound and style. A comparison of Page's guitar technique and Stonehenge might seem strange, but Burke's comments are apt:

> Stonehenge, neither for disposition nor ornament, has anything admirable; but those huge, rude masses of stone, set on end, ånd piled on each other, turn the mind on the immense force necessary for such a work. Nay, the rudeness of the work increases this cause of grandeur, as it excludes the idea of art, and contrivance; for dexterity produces another sort of effect which is different enough from this.[2] (p. 77)

Just as the "rudeness" of the boulders used in Stonehenge augments to their power and grandeur, the rough, grainy timbre of Page's overdriven electric guitar contributes a great deal toward the power of his style. The bright, biting sounds of Page's Fender guitars—for example, in his incendiary solos in "Good Times Bad Times" and the main riff for "In the Evening"—might be described as "rude" or "harsh" by Burke, yet these are precisely the tonal qualities that make Page's guitar sound sublime to our ears. Yet "rudeness" and "roughness" aren't only characteristics of Page's guitar tone; they are qualities that he cultivates in his very style of playing. Although Page is sometimes criticized by guitarists and critics for having 'sloppy' technique, this quality arguably contributes to the sublimity of his style; as Burke observed, "dexterity" produces an effect which is different from the sublime. Moreover, the roughness and power of Page's guitar sound and style perfectly complement Plant's voice, which shares the same qualities in songs like "Since I've Been Loving You," "Immigrant Song," and countless others. The classic duet during the free-form middle section of "Whole Lotta Love," in which Plant mimics Page's improvised phrases, is a classic example of this perfect pairing of their rough-hewn guitar and vocal styles.

Burke and "The Battle of Evermore"

One of Zeppelin's greatest musical achievements, "The Battle of Evermore" gives us deeper insight into the rock'n'roll sublime. One of the most striking aspects of this song is how it achieves great sublimity in a purely acoustic arrangement, without exploiting the inherently powerful elements of electric instruments or Bonham's

---

[2] Page can be as polished as any of the guitar gods of his era when he wishes to be. His solos on "The Song Remains the Same," "Stairway to Heaven," and the live version of "Since I've Been Loving You" (*How the West Was Won*) are just a few cases in point.

drums. The relevant Burkean features in this song include *darkness, overwhelming light, obscurity, difficulty, artificial infinity* and *intermitting sounds*. Burke's discussion of intermitting sounds helps explain the dramatic power of the song's introduction:

> A low tremulous, intermitting sound . . . is productive of the sublime. . . . I have already mentioned that night increases our terror more perhaps than anything else; it is in our nature, that, when we do not know what may happen to us, to fear the worst that can happen to us; and hence it is, that uncertainty is so terrible, that we often seek to be rid of it, at the hazard of a certain mischief. Now some low, confused, uncertain sounds, leave us in the same fearful anxiety concerning their causes, that no light, or an uncertain light does concerning the objects that surround us. (pp. 83–84)

One of the most inspired and spine-tingling moments in Zeppelin's entire *oeuvre*, the mandolin introduction to "Battle of Evermore" epitomizes some of the sublime qualities of intermitting sounds (even though, strictly speaking, it is not "intermitting"). Gradually fading into the song out of silence, the mandolin gives the impression of "confusion" and "uncertainty" because of its disorienting dissonant notes. For several measures it's unclear how these notes will resolve and, as a result, we are thrown into an anxious state of suspense; to paraphrase Burke, as listeners "we do not know what will happen to us."

The mandolin introduction leads into Plant's vocal, which intensifies the sense of anxiety through words that shroud the song in a foreboding darkness:

> The queen of light took her vows
> And then she turned to go.
> The prince of peace embraced the gloom
> And walked the night alone.

The ominous nocturnal imagery is continued two lines later in words that forecast the horrors of war: "The Dark Lord rides in force tonight . . . the darkest of them all." This pervasive darkness contributes dramatically to the song's sublimity. Indeed, according to Burke, "darkness" is one of the most powerful qualities of the sublime:

> To make any thing very terrible, obscurity in general seems to be necessary. When we know the full extent of any danger, when we can

accustom our eyes to it, a great deal of the apprehension vanishes. Every one will be sensible of this, who considers how greatly night adds to our dread, in all cases of danger. (pp. 58–59)

Throughout "The Battle of Evermore," Plant uses the words "dark," "darkness," and "darkest" six times, while "night" and "tonight" appear no less than seven. Clearly, Plant intuitively grasped Burke's insight into the powerful qualities of darkness.

This nocturnal gloom sets the stage for the fearful anxiety of people preparing for battle, uncertain of the outcome as they hear the terrifying sounds of the approaching enemy—the horses' thundering hooves in the valley below. A few verses later, Plant evokes more sublime sounds, singing, "The drums will shake the castle wall, / The ring wraiths ride in black." As we have seen, the sound of drums epitomizes the sublime. "Evermore" also emphasizes the sublime qualities of pain ("The pain of war cannot exceed the woe of aftermath") and great difficulty ("Tired eyes on the sunrise, waiting for the eastern glow" and "No comfort has the fire at night / That lights the face so cold"). The lyrics conclude with an example of the only case in which light, according to Burke, can be sublime: "Extreme light, by overcoming the organs of sight, obliterates all objects, so as in its effect exactly to resemble darkness" (p. 80). Illustrating Burke's insight, Plant closes the song with the following words: "With flames from the dragon of darkness / The sunlight blinds his eyes."

During the "outro," the mandolin and acoustic guitar parts of the song gradually fade while reiterating a simple melody, giving us the sense that the music and the violent, mythic world it describes continue on indefinitely, even after the song is over. This is a powerful example of what Burke describes as "the artificial infinite," an effect created when artists utilize repeating elements in a way that produces the illusion that the art-work continues beyond its actual ending.

> Succession and uniformity of parts are what constitute the artificial infinite. [To create this effect, it is] requisite that the parts may be continued so long, and in such a direction, as by their frequent impulses on the sense to impress the imagination with an idea of their progress beyond their actual limits. (p. 74)

Burke associates the artificial infinite with the sublime quality of obscurity, since the boundaries of obscure things are unclear, and *sublime language / Longinus.* (handwritten annotation)

we can't distinguish where they begin or end. With its gradual fade-in and fade-out, "The Battle of Evermore" dramatically suggests precisely this kind of obscurity. This technique for creating the illusion of "infinity" by means of a gradual fade-out is also used to great effect at the end of "Thank You," where John Paul Jones's reflective organ part, punctuated by single bass notes on Page's twelve-string guitar, suggests the undying, eternal love proclaimed earlier in the song's tender lyrics.

"Hammer of the Gods": Longinus's Sublime Thunderbolt

Although Burke's analysis of specific sensory qualities of the sublime is illuminating, it is limited by its formulaic approach. Any artist, poet, or musician might incorporate these qualities into an art-work—for example, by writing lyrics that discuss pain, fear, and death. But this is no guarantee that the art-work will be sublime in effect. What Burke seems to overlook is that there is no recipe for sublimity—as Kant famously notes in *The Critique of Judgment*, art isn't to be confused with cooking. Longinus's "On the Sublime"—a work much earlier than Burke's—takes a different approach that overcomes this problem.

Longinus's discussion of the sublime centers on poetry, but many of the qualities he describes can be applied to music and the creative arts in general. His definition is broad: "sublimity consists in a certain excellence and distinction in expression, and . . . it is from this source alone that the greatest poets and historians have acquired their pre-eminence and won for themselves an eternity of fame."[3] According to Longinus, sublime language is not merely persuasive or pleasing, but "entrances" and "transports us with wonder"; as he puts it, "a well-timed stroke of sublimity scatters everything before it like a thunderbolt, and in a flash reveals the full power of the speaker." Although a poet can learn the principles of the sublime and cultivate them in his writing, ultimately the sublime is a product of "nature" and "genius," a "gift" created under "the stimulus of powerful and inspired emotion" (pp. 101–08).

Longinus's definition of the sublime itself is somewhat vague and indirect; he focuses on how it is produced and how it affects

---

[3] Longinus, *On the Sublime*, in T.S. Dorsch, *Aristotle, Horace, Longinus: Classical Literary Criticism* (Viking, 1965), p. 100.

us, rather than on what it *is*. Yet we can gain a clearer sense of what he means via the quotations he uses as illustrations. (To fully appreciate the sublime qualities of these passages, they are best read aloud!) Longinus particularly likes to quote Homer's *Iliad*. For instance,

> And round them rolled the trumpet-tones of the wide heavens and of Olympus. And down in the underworld, Hades, monarch of the realm of the shades, leapt from his throne and cried aloud in dread, lest the earth-shaker Poseidon should cleave the earth apart, and reveal to the gaze of mortals and immortals alike those grim and festering abodes which the very gods look upon with abhorrence. (pp. 110–11)

Here's another example Longinus quotes from the *Iliad*:

> And as far as a man can see with his eyes into the hazy distance as he sits upon a mountain peak and gazes over the wine-dark sea, even so is the leap of the loudly-neighing steeds of the gods. (p. 110)

Although the quality of Plant's writing is uneven at times, at their very best his lyrics approach this kind of sublimity. Indeed, despite being separated by 2,700 years, it's striking how similar Homer's passages above are to Plant's heroic tales of war, set in a misty, mythical past.

Plant's account of how he wrote "Stairway to Heaven" provides a striking illustration of Longinus's theory of inspired sublimity. One evening Plant and Page were sitting by a log fire at Headley Grange, the house where they wrote and recorded *Led Zeppelin IV*. As Page fingerpicked the song's introduction on acoustic guitar, out of nowhere the words suddenly came to Plant.

> I was holding a pencil and paper, and for some reason I was in a very bad mood. . . . Then all of a sudden, my hand was writing out the words, "There's a lady who's sure / All that glitters is gold, / And she's buying a stairway to heaven." I just sat there and looked at them and almost leapt out of my seat. (Barney Hoskins, *Led Zeppelin IV*, Rodale, 2006, p. 94)

This is precisely the kind of spontaneous inspiration that Longinus considers essential to the sublime—verses that come to the writer *ex nihilo*, as a "gift," and whose greatness is immediately apparent. The sublimity of the song was also clear to the entire band the next day when they rehearsed it together for the first time. During this rehearsal the rest of the song's lyrics came to Plant in another flash of inspiration. Page recalls:

> . . . we were all so inspired by how the song could come out—with the building passages and all those possibilities—that [Robert] suddenly burst out with the lyrics. Then we all threw in ideas—things such as Bonzo not coming in until the song was well underway to create a change of gear—and the song and the arrangement just came together. (p. 95)

The greatness of the song was also immediately clear to fans when it was first performed live. According to Page, "We knew it was really something. . . . I remember we played it at the [Los Angeles] Forum, before the record had even come out, and there was like this standing ovation."[4]

Boogie with Kant

Combining the ideas of Burke and Longinus, we can begin to synthesize a more adequate conception of the sublime—one that accounts for the sensory qualities of an art-work, but also the more elusive qualities of creative genius and inspiration. What's still missing, however, is a more rigorous aesthetic theory explaining why we experience certain objects and art-works as sublime. Ideally, we would have a theory based solidly on "a priori" principles[5] that takes us beyond "recipes" for sublimity and such vague concepts as artistic brilliance and inspiration. Immanuel Kant's theory attempts to do just that.

In his groundbreaking *Critique of Judgment*, published in 1790, Kant seeks to anchor judgments about the sublime and the beautiful in the principles of human cognition. According to Kant, aesthetic judgments involve three mental faculties: imagination, reason, and understanding. *Imagination* is the faculty that forms an image in the mind of some finite, external object; thus, Kant sometimes refers to imagination as the faculty of "presentation." Imagination "presents" particular objects to the mind, whereupon

---

[4] Alan Paul, "Led Zeppelin," *Guitar Legends* (February 2004), p. 32.

[5] The philosophical term "a priori" refers to knowledge that doesn't depend on the evidence of experience. Mathematics is a good example of a priori knowledge.

they become accessible to the operations of the understanding. *Understanding* applies concepts to particular perceptual objects. For example, if someone hands you a guitar pick, the imagination presents this particular object to your mind as a raw, visual image with no linguistic concept attached to it—in this case, the image of a smooth, flat, quasi-triangular object. The next step occurs when the understanding subsumes this particular object under the general or universal concept of "guitar pick," whereby you make a judgment about what *kind* of object it is.

According to Kant, sublime objects present a problem: for, unlike the guitar pick, which can be presented to the understanding as a limited, easily definable object, sublime objects lack a clear, discrete form. On the contrary, they appear *undefined* or *limitless* in form. As a result, the imagination cannot present the sublime object to the understanding as an immediately apprehensible, discrete object, and therefore the attempts of the understanding to subsume the object under a concept are frustrated. Kant's examples of things we perceive as sublime include "shapeless mountain masses piled in wild disorder upon one another with their pyramids of ice" and "the innumerable number of Milky Way systems called nebulae, which presumably constitute a system of the same kind among themselves, and [which] let us expect no bounds." These are things of such great *magnitude* that they defy the capacity of the understanding to grasp them.

Kant also discusses things that are sublime with respect to their overwhelming *power*: for example,

> Bold, overhanging, and as it were threatening rocks; clouds piled up in the sky, moving with lightning flashes and thunder peals; volcanoes in all their violence of destruction; hurricanes with their track of devastation; the boundless ocean in a state of tumult; the lofty waterfall of a mighty river, and such like—these exhibit our faculty of resistance as insignificantly small in comparison to their might. (*The Critique of Judgment*, Hafner, 1951, p. 100)

Reading such passages, one senses that the great German philosopher may also have been a frustrated sublime poet! The key point is that, in their enormity and power, sublime objects evoke terror and awe in us.

Yet provided that such objects pose no immediate physical threat, they can also produce delight. Kant explains that, although the power and vastness of such objects are not amenable to our imagination or understanding, we *can* comprehend them by means of the wondrous faculty of "reason." Unlike the imagination and the understanding, reason operates independently of perceptual objects and consequently cannot be overwhelmed by them. Therefore, even though we cannot grasp the vastness of the Milky Way or the power of Niagara Falls through imagination and understanding, we *can* grasp such things through *reason*, which can supply us, for example, with mathematical measurements that can comprehend their vastness and power (math being a rational system that exists independently of the perceptible world). In this way, according to Kant, we can exult in the realization of the superiority of our reason even to such awe-inspiring objects, and this recognition of our mind's incredible power gives us pleasure.

Stairway to the Sublime

Applied in combination, the theories of Burke, Longinus, and Kant enable us to better understand the sublimity of Led Zeppelin's music. Let's look at "Stairway to Heaven" systematically to see more clearly how these philosophical ideas can illuminate it. Once again, here are the song's classic opening lines: "There's a lady who's sure / All that glitters is gold, / and she's buying a stairway to heaven."

These words approach the Kantian sublime insofar as the concept of a stairway reaching to heaven defies the imagination's faculty of "presentation": the precise location of "heaven" and the notion of a stairway so incredibly long as to be able to reach it frustrate our imagination's powers of visualization and, hence, our understanding. This is in fact the exact point of the lines: such a stairway could never be built; indeed, the very idea that it could be reflects the unrealistic materialism of the superficial lady the song describes. Yet the very impossibility of such a stairway existing is precisely what gives the image its sublimity.

The sublime Kantian qualities of indefinability and limitlessness are sustained after the acoustic section of the song ends and Page introduces a new, twelve-string electric guitar part, accompanied by Jones on electric piano. The harmonically rich and complex chords that Page and Jones play are clearly inspired, evoking images of flight and vastness (another Burkean sublime quality). It is one of those rare musical moments that induces goose bumps, even after hearing the song hundreds of times. Plant's words "and it makes me wonder" suggest a complementary kind of flight—that of the understanding—as it rises to the challenge of grasping an elusive truth that the lyrics never define.

In the next verse, Plant sings, "There's a feeling I get / When I look to the west, / And my spirit is crying for leaving." Here again, we have the Kantian quality of undefined vastness, with two concepts that surpass the mind's capacity for visualization: "the west," an immense, vaguely bounded region that far exceeds our field of vision; and the concept of a "spirit" longing to leave the singer's healthy, young body—another thought which strains both imagination and understanding. It's as if the undefined expansiveness of "the west" is so free and inspiring that the spirit seeks to leave the narrowly circumscribed vessel in which it is imprisoned so that it too can achieve this kind of boundlessness.

At the outset of the next verse, Bonham enters on drums, and Plant introduces a new sublime idea: "Your head is humming and it won't go; / In case you don't know, / The piper's calling you to join him." The nature of this "humming" is ambiguous; however, it may refer to an experience familiar to many Zeppelin fans—the humming in one's head that results from listening to very loud music! Yet Plant gives the mundane experience of tinnitus a provocative new meaning, suggesting that "the piper" (recalling Pan, the companion of Dionysus) is beckoning the listener to follow him. This is sublime, not in a Kantian or Burkean sense, but in a sense closer to Longinus's definition of the term, by virtue of the verse's sheer imaginative brilliance.

Soon afterwards, the music comes to a dramatic pause, and the band commences a bridge section that marks another sublime high point of the song. It's a kind of fanfare, sounded by the entire band and underscored by three rapidly-struck D chords, moving down to a C. Page employs two guitars in this section, each playing slightly different inflections of the chords, creating a complex effect of expansive power and grandeur—two of Burke's sublime qualities, but with an evocative magic that exemplifies the inspired brilliance described by Longinus.

A moment later, Page takes flight with the song's legendary guitar solo, a stunning composition in itself that, like Plant's lyrics, Page says was largely improvised on the spot. The searing tone of his Telecaster borders on the sublime quality of harshness—a pleasurably painful biting quality that complements the solo's jagged melodic lines. Page drenches the guitar in tape echo, giving his playing even greater drama and depth. Halfway through the solo,

Page repeats one short, dramatic figure no less than eleven times, giving us in effect another powerful example of the Burkean "artificial infinite." But this quality isn't merely abstract—it seems to express the agony of the soul previously described in the lyrics, desperately struggling to break free of its physical limitations. Moments later, the solo climaxes in one of the most awe-inspiring moments in the history of rock guitar: a lightning fast, repeated figure on the upper reaches of the fretboard, ending with a shattering high note —another perfect illustration of Longinus's "well-timed stroke of sublimity [that] scatters everything before it like a thunderbolt."

After the solo, Zeppelin launches into an intense, almost violent, hard-rocking section, with Plant in full-throated scream, while Page and Jones hammer power chords above Bonham's explosive drums. The effect is sublime in the Burkean sense of overwhelming power, while the lyrics partake of the Kantian and Longinean sublime as well. In light of Kant's analysis, we can better understand the power of the words, "Our shadows taller than our soul," which strain the imagination and the understanding with their implication that something immeasurable—the soul—can somehow be measured against a shadow (the latter being perhaps a Jungian archetype for the darker, instinctual part of the self). Yet we happily surrender to this logical impossibility because of the line's sheer brilliance. Imagination and understanding are similarly frustrated by the line, "When all are one and one is all," which implies that the boundaries of the individual are somehow breached, and all become "one," while the limited "one" encompasses the "all," thereby transcending its limits. The paradox epitomizes the Kantian sublime.

From Low to High Culture: Where's That Confounded Bridge?

As a category of aesthetic experience, the sublime has traditionally been reserved for art-works understood as "high culture," ranging from the Homeric epics to postmodern architecture. But rock'n'roll has been deemed too vulgar an art form to attain the heights of sublimity, and this quality has rarely, if ever, been recognized as an essential quality of the music. If, however, we understand that the sublime and the beautiful are the qualities on which the aesthetic value of the arts depend (as many critics concur), and if we can identify both qualities in the greatest work of bands like Led

Zeppelin (as I affirm they can be), then to relegate this music to the bargain basement of "low culture" is no longer philosophically tenable. On the contrary, understanding the profound and powerful elements of sublimity in Zeppelin's music enables us to recognize that the categories of 'high' and 'low' culture are little more than effete expressions of aesthetic snobbery, and that, when it comes to artistic expression, be it Renaissance painting, Romantic poetry or rock'n'roll, all are truly one and one is all.[6]

---

[6] I'm grateful to Scott Calef and to Shari Stone-Mediatore for their thoughtful readings of this chapter. It has benefitted significantly from their excellent suggestions.

2
When All Are One and One Is All

JEANETTE BICKNELL

One of the radio stations I listened to as a teenager was WRIF 101, a pioneering AOR radio station that broadcast out of Detroit, Michigan. I didn't like all of the music they put on the air, and some of the songs and bands sounded much the same. But the music of a few artists stood out, and Led Zeppelin was one of them. I could almost always recognize a track by them, and it was usually worth listening to.

Some singers and groups are better than others at offering listeners richer, more enjoyable experiences. While some musicians break new ground, others, though enjoyable enough to hear, are derivative. Some groups have an unmistakable and distinctive sound that is theirs alone; you'd never confuse them with a different group. Other groups kind of blend into one another and are hard to tell apart. Who but their keenest fans can tell the difference between Journey and Foreigner, or between Styx and Boston? (I can't.) But what accounts for the differences between a great, genre-busting band like Led Zeppelin and their followers? Granted, creativity in music, or in any of the arts, is mysterious, but there must be *something* that sets Led Zeppelin apart from so many other hard rock and heavy metal acts. What could it be?

An Inspiration Is What You Are to Me

Plato (427–347 B.C.E.) wrote a short dialogue called *Ion* which has had a huge influence on thinking about artistic creativity.[1] Ion was

---

[1] Plato, *Ion* in *Complete Works* (Hackett, 1997).

17

what the Greeks called a 'rhapsode'—a performing artist who recited or sang poetry to appreciative audiences. Ion didn't perform poetry he'd written himself; he specialized in reciting the poetry of Homer. In this he was like Zeppelin or any other band covering material written by other people.

At the beginning of the dialogue when he and Socrates meet, Ion has just come from a competition for rhapsodes where he has won first prize. Ion was successful and renowned in his day, just as Led Zeppelin was in theirs, and like the members of Led Zeppelin, Ion could sound a bit full of himself. Perhaps understandably, Ion comes across as rather vain when Socrates—a self-described "gadfly"—inquires about his profession. Socrates habitually infuriated Athenian citizens by asking them pointed questions and showing them to be ignorant or confused about those very things which they thought they knew best. Without being too obvious about it, Socrates does the same thing with Ion. (Perhaps, like Led Zeppelin, Ion would have done well to swear off giving interviews!)

Under Socrates's questioning, Ion is led to make a number of highly questionable claims about his skills and the nature of his art. For example, he claims to have lots to say about Homer, to understand Homer's mind, and even to know something about each of the many topics that Homer touches upon in his verse. Yet with further questioning, Ion comes to admit that when he speaks about Homer, what he says isn't based on knowledge or expertise at all. If Ion really was knowledgeable or skilled then he could speak intelligently about any poet, not just Homer, since other poets address the same themes as Homer. If Ion were knowledgeable about Homer's subject matter he would be equally knowledgeable about the other poets too, at least when they speak on the same topics. But Ion isn't really interested in any other poets; much less does he have anything to say about them. Nor does he really know much about the different subjects Homer discusses, such as chariot driving, leading armies into battle, medicine or divination. So Ion is like someone who sings in a Zeppelin cover band and claims to know all about their songs, but who can't explain what a "bustle in a hedgerow" is.

Yet there's no denying that Ion is good at what he does. After all, he won first prize in the competition. But then, what makes him a master of his profession if it isn't technical skill or some kind of knowledge? Socrates's answer is that Ion is the recipient of divine gifts. Just as poets like Homer are divinely inspired and even "possessed" by the gods when they compose poetry, so too are rhapsodes like Ion divinely inspired then they recite that poetry well. Neither poets nor rhapsodes are quite in their right minds when they write or recite poetry, and they don't have teachable skills that might be passed on to others. Consequently, on Socrates's view neither poets nor rhapsodes create the works and performances we attribute to them. Rather, they're mere conduits for the gods who take away their intellects and speak through them.

At the end of the dialogue Ion is left both confused and flattered. Perhaps his vanity prevents him from appreciating Socrates's irony. After all, Socrates's claim that poets and rhapsodes are divinely inspired is a backhanded compliment, at best. While being associated with the gods sounds like something good, it also implies that poets and rhapsodes themselves have very little to offer. They aren't knowledgeable or skillful in any important way and don't really deserve credit for what they do.

Ion was the first but not the only one to miss Socrates's irony in this instance. The British poet Percy Bysshe Shelley was a huge fan of the dialogue and even translated it into English, smoothing out the Socratic irony in a number of key passages. Shelley's translation of the *Ion*, published in 1840, influenced the romantic conceptions of art and poetry as the products of unconscious and mysterious inspiration. These same romantic conceptions have had an influence on some Led Zeppelin fans. Those who believe that Zeppelin's associations with the occult are in some way a cause of their power and originality are carrying on this tradition of creativity as otherworldly inspiration.

His Is the Force that Lies Within

The German philosopher Immanuel Kant (1724–1804) also gave an account of artistic creativity.[2] Kant wrote mostly about poetry and the visual arts, but what he said was applied to music as well. When we examine a work of art—imagine a painting—we understand that it is a painting and not the thing depicted. No one mistakes a painting of a horse for an actual horse, or a black and white graphic of an exploding zeppelin for a real one. But to make a graphic of a

---

[2] Immanuel Kant, *Critique of Judgment* (Hafner, 1951).

zeppelin look like or be acceptable as a zeppelin to an audience, the artist must follow certain rules or conventions. These rules are relative and vary across artistic and cultural traditions.

A painting of a horse from ancient Greece might not look exactly like one from eighteenth-century France, and one artist's rendering of a zeppelin might not look like another's. But if both are really good artworks they'll have at least one thing in common: when we examine them we'll forget that the artist worked according to artistic conventions. We'll be so absorbed in the painting that it won't cross our minds that the artist had to follow certain rules. Something similar happens when we listen to music. Zeppelin fans can distinguish their music from other music in similar styles, but they don't think about the "rules" of the various popular music styles. All of this raises further questions: where do these rules come from and why do they change from time to time?

Kant's answer to both questions is: artistic genius. Certain individuals have an inborn talent or natural gift for making art. Although immersed in an artistic tradition and capable of following all the rules of that tradition, these special individuals can make art that seems new and different. They can make art that is original. In effect, they break or ignore the rules of the current artistic scene and create new rules that other artists will follow in the future. Think of Jimmy Page using a bow to play the electric guitar, or how "Stairway to Heaven" lasts much longer than a standard three-minute radio hit. Zeppelin continued to break rules with "Stairway" when they refused either to release the song as a single or to record a shortened version for radio play. Later artists who come after the genius may be technically very proficient; but they will be followers rather than leaders. They lack that spark of genius that would allow them to make new rules themselves.

For Kant, artistic genius is rare and fundamentally mysterious. The genius doesn't himself understand how he comes up with his new ideas. Nor can he teach anyone else how to be original. We might say that the genius has a more productive imagination than others do, or that his imagination works in a different way. But these are just ways of restating the problem. What does it really mean to say that one person has a "better" or more prolific imagination than another person? What makes the genius different from other talented yet unoriginal artists? We can only wonder.

Lots of People Talking (about Creativity) and Few of Them Know

On the surface, Plato's and Kant's accounts of creativity seem different. In the first, the creative artist is inspired by external forces. He or she is merely a medium or conduit through which the muses or the gods communicate, and makes very little contribution to the process. In the second, the creative artist deserves all the credit. He has a mysterious gift that elevates his work above that of other artists, who are competent but must be content to follow rules. These competent but uncreative artists are like musicians in some cover bands. They're fine as long as they follow the rules and play someone else's material, but their own stuff just doesn't cut it.

Yet when we take a closer look, Plato's and Kant's accounts actually have a lot in common. First, both are intensely individualistic. It's not just that Plato and Kant assume that the artists in question will be individuals and not groups. They also write as if these individuals could work in isolation. The great rhapsode is picked out by the gods and inspired by them. That's all there is to it. The only social context the rhapsode needs is an audience to appreciate his performances. Kant's genius does need others to help him learn the existing artistic conventions. But his real talent only becomes apparent when he can transcend those conventions, and perhaps also transcend the surrounding social context.

Tradition—and by implication the people who embody those traditions—must be overcome if genius is to shine forth. This is one of the major sources for the stereotype of the great artist as a solitary genius, doomed to be misunderstood by those around him. However, thinking of creative artists in this way leaves us perplexed when it comes to groups such as Led Zeppelin. How could four solitary geniuses work together? Is the group itself some kind of "super-genius"? But if so, then we can't say anything about the way in which the group members interact with one another or create together.

Second, both accounts of creativity are predominantly mental or psychological. When a rhapsode is inspired, it's his intellect, not his body, that is taken over by the gods, who then speak through him. Similarly, the originality of Kant's creative genius is described in mental terms. It is not his physical mastery of technique that makes him a great artist. Many artists have mastered technique but genius is rare. What sets the genius apart is something about his mental faculties—his imagination is different from others', as is the way it interacts with the rest of his mind. Applying this model, we would have to explain what made Zeppelin creative without talking about Page's amazing guitar technique or Bonham's brute physical interaction with his drum kit.

Finally, both Plato and Kant present creativity and originality in art as fundamentally mysterious, not to say inexplicable. According to Kant, the genius himself doesn't understand the source of his creativity, and Socrates's reference to the muses or the gods only pushes back the question without answering it, since we have no knowledge of what makes the muses creative. Empirical research into the phenomenon of creativity seems to be a waste of time. Studying how creative artists actually work would apparently leave us none the wiser. If Plato and Kant are correct, there is no point in trying to figure out what made Zeppelin great.

It Really Makes Me Wonder

These two accounts of creativity—Platonic inspiration and Kantian artistic genius—have been hugely influential and still affect the way we talk about art and music today. Both also fit very well the Romantic conception of the artist as a solitary, misunderstood loner. For certain kinds of musicians—especially singer-songwriters like Bob Dylan or Joni Mitchell—these traditional models might have a place. But for thinking about the artistic and musical achievements of rock bands or other kinds of artistic ensembles, they fall flat. In fact, thinking about creativity in terms of these two accounts can seriously obscure what is musically and artistically significant about the work of creative ensembles.

There are at least two other things any decent theory of creativity would have to cover. The first is what some philosophers of mind have called the "extended mind" hypothesis. This is the idea that the mind isn't all in the brain (or the head). Human cognitive processing sometimes extends into other parts of the individual's body and even into the environment around him or her. Second, theorists need to take seriously the idea that creativity is a social and not simply individualistic phenomenon. Some creative works are best seen as emerging from the cooperation and conflict of a number of actors, rather than as the work of solitary geniuses.

The Piper's Calling You to Join Him

The idea of the extended mind was introduced to philosophers in a well-known article by Andy Clark and David Chalmers published in 1998.[3] The authors were impressed by the way the environment and things in it can sometimes support or even direct cognitive processes. Props—including body parts such as fingers as well as external props like notebooks, calculators, and computers—have long served as aids to cognition and memory. A guitarist might find that it's easier to remember how to play a song on the guitar if he or she actually has a guitar in hand. The fingers may "remember" what the mind forgets. Clark and Chalmers defended what they called the "Parity Principle." As Clark put it, "If, as we confront some task, a part of the world functions as a process which, were it to go on in the head, we would have no hesitation in accepting as a part of the cognitive process, then that part of the world is (for that time) part of the cognitive process."[4] In other words we can't conclude, simply on the basis of spatial location or metabolic structure, that something isn't part of the mind.

For example, there's a growing body of experimental work that underlines the importance of physical gestures to thinking and problem solving. Children who were told not to move their hands or gesture while solving math problems did worse on the problems than children who were encouraged to gesture. Researchers disagree as to what role the gestures play, but it seems clear that they have a cognitive function. In other words, the gestures are doing some of the mental work that we previously assumed was confined to the brain. Understanding gestures in this way can help explain why we gesture when talking on the phone although we realize the person we're speaking with can't see our gestures, and why even people who have been blind from birth gesture when they are talking to other blind people. It might even illuminate the compulsion to play air guitar when no one is around—*especially* when no one is around!

The idea that the mind might extend outside the head and even outside the body sounds pretty bizarre; but that isn't a reason to reject it. A lot of ideas that are now generally accepted as true

---

[3] Andy Clark and David Chalmers, "The Extended Mind," *Analysis* 58 (1998), pp. 10–23.

[4] Andy Clark, "Curing Cognitive Hiccups: A Defense of the Extended Mind," *The Journal of Philosophy* 54:4 (2007), p. 166.

sounded bizarre when they were introduced. According to the Parity Principle, if I work out a long division problem on paper rather than in my mind, the pen and paper constitute part of my cognitive process and part of my mind. Or think of musical notation as a cognitive prop that helps us to extend our "built-in" biological memory. Before the invention of musical notation, the only way to preserve a musical work was to preserve it in human memory. If everyone who knew a particular tune died the tune would be lost forever. But if the tune is written down it will be accessible as long as there are people who know how to interpret the notation. Imagine a musician (a piper?) who carries with him a book with the notation for all the tunes he can play. Rather than memorize every tune he knows, he can look them up anytime in the book. That way, when we all call the tune, he's never at a loss. It seems plausible to regard the book as an external memory storage device.

What does this have to do with creativity (or with Led Zeppelin)? If our idea of creativity is fundamentally mental or psychological and we conceive of the mind as being in the head, then we will pay the most attention to those processes that seem to go on *in the head*. We will tend to think that musicians' major creative activities will be thinking up lyrics and music, in the sense of working out tonal and rhythmic patterns and harmonic sequences. We will tend to downplay or even overlook the creative work that does not go on primarily in the head but with the aid of musical instruments. And yet, in an interview with Alan "Fluff" Freeman, Jimmy likened his relationship with his guitar to that of an actor actually becoming one with the role that he plays: when an actor "takes on the part within a play he becomes that person. I mean it's just a total involvement within it. And that's just how it is with your instruments. You're just totally involved with it. It's just a part of you, an extension of you, and yet sometimes maybe you're an extension of it. It's like driving a car. You're part of the machine."[5] So, when John Bonham works out a solo on his drum kit, or Jimmy Page plays around with different guitar hooks until he finds the right entry, the work they do on the musical instruments is in each case part of the creative thought process. And these small touches

---

[5] Transcribed from an unbroadcast interview for the King Biscuit Flower Hour recorded between late 1976 and April 1977. Available on a bonus CD accompanying Led Zeppelin's *BBC Sessions*.

are anything but trivial. They can make the difference between a good track and a great one.

Take, for example, one of my favorite Zeppelin recordings—"Babe, I'm Gonna Leave You," from their debut album. The song sounds like it might have been around forever, but was actually written by Anne Bredon in the late 1950s. Page knew and liked the Joan Baez version, and he'd played the song as a session musician with Marianne Faithfull. As Baez sings it, accompanied by a lilting acoustic guitar, the song has a definite folk sensibility. The Led Zeppelin version still contains elements of the folk sound, but there is much more going on. Page's arrangement inserts an instrumental bridge—drums and guitars—between each verse. Each time this is played, it is progressively louder and more intense. Robert Plant's voice is gentle at the beginning of the song, but grows stronger and more intensely emotional as the song progresses. As he continues, elements of mystery and menace can be heard in his voice. Whereas Baez's voice remains on a consistent level throughout her performance, Plant goes almost literally from a whisper to a cry. Led Zeppelin doesn't just cover the song; they transform it into something that is completely new and completely their own.

Led Zeppelin's version of "Babe, I'm Gonna Leave You" is a creative achievement that would in turn be copied by later groups. It's virtually part of the hard rock/heavy metal "rulebook" that bands must slow down and perform at least one heartfelt ballad. In more ways than one, "Babe, I'm Gonna Leave You" is the ancestor of Kiss's "Beth," Journey's "Faithfully," Foreigner's "I Want to Know What Love Is," Def Leppard's "Love," "November Rain" by Guns 'n' Roses, "Still Loving You" by the Scorpions, and "Bed of Roses" by Bon Jovi. The way "Babe, I'm Gonna Leave You" is changed in Zep's performance is not best understood as something that happened in the head of Page or any of the other members. Led Zeppelin did their major creative work together, whether in rehearsal, in the recording studio, or on stage in live performances.

The extended mind hypothesis can help us to understand the creative work that can come out of their playing together. If we think that creativity is limited to the head, then rehearsal and performance can only be a putting into play of musical ideas that have already been thought out. But anyone who has ever played music with others—whether in a garage band, string quartet, or high school marching band—knows that playing together is not like this. Depending on the type of ensemble and the setting, rehearsals and playing together are more or less controlled processes of trying things out, listening, adjusting, and then trying something else. Musicians do not think and then play; rather, they think with or through their instruments. Their instruments and their bodies are not the means by which they express musical ideas that have already been formed in their heads. Rather the act of playing an instrument has to be understood holistically and as itself a form of creative musical thought in action.

So Anytime Somebody Needs You, Don't Let Them Down

Led Zeppelin is a group, not a single individual. In some situations though it can be useful to talk about Led Zeppelin as a super-individual made up of its four members. This was particularly convenient, for example, when Led Zeppelin was sued by other musicians for plagiarism. Yet in other cases to talk about Led Zeppelin as a single individual is to risk obscurity. This is especially true if we want to try to understand the band's creative achievement—what made them stand out from other bands at the time and what contributes to their on-going popularity. I think that the band's creative output is best understood as an example of small-group collaborative emergence.[6] The concept of emergence allows us to recognize the social aspects of creativity and that Led Zeppelin was made up of four talented *individual* musicians who nonetheless achieved something extraordinary when they worked together.

Emergence is an important concept for a number of different fields, from biology to psychology to computer science. Emergence is anti-mechanistic; when you combine a number of different elements sometimes something new and unexpected arises. Emergent *effects* are always different from the various elements from which they arise, and somewhat unexpected. Emergent effects are not initially predictable from the knowledge of their components. A classic example is the wetness of water: hydrogen and oxygen are the causes, wetness the emergent effect. The wetness of water emerges from the mixture of hydrogen and oxygen.

---

[6] My main source here is R. Keith Sawyer, "The Emergence of Creativity," *Philosophical Psychology* 12:4 (1999), pp. 447–469.

A *property of a system* is emergent if it is not possessed by any single component of the system. Being alive is an emergent property of cells. To use a Led Zeppelin example, being awesome is a property of the solo on Stairway to Heaven, but not (necessarily) a property of any individual note. Nor could the awesome quality of the solo be predicted just from knowing that Page first bends the G string at the seventh fret, then plucks the high E string at the fifth fret (in other words, hits an "A"), and so forth. The emotional impact of the solo emerges from its components without being reducible to them, considered in isolation from their place in the whole.

An *emergent system* is one that displays new behavior or novel properties that could not have been predicted from a complete description of the individual components of the system. One of the key ideas here is that understanding the base level does not necessarily mean that you will understand the higher levels. Understanding which notes Page plays on the guitar does not allow us to predict what the music will sound like. Emergence can occur at many levels of organization, from the molecular level to the interpersonal or social level to the geopolitical level. *Collaborative* emergent phenomena are those that result from the collective activity of social groups where there is no one formally directing the group and no structured plan is followed. Examples include everyday conversation, brainstorming sessions, discussion seminars, improv theatre and musical improvisations.

R. Keith Sawyer, a psychologist who studies creativity, stresses that although collaborative emergence results from the interactions of individuals, these phenomena cannot be understood by simply analyzing the members of the group individually. Sawyer gives the example of improvisational theatre performances in which actors create dialogue on stage without a script. As he says, "the performance that results is truly a collaborative creation; the performance cannot be understood by trying to reduce it to a study of the psychology of individual actors" (p. 449). Sawyer explains that as each actor improvises a line of dialogue, one possible path for the action is chosen and other potential paths are closed off. As the improvisation continues, there is a changing dramatic emergent—a shared understanding of what has been established and what is going on. The actor's further speech and actions must be appropriate; that is, they must proceed within the frame established by the emergent drama. But it is worth noting that this shared frame is itself an emerging social product that has been created, bottom-up, by the actions of individual actors.

I hope that the implications for musical creativity (and for Led Zeppelin) will be obvious. In trying to understand Led Zeppelin's creative achievement we need to look not only at their individual talents and skills but also at how they worked together. The music of many groups is better than what is produced by the solo efforts of their most talented member. On the other hand, a group might have very talented individual members but—for reasons of ego, personality, or temperament—be unable to work together effectively for very long. The Jeff Beck Group and the latter-day Yardbirds are good examples. Led Zeppelin was exceptional in being made up of four supremely talented musicians who were nonetheless able to work well together. (Plant called their union, "a very strange, four-quadrant marriage.")[7] To understand the creativity of Led Zeppelin, it is not enough to know that Page was an amazing guitarist and arranger, Bonham was probably the best rock drummer ever, Plant was a superb vocal communicator, and John Paul Jones was a talented multi-instrumentalist. Almost everyone who writes about Zeppelin says something about their "telepathy"—their almost spooky ability to understand and anticipate one another's musical moves on stage. Jimmy Page, discussing the way the band worked together in performance, told David Fricke that "Robert could come in at any point [with a vocal idea], and by the time he got halfway through the first line, we'd know what he was going for. And we'd be there with him before he finished that line. That's how *on* it all was. Of course, we had the benefit of knowing each other so well musically—and also the fact that this band continued on, year after year, tour after tour, album after album. We could take more and more chances with each other onstage."[8]

What the four members of Zeppelin achieved together cannot be appreciated or understood simply by analyzing their respective individual contributions. Their music and their unique sound

---

[7] Chuck Klosterman, *Chuck Klosterman IV: A Decade of Curious People and Dangerous Ideas* (Scribner, 2006), p. 97.

[8] David Fricke, "Robert Plant on the Led Zeppelin Rehearsals: The Band Has 'Done It. It's There'." *Rolling Stone.* On-line exclusive, December 13th, 2007. www.rollingstone.com/news/story/17574852/robert_plant_on_the_led_zeppelin_re hearsals_the_band_has_done_it_its_there/1. Accessed April 28th, 2009.

emerged from but cannot be fully explained in terms of each member's individual actions. To fully understand what set them apart we would need to delve into how, exactly, they worked together. This may be difficult but at least it gives us a place to start. And there's a big difference between claiming that something is very difficult to explain and claiming that it is fundamentally inexplicable.

For me, one of the recordings that best exemplifies the way that the four members of Led Zeppelin together could make music that was greater than the sum of its parts is their recording of "When the Levee Breaks." Rock writer Chuck Klosterman's description of this track is particularly apt: "Drums from God, lyrics from the Depression, guitars that go everywhere, guitars that go nowhere, and the sonic weight of a thousand woolly rhinos falling from Skylab" (*Chuck Klosterman IV*, p. 92). A great many elements go into making "When the Levee Breaks" a great track. The enigmatic lyrics are both anachronistic and timeless, and Plant sings them with total conviction. Yet I think many would agree that Bonham's drums are particularly important in making the track the great work that it is. Indeed, he is roundly recognized as having set a new standard for recorded drumming. But while Bonham does the actual drumming, the sound produced is not due only to him. Page and recording engineer Andy Johns came up with idea to put the drum kit in a stairwell and record it through overhead microphones. This, together with the technique of feeding the sound through a guitar echo unit and compressing the hell out of it gives the track its characteristic sound. This decision to try for a certain sound in the drums shaped the overall character of "When the Levee Breaks" because every additional musical decision made by any member of the group had to be appropriate within the frame of the emergent drum groove. The drum groove—together with each additional musical decision—opened up new possibilities but closed off others. Each musical decision helped shape the track.

Bring It On Home to You

What would Plato and Kant have made of Led Zeppelin's creativity? Plato condemned the popular art of his own day, and it seems unlikely that he would have approved very highly of ours. Kant seemed not to have cared much at all for music. (There are reports that he tried to get the warden of a nearby prison to prevent the inmates from singing hymns—the sound interfered with his concentration!) But more important than the personal artistic taste of either thinker is the fact that their theories of creativity (and the theories of the many thinkers whom they influenced) falter when faced with the example of Led Zeppelin. The account that Plato offers, that artists are inspired by the muses or the gods, in the end amounts to another way of saying that their creativity is a mystery that cannot be explained. Maybe, ultimately, it is; but shouldn't we at least make an attempt at explanation before we conclude as much? Kant's account of the creative artist as a solitary genius is maybe even less helpful in making sense of Zeppelin. Yes—the band qualifies for artistic "genius" for the way they broke rules and changed popular music. But they didn't do so by "overcoming" musical tradition. Rather, they drew on and transformed the British Blues tradition that was their immediate musical context and which was itself inspired by African-American musical traditions. Later work by Zeppelin is even more "multicultural" in drawing on a number of different musical influences. Think of "Kashmir" and "D'Yer Mak'er", for example. When it comes to the band members themselves, it makes no sense to think of them as four musicians, each reluctantly drawn from a more worthwhile solo project to make music together. While Jimmy Page, Robert Plant, John Bonham and John Paul Jones were incredibly gifted individuals, it was their interaction as a group—the co-operation, conflict, and competition that arose from that interaction—that allowed each to do what was undeniably their best work.[9]

---

[9] For discussion and comments on earlier versions of this paper, I'm very grateful to Scott Calef, Ted Gracyk, and Ian Jarvie. I would also like to thank Hollis Bowman for research assisstance.

3

The Song Remains the Same, But Not Always

THEODORE GRACYK

> Expressive content is personal, individual, specific, unique. It cannot be borrowed. If it is not spontaneous it is not sincere, hence not, in the long run, convincing. But intellectual content is all borrowed.
>
> —VIRGIL THOMSON

Led Zeppelin has been many things to many people. However, if there's one thing that their dedicated fans know about the collective interplay of Jimmy Page, Robert Plant, John Paul Jones, and John Bonham, it's that they played rock, not pop.

Rock music is often distinguished from mere "pop" music by saying that rock requires sincere self-expression (and pop doesn't). Media studies professor Keir Keightley says that "genres and performers that are thought to merit the name 'rock' must be seen as serious, significant, and legitimate in some way."[1] Musicologist Simon Frith agrees that when musicians avoid "self-exposure," so authenticity "is not an issue," the result is pop, not rock.[2] Rock musicians are supposed to be personally invested in their music, which generally requires composing, arranging, and performing original music. In contrast, pop stars can simply enter the studio at the end of the hit-making process and plop their vocal track on top of whatever the "hot" producer has assembled for them.

---

[1] Keir Keightley, "Reconsidering Rock," in *The Cambridge Companion to Pop and Rock*, edited by Simon Frith, Will Straw, and John Street (Cambridge University Press, 2001), p. 109.

[2] Simon Frith, "Pop Music," in *The Cambridge Companion to Pop and Rock*, p. 94.

Pop stars don't have to "mean" it, but rock musicians do, which is why Eric Clapton took the high road and quit the Yardbirds when he was expected to contribute guitar to a pop song, "For Your Love," written by an outsider and brought to the group as a potential hit single. This higher standard for rock music looks back to Buddy Holly and Chuck Berry and then, in the next generation, to the Beatles and the Rolling Stones. Most of the music performed by the Beatles was by Lennon and McCartney. Most of the music performed by the Rolling Stones is by Jagger and Richards.

So the prevailing standard of rock integrity says that original songwriting is necessary for sincere self-expression. On the model of the Beatles and the Stones, the quality of a band's original material is the true test of any rock band. So it is not enough that Zeppelin had a near-telepathic musical interplay. To be a great rock band, the originality of their *sound* (the musical juggernaut that died with Bonham) must serve as the vehicle for original *songs* (which, if best when played by the founders, might be learned and performed by anyone). Following this logic, the essential Zeppelin emerges when Plant verbalizes his Viking and *Lord of the Rings* fantasies over Page's riffs. I admit that what I've just presented oversimplifies things by ignoring the fact that Jones originated a number of their classic riffs. However, it's the sort of narrative that many fans construct in order to justify Led Zeppelin's status in the rock Pantheon. ("Pantheon," if you're wondering, is basically the Roman Valhalla.)

The interesting point is that the band's critics rely on the same basic logic of self-contained creativity when they criticize Zeppelin. Their critics like to point out how much of their music derives from uncredited yet identifiable blues and rock sources.[3] But does this really matter? It's not as if the Beatles and the Stones composed everything they performed. In fact, part of the fun of Zeppelin concerts was the diversity of obscure "cover" songs that appeared in the middle of their epic performances of "Whole Lotta Love." Yet I

---

[3] For example, see Will Shade, "The Thieving Magpies: Jimmy Page's Dubious Recording Legacy, Part 2," *Perfect Sound Forever*, www.furious.com/perfect/yardbirds2.html, accessed December 15th, 2008. Given that Will Shade is the deceased leader of the Memphis Jug Band, the author's name is likely a pseudonym. The best academic examination of Zeppelin's musical borrowings is Dave Headlam, "Does the Song Remain the Same? Questions of Authorship and Identification in the Music of Led Zeppelin," in *Concert Music, Rock, and Jazz Since 1945: Essays and Analytic Studies*, edited by Elizabeth Marvin and Richard Hermann (University of Rochester Press, 1995), pp. 313–363.

think that I speak for most fans when I say I wasn't holding my breath in anticipation of a whole album devoted exclusively to their favorite 1950s rock'n'roll. No matter how well performed, the result would have been a letdown. "Boogie With Stu" is great fun on *Physical Graffiti,* but Led Zeppelin's achievement is partly based on their having created *their own music,* so much theirs that they could play it in a way that no one else ever could.

So how much of the music performed by Led Zeppelin was composed by its members? Was it their best music? How self-contained was the band? Zeppelin's stature as a rock band seems to hinge on our answers to these questions.

However, philosophy is nothing if not an activity of questioning what everyone takes for granted, and my goal in this chapter is to question what it means to say that some of the music played by Led Zeppelin is theirs, and some is not. More to the point, I want to ask why it matters.

The Authorship Issue

Let's begin with the obvious point that a song involves the interplay of two components, words and music. Consequently, changing either component can change the identity of the song that's performed. But how much change is enough to make this happen? At one extreme we find Nelson Goodman's proposal that the alteration of a single note changes the identity of the music.[4] But this proposal ignores the reality of music as a performing art. It gives musicians no latitude for interpretation in performance—for launching into "Let's Have a Party" in the middle of "Whole Lotta Love"—and it implies that Led Zeppelin never performed any song more than once!

So how much can change in performance while retaining identity? And how much do you have to change someone else's music in order to claim that it's yours?

The practical relevance of these questions is their bearing on the issue of Zep's "borrowings" or appropriations from existing songs and song arrangements. There's no doubt that Zeppelin was sometimes slow to acknowledge that some of their music, lyrics, and arrangement ideas were borrowed from other musicians. Sometimes

---

[4] Nelson Goodman, *Languages of Art: An Approach to a Theory of Symbols* (Hackett, 1976).

this was mere sloppiness; Page found the song "Babe, I'm Gonna Leave You" as the opening track on a Joan Baez album, *In Concert Part 1*, where the song was mistakenly credited as "Traditional" (that is, as a song old enough to be in the public domain). However, this was an error. Anne Bredon had only recently composed it when Baez heard it from someone else and adapted it. Baez was ignorant of Bredon's authorship when *In Concert* was being prepared for release. Trusting the erroneous claim of "traditional" on Baez's record, Page assumed that he owed no one any money for using the song. Once Bredon contacted Led Zeppelin, she received her proper credit (and, presumably, payment).

Although the failure to credit Bredon was an honest mistake, it is unlikely that we can be quite so charitable about Page's persistent failure to acknowledge Jake Holmes's "I'm Confused," a song he reworked into "Dazed and Confused" when he was with the Yardbirds. Similarly, Page did not write "Black Mountain Side," but rather arranged the music of a traditional folk song, "Black Waterside." The most original thing about "Black Mountain Side" is the decision to use an Indian tabla drum for percussion; the guitar arrangement derives from Bert Jansch's arrangement of the traditional song. Yet Zeppelin has never acknowledged that it was an arrangement of a public domain piece, much less that Jansch had a hand in the arrangement. And then there are the blues covers. As many fans know, Willie Dixon had to file lawsuits in order to get his songwriting credit and royalties for "You Need Love" and "Bring It on Home," which are identifiable source material for "Whole Lotta Love" and "Bring It on Home" on *Led Zeppelin II*. Howlin' Wolf likewise sued to get royalties for his unacknowledged contribution to "The Lemon Song."

These cases show that the group was initially dependent on outside sources for some of their songs, and that they were slow to broadcast their dependency. However, these facts do not diminish their other early achievements, which center on musical arranging and playing rather than original songwriting. The arrangement of "Babe, I'm Gonna Leave You" is, for me, that album's best example of the hard-soft musical dynamic implied by the oxymoron of the group's name. Delicate passages of voice and acoustic guitar give way to instrumental bombast and intensity.[5] Apart from some

---

[5] John Paul Jones insists that a balance of "heavy" and "light" elements was

of the music that Jeff Beck made with Rod Stewart and Ron Wood, there was nothing else like it in popular music—even there, Beck emphasized contrasting dynamics of different songs rather than extreme dynamics within the same song. Although rock critics today tend to associate this soft-loud-soft dynamic with groups like Nirvana and the Pixies, it really harks back to Zeppelin.

If Led Zeppelin's debut album announced the emergence of an interesting and powerful musical group, rather than a fully self-contained and inventive creative partnership, they subsequently developed their songwriting abilities. On the second album, the four songs "Thank You" through "Ramble On" are unquestionably their own creations. Overall, *Led Zeppelin II* sets the pattern for the majority of the remaining albums—most of the songs are originals but there is a fair share of homage paid to influences through the inclusion of "covers" and rearrangements of existing music. *Houses of the Holy* and *In Through the Out Door* obviously violate this pattern by featuring only original material, but even here there are overt stylistic nods to other musicians in "The Crunge" and "Hot Dog."

Led Zeppelin's continuing reliance on existing music is not an artistic weakness. No musician is completely original—a completely original artist, warns Immanuel Kant in his influential discussion of genius, produces unintelligible nonsense.[6] True genius, according to Kant, is the ability to inspire a school of imitators. As such, our ability to hear Led Zeppelin in a host of subsequent bands (from Soundgarden to the White Stripes to Whitesnake to Kingdom Come) is evidence enough that Led Zeppelin had at least some measure of genius. After all, no one is reminded of Willie Dixon when listening to Whitesnake. Zeppelin always transformed their borrowings, and through this process of borrowing and reworking, forged a distinctive musical identity.

Their Masterpiece?

Because they're English, it's ironic that Led Zeppelin's recording of "Stairway to Heaven" is recognized as having received more American radio airplay than any other recording, ever. Yet overexposure does not obscure the fact that "Stairway to Heaven" is the

---

essential to their music; see Susan Fast, *In the Houses of the Holy: Led Zeppelin and the Power of Rock Music* (Oxford University Press, 2001), p. 80.

[6] Immanuel Kant, *Critique of Judgment*, §50.

quintessential Zeppelin song. Composed by Page and Plant, its balance of the pastoral and the volcanic, of acoustic and electric, of restraint and bombast, make "Stairway" the perfect embodiment of the group's multiple talents. Yet is "Stairway to Heaven" really any more *theirs* than one of their cover versions—more theirs than, say, "Boogie With Stu" or "The Girl I Love She Got Long Black Wavy Hair"? Some of their detractors think that its achievement is lessened by the fact that the descending motif of the song's opening acoustic theme is adapted from a segment of "Taurus," an instrumental by the rock band Spirit. In Page's defense, he altered what he borrowed, enriching the chord sequence and resolving the musical line differently than did "Taurus" composer Randy California. Ironically, Led Zeppelin's history of unacknowledged borrowings suggests that "Stairway to Heaven" would *not* be quintessential Zeppelin without an element of appropriation. It would hardly reflect their total strengths and weaknesses if it were *wholly* original.

Given their cavalier attitude toward musical appropriation, Led Zeppelin's response when they first found themselves on the receiving end of musical appropriation is fascinating. In 1978, an obscure band from San Francisco, Little Roger and the Goosebumps, borrowed from "Stairway to Heaven" and created "Gilligan's Island (Stairway)." Released as a 45-rpm single on Splash Records, it was one of a string of parody records created by the team of Roger Clark and Dick Bright. They worked together in a comedy-musical act with a regular gig in San Francisco. In some circumstances they were known as Dick Bright and His Sounds of Delight Orchestra. Other times, they were billed as Dick Bright and the Hi-Balls. To make matters more confusing, their earlier 1976 tribute disc to the Kinks, *Kinks Sides*, attributed one song to the Sounds of Delight Orchestra but two others to the Goosebumps.

"Gilligan's Island (Stairway)" gained immediate national airplay. It falls squarely into the tradition of rock'n'roll novelty songs. Clark and Bright edited the *music* of "Stairway to Heaven" into a manageable three and a half minutes—something that Zeppelin had refused to do, so that the original song's radio success was independent of its status as a Led Zeppelin single.[7] Over the highly rec-

---

[7] Several versions of the Zeppelin-Gilligan combination circulate on the Internet. Ironically, given the issues of authenticity and imitation, a number that are offered as the Goosebumps "original" are imitations, recorded years later by others.

ognizable music, a voice enters in a fairly good imitation of Robert Plant. (The vocal was contributed by John Means, a San Francisco comedian whose stage name is Dr. Gonzo.) However, instead of the familiar words, "There's a lady who's sure all that glitters is gold," he shatters our expectations by singing something else: "Just sit right back and you'll hear a tale." While this line may be unfamiliar to many people today, it opens the theme song of a popular 1960s situation comedy, *Gilligan's Island*. In the 1970s, the show's ninety-eight episodes were frequently seen through their continuing syndication. It's quite possible that more people knew the TV program theme song, written by George Wyle and Sherwood Shwartz, than knew "Stairway to Heaven." Roger Clark cleverly combined the melody sung by Robert Plant with the words of the first three verses of the TV theme, proceeding with their seamless marriage until words and music arrive at their dramatic climax. But now "And she's buying a stairway [dramatic pause] to heaven" is replaced by "And they're here on Gilligan's [dramatic pause] island," and the pretentious Led Zeppelin anthem deflates into triviality, the mystical into the ridiculous.

Today, most fans would call this a mash-up.[8] If you've never heard this recording, it's probably because Led Zeppelin threatened a copyright infringement lawsuit against Splash Records unless they stopped distributing it. Lacking the money to fight Zeppelin in court, the Goosebumps complied and killed it. (There was not, as is often reported, an actual lawsuit.)

The Gilligan-Stairway hybrid is interesting for two different reasons. First, it seems to make hypocrites of the members of Led Zeppelin, who would not permit others to engage in the same musical appropriation that defined their early career. However, that's not itself a philosophical issue. What's philosophically interesting is the way "Gilligan's Island (Stairway)" illustrates a situation

---

Versions that run less than three minutes are not the real deal. My vinyl 45 has three minutes and twenty-two seconds of music. A musical coda follows the final sung phrase, "Gilligan's island." The re-recordings do not have the coda. The Goosebumps do a better job imitating Zeppelin than do their imitators.

[8] Unlike recent mash-ups, which take recorded music and combine it with recorded vocals from another source, the Goosebumps had to recreate everything from scratch by actually playing and singing it themselves. Furthermore, the Goosebumps preserve the Led Zeppelin melody for the vocal, not feasible with a mash-up of two recordings.

discussed by Eduard Hanslick, a nineteenth-century music critic who wrote an influential book on the value of music.

Hanslick's Thought Experiment

Hanslick offers the following thought experiment:

> Take any dramatically effective melody. Form a mental image of it, separated from any association with verbal texts. In an operatic melody, for example, one which had very effectively expressed anger, you will find no other intrinsically psychical expression than that of a rapid, impulsive motion. The same melody might just as effectively render words expressing the exact opposite, namely passionate love. . . . Has the reader never heard the fugato from the overture to *The Magic Flute* performed as a vocal quartet of quarrelsome . . . shopkeepers? Mozart's music, with not a single note altered, suits the low-comedy words almost alarmingly well, and we must laugh at the comedy just as heartily as we enjoy the seriousness of the music in the opera house. (Eduard Hanslick, *On the Musically Beautiful*, Hackett, 1986, pp. 17–18)

Take some serious music, such as a melody from Mozart's opera, *The Magic Flute*, or take an angry song from an opera. For centuries, musicians have had fun by setting new words to familiar music, so that the new words conflict with audience understanding of what was previously expressed by the familiar music. Through this juxtaposition, serious music can create humorous songs and angry music can be used to express any passionate feeling, including love. Surprisingly, the music works equally well either way! Hanslick's best example is G.F. Handel's recycling of his own music. Handel wrote a set of songs for Italian lyrics focused on lust and desire, then used the same music many years later when he did a rush job writing his religious masterpiece, *Messiah*. Music originally written to express criticism of a lover became, "unchanged in key and melody," Handel's music to convey the joyous excitement that accompanies the Messiah's birth in "For Unto Us a Child Is Born" (p. 19). *Messiah*, of course, consists of musical settings of Bible verses; the highly emotional refrain of "For Unto Us a Child Is Born" is a setting of Isaiah 9:6.

It should now be obvious why I quoted Hanslick. Bright and Clark pulled a Handel! Where Handel took a Bible text and set it to music that should have been incompatible with it, Bright and

Clark took the trivial words of a TV theme song and set them to one of the most epic, serious, and uplifting pieces of music of the rock era. Like the Mozart melody adapted into an exchange among four quarrelsome shopkeepers, the result is hilarious. However, the important point is that the words fit the music, and the music fits the words. Just as ordinary listeners will find nothing amiss in Handel's "For Unto Us a Child Is Born," anyone who doesn't already know "Stairway to Heaven" will experience no immediate disconnect between music and words in "Gilligan's Island (Stairway)." The music sounds as if it's been carefully crafted to provide just the right support for the words. The music is peaceful as the ship sets sail, and then becomes stormy and turbulent as "the weather started getting rough." (The sound of thunder is added to heighten the effect.) Where Led Zeppelin invest their full fury into the music leading to the line "To be a rock and not to roll," Dick Bright reaches the same point with the beaching of the ship, with the lyric, "On this uncharted desert isle."

Hanslick invites us to consider why such cases surprise and amuse us. After all, it's not as if Plant sat beside Page as they co-wrote "Stairway." Plant contributed the words *after* the music was written, which, for its part, was constructed from separate bits of music that were not originally intended to work together—a lesson already demonstrated by the presence of Spirit's "Taurus" in "Stairway." That, in fact, is the first of Hanslick's two points in asking us to think about such examples. Put aside your amusement over the prank or your outrage that your musical heroes have been skewered. Hanslick asks us to use our "capacity for abstraction"—in other words, to philosophize (p. 16). If different words can work equally well with a single piece of music, then the music's emotional power is determined by its *interaction* with each set of words. We might suppose that a song's expressive power is primarily due to some intrinsic property of the music, but that is false. If we find that different emotions are expressed when different words are set to the same melody, then each *song's* expressive power is due to that interaction. However, if the interaction of the two elements (words and music) creates an expressive effect that is absent from either on its own, then the music alone does not have any particular expressive power at all! By itself, the music is neither angry nor happy, neither spiritual nor carnal.

Hanslick is calling attention to a mistake that philosophers recognize as the fallacies of division and composition. Fallacies are common reasoning errors, and the errors of division and composition are the common mistakes of thinking that what's true of a part is true of whatever it's a part of (composition), and that whatever is true of an object is true of each of its parts (division). Examples quickly demonstrate why these assumptions are foolish. After all, "D'yer Mak'er" is reggae and it's on *Houses of the Holy*, but that doesn't mean that *Houses of the Holy* is a reggae album! Going from whole to part, I can enjoy *Houses of the Holy* without loving every song ("The Crunge" doesn't do all that much for me). So when we explain the emotional power of a song—that is, the combined whole of music and words—by pointing to what happens in the musical component, we should be on guard for the fallacy of division. If the song feels emotionally changed when we change the lyrics, then it's illogical to suppose that one part, the music, is the emotional engine driving things. Our examples of different lyrics for the same music suggest that the words, not the music, are the determining factor in our understanding of its expressive features. Not that they are the *only* factor, for that conclusion would itself be a fallacy of composition. But our examples suggest that the lyrics are the most important contributing factor in arriving at a determinate identification of what's expressed.

Hanslick uses a metaphor of visual representation in order to clarify his point about the interaction of words and music. "In vocal music," he proposes, "the music adds colour to the black-and-white design of the poem." The music adds to the words, and thus good music "could transform a mediocre poem into a fervent manifestation of feeling." We can confirm Hanslick's insight by examining the lyrics that got Zeppelin into trouble with Willie Dixon and other blues musicians. On paper, as a poem, there isn't much emotional drama in Dixon's words for "You Need Love." Better yet, consider Bukka White's words for "Shake 'Em on Down" (one source for Zeppelin's "Hats Off to (Roy) Harper"). As sung by Plant, accompanied by Page's slashing slide guitar, the same words are frenzied, bitter, and vengeful. Here we see the point of Hanslick's analogy between music and drawing. A drawn outline gives us the idea of the thing it represents, but it takes the addition of color to bring it to life for us. The phrase "shake 'em on down" is a bare outline of what's happening—it's a threat aimed at others—but we need supporting music to fill it out, to move us with the anger of that threat.

This proposal is curious, given that examples like "Gilligan's Island (Stairway)" and Handel's "For Unto Us" show that the music is emotionally neutral. By itself, music does not possess features that can be decisively labeled as bitter or vengeful, sad or hopeful, spiritual or earthbound. So how does music give emotional power to lyrics that are, taken by themselves, simplistic and trite? Hanslick realizes that he owes us a positive theory of how the music enhances the words.

Hanslick's explanation relies on the insight that each composition of tonal music normally possesses a distinctive form, a tonally moving form. The important point is that we hear successive musical pitches as a display of movement, as when a melody line is heard as moving up or down. Motion, in turn, possesses dynamic qualities (p. 20). A motion can speed up, as when the hard rock section of "Stairway to Heaven" has a faster motion than the opening, acoustic segment. Music can saunter (the opening of "Down by the Seaside"), race along ("Hot Dog"), or stagger (the main riff of "Black Dog"). Among its other dynamic qualities, music can also thicken and thin, and gain force and weaken. In relation to its purely musical dynamics, music "can be called charming, soft, impetuous, powerful, delicate, sprightly" (p. 10). Because emotions are experienced as having parallel dynamic qualities, combining a musical dynamic with a lyric that conveys a particular emotion produces a heightened experience of the lyric's emotion. In this way, the musical motion "animates" the ideas provided by the words, and a sketchy lyric is experienced in a setting that makes it experientially rich and powerful. In other words, all competent listeners will perceive music's distinctive characteristics of motion, but these are not apprehended as distinctive emotion unless we receive additional, textual cues about which emotion is being represented.

So Susan Fast is either mistaken or speaking very loosely when, analyzing "Stairway to Heaven," she unpacks its construction to reveal the musical details that create its distinctive "affective character" (*In the Houses of the Holy*, p. 63). Analyzing the opening acoustic section, she claims that the music's plaintive character "is important to the narrative, encoding the weightiness of and uncertainty of spiritual journeys. In other words, this musical construction signifies struggle."[9] But, as Little Roger and the

---

[9] *In the Houses of the Holy*, p. 63. In contrast, Keith Shadwick hears "warmth and peace" in the same opening section. Keith Shadwick, *Led Zeppelin: The Story of a Band and Their Music 1968–1980* (Backbeat, 2005), p. 159.

Goosebumps demonstrate, the musical journey need not be a spiritual one. It might be a sightseeing trip from a tourist port! And the perceived uncertainty may just be some dark clouds on the horizon. The supposed "weightiness and uncertainty of spiritual journeys" derives more from Plant's words than from Page's descending cadences.

Get over the joke value of juxtaposing Zeppelin's music and the Gilligan lyrics in "Gilligan's Island (Stairway)" and you'll find that, as Hanslick predicts, the story of the Minnow's voyage now has considerable drama and emotional wallop. Wedded to lyrics about bad weather, the same musical motion that powerfully conveys a spiritual journey is equally good for conveying the physical peril of the Minnow's crew and passengers.

Authorship through Transformation

Still, Hanslick's main point is that if music and the words are distinct entities, then composing and songwriting are very different arts. The fundamental art of music is the art of composing instrumental music, in which the composer's thoughts and ideas "are first and foremost purely musical ideas" (*On the Musically Beautiful*, p. 10). In other words, the composer is preoccupied with combining musical elements in a way that makes musical sense without guidance from a text. The art of composing songs is a different art. Whenever a singer is singing words, those words provide a direction for audience interpretation, so the audience's interpretation of the musical element will be different depending on which words are set to that music. In short, Page and Jones were Zeppelin's principal composers, and Plant was the principal songwriter.

At this point, some readers will worry that I'm just imposing my own views on the band and its music. Discussing the derivation of "Whole Lotta Love" from "You Need Love," Page says, "I always tried to bring something fresh to anything that I used. I always made sure to come up with some variation. I think in most cases you would never know what the original source could be. Maybe not in every case, but in most cases." In other words, they transformed any music they borrowed. It was the lyrics that got them into legal trouble: "most of the comparisons rest on the lyrics. And Robert [Plant] was supposed to change the lyrics, and he didn't always do that, which is what brought on most of our grief. They couldn't get us on the guitar parts or the music, but they nailed us on the lyrics."[10]

If Plant had written original lyrics for "Hats Off to (Roy) Harper," no one would ever have said that it derives from Bukka White's version of "Shake 'Em on Down." Their shared blues elements are so basic and generic that the specifically *musical* link to White's song is non-existent. Similarly, "Boogie With Stu" can be linked to Ritchie Valens's "Ooh! My Head" *only* because Plant appropriated Valens's lyrics. Change the words and no one could say whether any particular 1950s song was the actual inspiration. Most telling, I think, is Dixon's lawsuit over the appearance of his lyrics for his 1962 song "You Need Love" in "Whole Lotta Love." Zeppelin settled out of court, acknowledging Dixon as co-writer. However, give a listen to Muddy Waters's 1962 recording of "You Need Love." Aside from the swirling organ, it's a pretty standard Chicago blues performance. Omit the words from "Whole Lotta Love" and, again, no one would ever link the Zeppelin riff and rhythm to the Dixon song. Where Waters struts, Zeppelin churns. (The actual musical connection appears to be a third song, the Small Faces version known as "You Need Loving," where Steve Marriot's vocal clearly influences Plant's delivery of some lines of the Dixon lyric.)

Suppose we ignore what Plant is singing in these appropriations and concentrate on Page, Jones, and Bonham. Focus on the music, not the lyrics. In each case where we can identify borrowed musical materials, Zeppelin's *music* diverges from the known source material. In many cases, the musical trio of Page, Bonham, and Jones is playing their own version of what is otherwise a generic blues progression. Remove the words and Zeppelin's blues *music* can never be confused with that of Muddy Waters or Sonny Boy Williamson. Their non-blues borrowing are equally distinctive. With two exceptions, they rearranged the material beyond recognition. That leaves only the two serious cases of non-lyric, *musical* borrowing—the clear similarities between "Stairway" and "Taurus" and between "Black Mountain Side" and Jansch's "Black Waterside." Even here, they are musically reworked. Zeppelin's arrangement of borrowed music is always distinctive.

---

[10] As quoted in Mick Wall, *When Giants Walked the Earth: A Biography of Led Zeppelin* (Orion, 2009), pp. 149–150.

Because the real problem of "theft" lies in the words that Plant sings, let's return to Hanslick's point about what happens when a distinctive musical element is wedded to an existing lyric. Both are transformed. And just as new words alter our interpretation of existing music, changing the music will enhance or diminish the feelings identified by familiar words. Either way, the new entity is never merely a sum of its parts. Led Zeppelin may have objected to Little Roger's "Gilligan's Island (Stairway)" (or at least some of them did), but it's a wonderful example of how their own music works. Much of the time, musical creativity and success have far less to do with a narrow understanding of authentic and sincere emotional expression (spontaneous originality) than with musicians' abilities to breathe new life into our shared musical past. Whenever Plant borrowed the emotions of others by borrowing the rudiments of songs, their collective genius was to reinvigorate and animate those emotions.

Authentic Rock

Because Plant is clearly borrowing whole lines from other songs, a number of Led Zeppelin's compositions are not entirely original as songs. Nonetheless, the unique *musical* interplay of Page, Bonham, and Jones—and, yes, Plant—produced something genuinely new. Songs have both words and music, leading to important interactions between the specifically musical elements and the meanings of the words. Aesthetically original and powerful music may arise in this interaction, which does not require completely original material in the music and words. We should therefore resist the temptation to think that the features that we value in the combined whole are directly contributed by either the words or the music. Conversely, Led Zeppelin's lack of originality in some of Page's music and some of Plant's lyrics does not translate into a lack of originality in the musical interactions to which they contributed.

Three additional conclusions now follow. First, Zeppelin fans who think that originality and creativity are important features of rock music can defend their heroes in good conscience. Despite their borrowings, "Whole Lotta Love" is not "You Need Love," "Hats Off to (Roy) Harper" is not "Shake 'Em on Down," and "Stairway to Heaven" is not "Taurus." Second, we must reject the idea that emotionally powerful music requires a tight connection between sincerity, originality, and personal self-disclosure. Borrowed words and musical ideas can reduce the originality of a part without reducing the emotional wallop of the whole.

I don't know how sincere Plant is when he sings the borrowed line, "Squeeze me, babe, 'till the juice runs down my leg," in performance after performance. What I do know is that Led Zeppelin regularly supplied the musical motion to make it worth hearing. Finally, that last point challenges the idea that self-exposure and authenticity make rock different from pop music. Don't get me wrong: I'm not trying to do away with the distinction between rock and pop. When we look up "rock" in the dictionary, we ought to see a picture of Led Zeppelin. But their place in the rock Pantheon shouldn't be tied to a one-size-fits-all story that takes too narrow a view of creativity and casts doubt on the legitimacy of musical borrowings.

4

Black Dog: A Mood Mix

LUKE DICK

I can't help air drumming when John Bonham plays. It's nearly impossible to resist. I have to admit that having my arm twisted by the Zep, being compelled to furrow my brow and bob my head to the grinding, pounding, and wailing of some British blokes, seems rather adolescent for a grownup. But this music is powerful stuff, and at the end of the day, I don't really care that such a gesture is primal (and perhaps even juvenile), as some part of me truly does identify with it. The music seems to occupy a place in my life—only a sliver of what it once did, but, nonetheless, the fact that Led Zeppelin is even a small part of my iTunes database is telling.

Especially for music lovers, our musical tastes say something definitive about us, and ultimately, I believe that Zeppelin's existence in my musical world says something about how the world is for me. I believe so firmly in the connection between one's musical tastes and the significant truths about one's being, that I would forbid my daughter to marry any man who would give her a mix of only Led Zeppelin tunes. You see, there is a peculiar connection between a male and Led Zeppelin. Ladies, forgive me as I limit the rest of the essay to the simple scope of male experience. It's wishful thinking to believe that I could ever tell a woman anything she doesn't know about a man. I still invite all of you to indulge the black dog . . .

Got a Flame in My Heart

The array of music one listens to as a thirty-year-old man is usually not the same one listened to as a fourteen-year-old boy, nor as a

47

six-year-old boy. Songs most often *don't* remain the same. However, at any point in our lives, tastes are indications of something. As a teen, music becomes a litmus test of sorts, and having Led Zeppelin among the bands you love indicates something to others—it's the basis for a conversation that runs deeper than the conversation at hand and deeper than the grooves on an LP. As a teen, if someone disliked Led Zeppelin or any other music that you might have liked, they were suspiciously different in some way. They might be allies, but they were not in your inner circle. As a Led Zeppelin fan, you may get along with a Garth Brooks fan, but there is some wedge between you. I believe this wedge has something to do with emotion.

Music lovers often talk about an "emotional song" or a "moody" band. On some primal level, we have an understanding of what these terms mean when we use them, but philosophers are supposed to be concerned with precision, and I want to unpack some of these loaded words. So, let's attempt to wrap our minds around the mystique of unique musical experience that is Led Zeppelin.

I think it's worthwhile to discuss what is happening in the emotional experience of the song "Black Dog," as well as what we mean when we call Led Zeppelin (or any band, for that matter) "moody" and how this experience relates to the overall human experience. This will require me to talk about a few dead fellows and what they thought about these essential qualities of human experience. Stay close by, since the crypt we are about to enter is as cryptic and musty as the music that rises from it. You may even want to put on your copy of "Battle of Evermore" for this part.

There are many ways to discuss the subject of emotion. For instance, physiological explanations focus on the body's physical responses to emotional stimuli. Similarly, neurological explanations describe the emotion in terms of chemical secretions and electronic impulses in the brain. In the context of evolutionary biology emotion might be discussed in terms of its role in developing the species. For our purposes, I intend to talk about the emotion from the perspective of phenomenology. This means that I will describe emotion from an experiential perspective.

Our first-hand experience of emotion is our primary mode of knowing it. That is, we listen to music, and it simply moves us in some way. We do not say to ourselves, "Man, my brain chemistry is really changing and synapses are firing in an intriguing sequence," which would suggest some kind of direct knowledge of our own neurological events. No, without any reflection on our part, music affects our everyday experience, even if we are oblivious to the physiological and chemical happenings, which are the nuts and bolts behind our experience. So, discussing the physiological or neurological details is quite unlike discussing the actual experience of the emotion. One simple experience of Zeppelin is that it rocks, and we want to turn it up loud and bob our heads when we listen. A description of this and other emotional experiences is valuable in understanding how we connect with music subjectively. Yes, the brain chemicals and evolutionary functions are part of the story of emotion, but our subjective experience of emotion is a significant aspect, as well. The phenomenological approach to emotion is a means of describing what our cognitive and physiological processes feel like under emotional affectation. For the philosopher, after we've described various emotional experiences, we can extract concepts about our emotional experience and describe it carefully so that others can understand what we all feel—sort of an objective subjectivity. There are some rules about how to create such descriptions, but it's easier to show you than to explain them. It's a dance you learn by doing it. This is the phenomenological approach. Of course, since philosophers can't agree on very much, there are several ways to do phenomenology, and different rules depending on who's singing lead, but I'll stick with just a couple of ways of doing it that got a lot of airplay back in the day. With me so far? Okay, let's push on in search of the black dog . . .

We have a common understanding of the terms, "emotion" and "mood." I'm going to be a little clearer and introduce a new term, affectivity. I've always marveled at the diversity of interpretations of "Stairway to Heaven," and it's arguable that there is value in artistic ambiguity. BUT, unlike lyrical interpretation, we all need to be on the same page here when we're doing phenomenology. My goal is for what I say to register similarly with all of you. That said, think of affectivity as that vast set of mental and physical processes that make it possible for us to be moved in the way that we are moved by things like Led Zeppelin—or anything else, for that matter. Let me demonstrate: Say you've just walked out of the used bookstore with a pile of good, dusty hardbacks. You are sitting alone, outside the local coffee shop, perusing the used copy of Schopenhauer you just bought. You've got your headphones on, air drumming to "Levee Breaks," in a thunderous state of trance. This compulsion to bob my head and air drum knows no bounds, public or not. Some chump walks up, asks what you're listening to, then gets in your face, insults Jimmy Page's guitar playing, and tells you that you're lame for ever falling for the drivel of Led Zeppelin, claiming instead that Muddy Waters is far superior: "Led Zeppelin is such a derivative band. They constantly rip off blues licks. They can NEVER be authentic in the way that the people they rip off are."

You hear all this, and instantly become moved to anger. You feel your face get hot. You are compelled to argue. Your Schopenhauer gets knocked to the ground as the argument heats up. Perhaps you even want to invoke the spirit of John Bonham and bring down the hammer of the gods upon this knucklehead, or at least some knuckles. You are ultimately affected by that person. Five minutes ago, you were in one affected state (remember the trance?), but NOW, this person is in your face, questioning your judgment of Bonzo as the musical equivalent of Thor, and you have transitioned to another affective state (a state of anger). *Affectivity*, then, broadly applies to this entire situation of being moved by something or someone, from one overall mental and physical state to another. Now, let's wake the dead and discuss emotion and mood, both of which fall under the umbrella of affectivity.

Muddying the Waters

Jean-Paul Sartre (1905–1980) was a phenomenologist, approaching the emotions through first-hand accounts of these experienced phenomena. In *The Emotions: Outline of a Theory*, he speaks of the emotions as unreflective ways in which we relate to objects in the world.[1] He says "unreflective," because becoming angry with the Muddy Waters-partisan required no reflection. Emotion just happens to us, overtakes us. We need not reflect or think about the situation, we are simply affected. In this case, we find ourselves becoming angry because our taste is insulted. The idea that we "become" angry towards a person or thing is significant to Sartre. The drastic change in how we might view the Muddy Waters-partisan pre and post anger prompts Sartre to refer to our emotions as having "magical" qualities. It seems bizarre to call emotion "magi-

---

[1] Jean-Paul Sartre, *The Emotions: Outline of a Theory* (Philosophical Library, 1948).

cal," but think of how affectivity changes when you listen to the songs "Black Dog" and "Going to California," back to back. This change alters your affective state. Your emotional orientation towards Led Zeppelin's music changes from song to song. You are moved differently. Why? And why so quickly? It's just noises, disturbances of the air in the vicinity of your ear. Why should *that* alter your whole mood? It seems like magic.

Sartre also focuses on the fact that emotion has to do with particular objects. That is, we're not just angry, but rather, we're angry at a particular thing. In the example above, our emotions are directed at the Muddy Waters-partisan (who should get out of our face if he knows what's good for him). This person is what Sartre would call the intentional object of our anger. For Sartre, the emotions affect how we think of the object. So, each emotional event is directed at a particular object. In this case, the object is the Muddy Waters-dude, who has a shrinking life expectancy. I mean, it's pretty weird, right? I made him up and I'm actually pissed off at him. And if you come along and ask me a question right now, I may transfer all that animus to you, so stay clear until I finish this part. The point is that an intentional object can be something right in front of me, or it can be something I'm imagining, since I have an image either way, and that's really the object that corresponds to my affectivity.

Our emotional apprehension of an object can change with the slightest twist. So, imagine again that your favorite band has just been vehemently insulted in the most heinous way, your artistic taste called into question by some cajoling stranger. Can you picture the stranger? Try to imagine being offended in such a situation, envisioning precisely those words you could not handle some clown saying about your band. But now, what if the Muddy Waters-lover is . . . a beautiful woman? I'll bet that changed your emotion toward the scenario, didn't it?! What's more, as she insults your music, her alto voice coolly washes over you in warm waves with dizzying authority and cinnamon gum on her breath. She tells you that regardless of the fact that she finds Zeppelin inferior, she still finds you irresistibly sexy, AND she just bought a new summer dress in which she wants to meet you for dinner, AND she gives you an address and phone number. God, she smells good, and you love her half-smile and how the edges of her mouth make the slightest wrinkle. Without another word, she whips around, her hair kicking up like a black skirt on a flamenco dancer. In one fluid motion, she walks away, leaving you in the phantom-wake of her perfume, with no choice but to watch her put one shapely leg in front of the other until she's out of sight. As you trace the outline of each step, it takes every ounce of will to keep your mouth closed. That was magic, no? How quickly an offensive git can be transformed into a ravishing woman. Since you have a few days until you get to meet her again, go ahead and gather yourself. You happen to press "play" on your iPod just in time to hear the pre-noise of "Black Dog." You pick your Schopenhauer up off the ground, and before Plant wails, you can't help but notice Jimmy Page's mysterious, dizzying sound is reminiscent of the fixed daze you are now in.

Hey, Hey, Mama, Say the Way You Mood

Before all of this happened, even before you had put on your headphones, you were sitting there, maybe even minding your own business, but probably not. Judging by the fact that you like Led Zeppelin, you probably picked your table for its vantage point, and you'd already been checking out the "talent" coming in and out of the café. You just weren't yet angry at anyone. You weren't yet in the emotional state brought on by "Levee Breaks." That doesn't mean you were devoid of all affectivity. Your mental and physical processes are such that they ALWAYS have an affective condition. Every object in your world, everything you see, touch, taste, hear, and even the thoughts you have are affected by emotion. The particular way in which your world is for you at any given moment is what Martin Heidegger (1889–1976) calls your mood. According to him, we are always in some kind of mood; that is, we are never moodless.[2]

Heidegger talked a bit about the mood of Angst, and he said moods provide our orientation toward death or "non-being." One gets the impression that he may even have actually invented the "pissy" mood, but that's just a bit of history in any case. Heidegger was not renowned for his social skills. For our purposes, we know what we mean by saying we are in a "good mood." Everything in our world seems better, and there's a pervasive "goodness" about

---

[2] Martin Heidegger, *Being and Time* (State University of New York Press, 1996).

all the people, places, and thoughts we encounter. Coffee tastes particularly good, traffic doesn't bother us nearly as much, the air smells sweeter. Moods change the quality of all things that you might experience. Mood is the affective veil through which everything is filtered. Now we understand basic notions of mood, such as "good mood" or "fearful mood," but I think that there are perhaps infinite variations of moods that we slip in and out of. For example, there's a slight difference between *worrying* about something and *fretting* about it. It's easy to step over the line of worrying and into fretting (which has the sense of being pointless or excessive worrying, given the object). Life rarely appears to us in static form—that is, our moods change, and we have the possibility of more-or-less infinite varieties. There may be seventeen shades of affectivity between worrying and fretting that don't even have names. There might be eighteen; or a hundred. As individuals we experience a multitude of moods, and these peculiarities are difficult to pin down in words. That is, it's really hard to name what kind of mood we're in, other than a few easy ones like "good" or "bad." I think really popular music, like Led Zeppelin, embodies particular moods that cannot be expressed by one simple adjective. There's a close kinship between my "Black Dog" mood and my "Whole Lotta Love" mood, and they are closer to each other than either is to my "Going to California" mood, but it isn't easy to state why. I expect you get my drift, though. And our moods shift and vary within the course of a single tune.

What does it mean, then, to say that Led Zeppelin, as a whole, has a *mood* about it? It makes sense, vaguely, to say that, I'm sure. It means that the music of Led Zeppelin conveys a certain way of experiencing the world, in general. In some sense, their music comes at the world in its own way. The sounds and lyrics of Led Zeppelin convey a particular way of being in the world. Similar to when you wake up and find yourself in, say, a bad mood, the music of Bonham, Plant, Page, and Jones finds itself in a unique mood, a mood that we can make sense of with enough experience. These fellows may not have been explicitly aware of the mood they created as they were creating it, but they probably felt it, lent their own individual experience to the mood through their respective contributions to the music. There IS such a thing as the Zeppelin mood, and it is made manifest by the way that these young men collectively created noise. This noise has a particular stylistic direction, and it conveys a mood more so than it conveys any particular message. You see, good popular music—from Beethoven to Led Zeppelin—has much greater power to articulate moods than language alone. When we reach for the iPod, we are reaching for an altered mood, and we know what range of moods are available to us when Led Zeppelin appears in the menu, even if we can't fully describe it.

So, my point is that music can articulate specific moods, but also general and vague ones. When we listen to Led Zeppelin, we identify with the mood of these songs. Through every sound, every strike of the drum, every wail and whimper, we identify with and validate the general mood of Led Zeppelin. So, how would we begin to describe and characterize those qualities that make a Zeppelin mood with which we identify?

Gonna Make You Burn, Gonna Make You Sting

"Black Dog" is a great title for a song, in that these words alone conjure an image and embody a mood. Paired with the music and lyrics the title can occasion all sorts of imaginings. For our purposes, we're going to focus on how the Zeppelin mood deals with sexuality, as sexuality is certainly a focal theme in many Zeppelin songs. In the technical terms discussed, we're figuring out how the Zeppelin mood affects the view of an intentional object, namely a woman. Put another way, the affectation in regard to women in "Black Dog" is a particular emotional instance of the Zeppelin mood.

With regard to women, in many of Zeppelin's songs, and certainly in "Black Dog," the emotion is one that growls, prowls, pounds, and salivates. I'm fairly certain the black dog of the title is meant to refer to the woman that leaves the character Plant creates. But I'm also convinced it's the other way around, as the band becomes more wolf-like with every note they play. Plant never so much as utters the words "black dog," during the tune, but the black dog is there. You can hear the pant and snarl. You can hear the dominance. You can hear him put one paw on his bitch as he sings during the breaks: "Oh, baby, oh baby, pretty baby, tell you what, you do me now."

In between verses, the instrumental rhythm bludgeons and bruises with each accent. It's really no wonder parents considered this music subversive. This is not Muddy Waters's "Mannish Boy." No, this is sexual pathos of a canine variety, and it comes in the night, when all you can see are its white fangs and the reflections in its eyes. That's one aspect of what we feel when we listen. This music is a derivative of blues, but it's altogether different in its mood. Muddy Waters may have cursed women in his songs, but with every cracking of Bonham's snare, the mood of Led Zeppelin gives them a whipping that burns and stings. It presses the edges of both our bodies and our imaginings. We quietly wonder: "Am I allowed to feel this way? Is this a sin?"

Big-legged Woman Ain't Got No Soul

Arthur Schopenhauer (1788–1860) could have very easily been Led Zeppelin's manager, as he had business in his bones, as well as a very "Black Dog-ish" emotional affectation when it came to women, evidenced by his essay appropriately entitled "On Women." His prevailing mood seemed to be a misanthropic one, rather than a predatory one, and his social skills were such as to make Heidegger seem like the very picture of graciousness. Schopenhauer says, "Only a male intellect clouded by the sexual drive could call the stunted, narrow-shouldered, broad-hipped and short-legged sex the fair sex: for it is with this drive that all its beauty is bound up."[3] This animalistic desire to sweat and groove, Schopenhauer believes, is man's will driven by man's biological nature and not owing to the reality of a woman's beauty. To hear Schopenhauer tell the tale, women are essentially devoid of beauty, and, due to their all-pervading vanity they are incapable of even recognizing it. Makes you wonder what that says about the men that women choose, eh?

Before you sits the used copy of *Essays and Aphorisms* by Schopenhauer, and apparently, a woman had owned it, because in the particular essay, "On Women," there were some rather "colorful" remarks after each paragraph, written in what seems to be a woman's handwriting.[4] Together with the comments, the essay reads similarly to the story in "Black Dog." There is certainly insight to be gained from the parallels:

> **SCHOPENHAUER:** One needs only to see the way she is built to realize that woman is not intended for great mental or for great physical labour. (p. 80)

---

[3] Arthur Schopenhauer, *Essays and Aphorisms* (Penguin, 1970), p. 85.
[4] True story, folks.

COMMENTATOR: In a man's world, pig.

SCHOPENHAUER: Women are suited to being the nurses and teachers of our earliest childhood precisely because they themselves are childish, silly and short-sighted, in a word big children, their whole lives long . . . (p. 81)

COMMENTATOR: Large pig.

SCHOPENHAUER: In the girl, nature has had in view what could in theatrical terms be called a stage-effect: it has provided her with super-abundant beauty and charm for a few years at the expense of the whole remainder of her life . . . for just as the female ant loses its wings after mating, since they are then superfluous . . . so the woman also loses her beauty . . . (p. 81)

COMMENTATOR: Oh, fuck you, Schopenhauer!

SCHOPENHAUER: They are sexus sequior, the inferior sex in every respect: one should be indulgent towards their weaknesses, but to pay them honour is ridiculous beyond measure and demeans us even in their eyes. (p. 86)

COMMENTATOR: Prick! I'm glad you had no wife or children.

Zing! Schopenhauer is said to have had a few lovers, but I think it's safe to say that the notches on his bedpost were nowhere near the number of even a Zeppelin roadie. Similarly, Schopenhauer was accused of assaulting a woman and lost a lawsuit, requiring him to pay her a monthly sum of money until her death. Regardless, Schopenhauer ends up alone, and his essays can be perceived as either actual philosophy or affected rationalizations of his own biases—or both. Similarly, after all the virile gyrations, somehow Plant's character in "Black Dog" gets cleaned out by this woman and ends up alone, too. She steals his car and wallet and leaves his bills and heart on the floor. This affectation doesn't seem to be working out for either of these fellas. Sounds like the women win, right?

According to Schopenhauer, this is precisely what women do. They use men as instruments for their own well-being, for their own ends and for the propagation of the species. They do this naturally, he believes, and he feels that their very nature is parasitic. Plant's character in "Black Dog" is left out to dry, as well, so now he's holding out for a "steady rollin' woman." Schopenhauer does-n't believe such a thing exists, and if you take into account the lyrics of "Livin' Lovin' Maid," it's difficult to believe that Plant is concerned with finding such a thing, either: "Livin, lovin, it's just a woman," right?

You've been listening to Zeppelin, yelling along even. Three days have passed and it's time to meet your new lady friend, the one who muddied your waters. So, what are you going to do with your own black dog? Part of you wants you to bear your canines, but something tells you that dogs can be dangerous? Inevitably, you check your watch, read the address again. . . .

Steady Rollin' Woman Gonna Come My Way

So, there you are, standing outside the door, waiting anxiously for your date. By now, you've had several phone conversations, and you know she is a neurologist. She actually loves Led Zeppelin and Muddy Waters. She's intent on making her own way in the world, but she's also interested in what you do and likes that you're intent on your making your own way. She's not so fond of Schopenhauer. She'll let you hold the door, but only if you let her pay the bill this time. She enjoys her femininity as an aspect of her personhood, just as she enjoys wrapping her small arm around your big one as you walk down the street after dinner. Her only proviso for the date is that you exchange 6-song mix CDs.

Yours: 1. "Black Dog," Led Zeppelin, just to be cheeky, and because it rocks. 2. "Blackbird," to continue with the black theme, and because this song is an airier mood of mysterious hope. 3. "Black Eyed Dog," Nick Drake, still on the black theme, because you can tell she likes the rain, as well as rainy day music. 4. "Oh What a Beautiful Morning," Ray Charles and Count Basie, because it just feels like the giddiness of a new day, and she needs to know you dig soul. 5. "Hatienne Cherie," Angus Martin, because there's nothing like a love song sung in French and stylistically performed reggae-style. Show her you're worldly and that you may want to say nice things to her, but you're subtle and intelligent enough to say it in another language, at least for now. 6. "Galway Girl," Steve Earle's version of a traditional Irish song, because she's Irish, feisty, and because he sings, "Her hair is black and her eyes are blue."

You see, there is something significant about how we connect to musical moods. If we actually care about music, our music collections become representations of the moods that strike chords within us. We identify with uncountable varieties of moods. Our identification also changes as we change. From youngster to teen to adult, I passed from cassette to CD, CD to iTunes, and my music collection changed. Where I once owned every Guns-n-Roses bootleg, now I have only a few songs in my collection. "Thriller" is in there, because it grooves, but I no longer re-enact the zombie video, as I did as a five-year-old. CSNY's "Our House" is there, because there is something I love about seeing new flowers in a vase, because I was fond of it as a child, and because I'm still my mother's son.[5] Harry Nilsson's "Coconut" is there, because sometimes there's no other explanation for life than it's surreal—best to have a good laugh. After all, mixing a lime with a coconut seems to be as good an answer as any to life's woes, sometimes. Led Zeppelin "IV" is there, too, along with many, many other varieties of mood. These moods partly manifest my own emotional understanding and connection to our world.

Now, I'm not a teenage boy anymore. I am a father, and nothing can make you reflect about the female experience quite like having a daughter. The care put into raising little girls also lends some keen insight when it comes to the male-female relationship. After all, every woman is somebody's daughter. I said earlier that I would never want my daughter marrying someone with *only* Led Zeppelin in their iPod. I think now you know why that is, and I think most anyone in their right mind would agree. Mood manifests itself in every personal relationship in our lives, and our musical tastes reflect our spectrum of moods and thus can indicate certain truths about us. It is a good exercise in practical ethics to judge whether you're good enough to marry someone's daughter—whether or not your spectrum of moods would be conducive to having a life with someone's daughter. In fact, since most of you reading this aren't women, this exercise is a great moral benchmark for self-improvement. So, now, knowing what I know, let me turn the benchmark against myself, and, as a father, ask of the three males here (Schopenhauer, Plant/Zeppelin, me): who is worth marrying?

---

[5] Though, I never knew if it was the flowers or the vase that she bought today.

Tell Me No Lies, Make Me a Happy Man

Despite the radical tone of both Schopenhauer and Zeppelin, they're both like train wrecks, in that you just can't look away. They are mesmerizing, powerful, and dangerous. In the case of Schopenhauer, we have the luxury of looking at the intellectual accomplishments of women in contemporary society to elucidate his ignorance. Despite this, it's hard not to marvel at this train jumping its track through the course of his essay. From our own affected place in the world, there's a certain pleasure we get as the train cars begin spilling old European notions of sexual roles. Interestingly, Schopenhauer actually says a few things about the female of the species that hold to this day regarding normative differences in cognitive styles; however, Schopenhauer's mood is such that he portrays these differences as instances of superiority/inferiority, when, at the end of the day, it seems that biological differences in men and women correspond to one another symbiotically.

It's said that Schopenhauer's mother was dismissive of him. She was a literary figure of the time, as well, and it has been postulated that she drove his father to suicide. The truth of the details isn't that important here. What is important is that one's affectivity has bearing on one's opinions. Even the all-objective philosopher, standing above the river and observing "true reality" could scarcely shake being human. To be human means to have affectivity, to have your own particular orientation towards all the possible objects in the world. I beg you to wonder about MY affectivity—and anyone else's, for that matter. Consequently, I would certainly not want my daughter marrying Schopenhauer.

As for Zeppelin, this is another primal force that we just can't seem to part with, for one reason or another. Perhaps at some level we accept that masculinity entails some predatory impulse, or perhaps it's because we just can't part with air-drumming, Zeppelin has some quality that gives them staying power. I'm inclined to think it has something to do with their distinct mood. That mood is certainly radical, decisively male, and not very conducive to marriage and raising a family. I know what rock-'n'-rollers do for fun, and it often results in a necessary penicillin shot. Unless you're Yoko and John or Paul and Linda, chances are slim that you'll stay out of the National Inquirer for some salacious scandal. Most rockers write love songs for at least half a dozen women. I will not give my marital blessing for such a small probability that my daughter is a rocker's last hurrah. Ramblin' men are generally not good sons-in-law.

Now, knowing the pains of and worries of a father, based on my own mood mix, would I be willing to endorse myself as a viable candidate for a suitor? I mean, that IS a great mix. It's got plenty of diversity. There's charm, and care, and thought, all good qualities, and it's got enough testosterone to produce some grand-babies (though it sometimes makes me dizzy to think of such things). Hmmm, . . . Ultimately, I think I need to witness several more mixes and know several more moods before I could ever (if ever I could) make that decision. I suppose I'll just have to do my best to raise a daughter who will both listen to her father's (perhaps) prudent advice and develop her own intellect, independence, and judgment when it comes to such crucial matters. Luckily, I have a few years to go before I have to worry about the black dog coming for her. The one pressing matter is what my lady friend's father thinks of my mix.

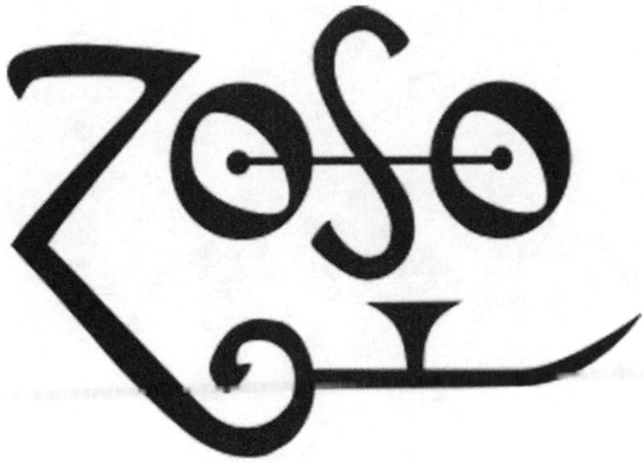

5
Sometimes a Guitar Is Just a Guitar

RICHARD E. WILSON and EMMA L.E. REES

Mechanic Chris Donald loves his work—he has sex with cars. And he admitted last night: "Some men like boobs and bums, but I much prefer curvy bodywork." Chris, 38, has a recognised psychological condition that makes him physically attracted to motors. He has had sex with more than 30 different models in 20 years, plus two motorboats and a pal's jetski. Chris, who does have a girlfriend, confessed: "A nice car for me is a feast for the senses. It's about smells, feelings and tastes. If I see a gorgeous Mercedes I know I'd love to jump into bed with it."

—*The Sun* (British daily tabloid newspaper), 9th March, 2007

When doing research for this chapter we encountered a whole new world of 'hobbies'. We don't think of ourselves as particularly naive but we were shocked to find numerous sites on the Internet aimed at people who are 'mechaphiliacs', that is, who have sex with cars.

We aren't going to provide some kind of shock revelation about the *actual* sexual preferences of the members of Led Zeppelin, and nor do you have to eye your treasured Buick with suspicion, but what we do want to do is to explore the realm of the fetish, as Sigmund Freud defined it, in relation to Zeppelin's lyrics. While John Bonham's love for the motor car was certainly platonic, what we can identify in Zeppelin's songs is a tendency to substitute other items (cars, pots of honey, pies, gardens . . .) for the female body. Freud called this method of substitution 'fetishism'. What's more, this inclination continued a long musical tradition of such representations.

63

What Is and What Should Never Be

Freud almost had a fetish for his theory of the fetish. He kept returning to it, publishing an essay on it in 1905 in *Three Essays on the History of Sexuality*; addressing the Viennese Psychoanalytic Society about it in 1909; and writing another essay about it in 1927.[1] Maybe he should have talked to someone about that. Anyway, in Freud's theory a little boy looks at a little girl and is horrified to discover that she does not have a penis. In the little boy's mind this absence is a lack which can only have come about as the result of some kind of calamitous accident. In other words, he believes little girls to be castrated boys. Pretty terrifying stuff for the little boy. The little girl is, therefore, a terrible warning to him. He can't look at the little girl's genitals without fearing that he, too, might be castrated. He transfers his desires, therefore, to a thing which he *associates* with the female genitals, but which is not actually them. This 'thing' is the fetish object. It's a substitute, a safe item or talisman which means the boy need not confront his fears about castration because his focus is on the fetish object, not on the girl's 'castrated' genitals. It's important, however, not to take one's eye off the ball too much (if you'll pardon the expression): on *Presence*, the song "Royal Orleans" tells the story of John Paul Jones's dalliance with a woman who turned out to be most definitely *not* castrated. She was a he. With whiskers. Oops.

Back to Vienna. As the boy grows up he should, according to Freud's ideas about sexual maturity, begin to understand more fully the woman's 'lack', developing a healthier relationship with his father whom he no longer regards with an Oedipal rage or jealousy, but with whom he instead identifies. (Mythical Greek king, Oedipus, unknowingly killed his father, married his mother, and blinded himself in an act of symbolic castration.) Freud argued that when the boy fails to resolve his psychological rivalry with his father, and fixates instead upon his mother, he has an 'Oedipus Complex', and will remain tied into an intense relationship with his primary caregiver, the mother. She, by virtue of being female, is seen as 'castrated' and both enthralling and terrifying to him. So, he has to look away from her castrated state and, as we have said, his

---

[1] See Sigmund Freud, *Three Essays on the Theory of Sexuality* in *The Standard Edition of the Complete Psychological Works of Sigmund Freud* (Hogarth, 1953), Volume 7.

focus becomes the fetish object. In his 1927 essay Freud thought that the choice of fetish-object was made on the basis of what the male child saw in the last moment before the traumatic sight of the 'castrated' genitals. Hence the prevalence of fetishes for feet, shoes, or stockings—in other words, the last item seen while mother could still be believed to be reassuringly phallic.

One young man discussed by Freud in his 1909 talk was more excited by the clothes a woman wore than by her body. The man refused to recognize female sexual difference—the focus on her *clothes* meant that he did not have to look *underneath* and see her 'castrated' self. The packaging of *Physical Graffiti* invites us to do precisely this, however: to look underneath. The die-cut brownstone windows turn us into voyeurs as through one we glimpse a striptease; in another a woman is literally turned into an object as she stands in for the supporting strut of a harp; elsewhere a woman in bondage gear is depicted from the neck down; and a cheerily seductive woman is caught in the act of removing her black stockings.

What is perhaps most provocative about the cover is the way in which the band members themselves invite our gaze and play with sexual ambiguity as they appear in drag: Jimmy Page blows a kiss from behind a huge yellow feather boa; a skirted Robert Plant drapes himself in furs; and a heavily made-up John Bonham closes his eyes, apparently naked apart from a fetching silk turban, and seemingly oblivious to the fact that he's sharing the frame with a grinning Page still wrapped in his boa. We could go on all day about the album sleeve images—the phallic zeppelin plummeting to earth; the young woman trampled underfoot by a giant; the tailor doing what is technically known as 'copping a feel' as he takes an inside leg measurement—but we won't. That would be fetishistic: we wouldn't be listening to the music itself, but would be dazzled instead by an associated substitute. Enough already with the 'clothes' of *Physical Graffiti*! On with the body underneath (the music. Pay attention. We're being metaphorical).

Soul of a Woman was Created Below

Before looking at the fetishism of *Physical Graffiti*, we need to think about the connection between fetishism and misogyny. Freud assumed that male adults, while knowing rationally that the female adult's body is *not* the site of some terrible trauma which resulted in her penis being cut off, still hang on to an element of that belief. So, many men find many women frightening. At the same time that heterosexual men desire women, deep down they are frightened little boys cupping their egos protectively in their sweaty little hands. It's not too much of a stretch, then, to see how Freud's castration complex might lead to a general deep-seated fear and distrust—even hatred—of women. This 'misogyny' is exhibited in many ways in everyday life. One way is by making women into objects (as is often done in pornography and advertising); another, the fetishistic route, is to make objects—at least symbolically—into women. Either process denies women individuality and power. They are instead passive, voiceless, even mechanized. Where they are not objectified they are a source of terror and mistrust.

Several songs on *Led Zeppelin I* are meditations on the unreliable, sexually promiscuous and generally devious behavior of women. In fact, so common are such activities that they are *natural* to women, somehow part of their physical make-up. It's on this album, of course, that we actually hear, in a deliciously medieval image, that women's souls are made in Hell ("Dazed and Confused"). Their nether regions hail from the nether regions, if you like. Robert Plant's no Shakespeare, although some of you reading this will dispute that, but his suggestion that women are devils does recall a misogynist tradition traceable back to the Bard.[2] "Down from the waist / They're centaurs, though women all above," rants crazy King Lear: "But to the girdle do the gods inherit; / Beneath is all the fiend's. There's hell, there's darkness, there is the sulphurous pit."[3] So, she's just a devil woman: "Soul of a woman," laments Plant, "was created below." Freud wouldn't have been surprised by this. Plant and Shakespeare both seem preoccupied with going down. Behave. We mean "going down to hell." Not only is the woman from hell, but her sexuality is like hell: steamy and scary. "Below" refers both to Satan's abode and to the woman's genitals—which in turn gives a whole new frisson to "the devil's in his hole" ("Achilles' Last Stand").

---

[2] Others of you will point to the song's origins, a Jake Holmes number played live by the Yardbirds in March 1968. Relax. We know.

[3] Shakespeare, *King Lear* (London: Routledge, 1997), Act 4, Scene 5, lines 121–25.

If the native unreliability of the woman doesn't altogether rule out men and women having relationships, then such relationships need, the album's lyrics suggest, to control her naturally roaming eye. In "You Shook Me," the influence is the Blues as much as it is the Bard: when Led Zeppelin revived Muddy Waters's version of Willie Dixon's and J.B. Lenoir's song, the overriding suggestion was that marriage was the only way to tame a woman.

There's an irony in this album's misogyny, especially as it's demonstrated in "Babe, I'm Gonna Leave You." The idea of calling a loved one 'babe' or 'baby' is in itself an interesting move, since it removes maturity from the object of affection. It infantilises "woman" who is promised that "one day" she will be reunited with him and they'll "walk through the park everyday." Plant justifies his abandonment of his "baby" because of his wanderlust, and, contradictorily, his being called "back home." We need to be careful in this analysis, however, as it was originally a woman, Anne Bredon, who wrote the song, and it had already featured as the opening track on Joan Baez's 1963 LP, "Joan Baez in Concert, Part 1." However, a very similar sentiment is expressed in "I Can't Quit You Baby," which is another 'tribute' to the corrupting, fearsome power of female sexuality: Plant cries out to his mistress that he must try to escape her to return home.

The elusive, if not impossible, nature of the ideal woman can at times be quite poignant in the band's lyrics on other albums, as suggested by the "girl with love in her eyes" of "Going to California." The ideal woman here is again portrayed as a "girl," that is, made infant-like and so subservient to the male. This transformation of the sexually active and, therefore, sexually aggressive, female into an idealized, controllable 'child' or 'baby' is another facet of fetishism running through the band's lyrics. Indeed, this figuring of the 'child' woman was evident in the practices of the band and their entourage in their heyday. Bob Hart, a journalist covering the 1973 US tour, commented on how badly groupies were treated, and on how some of the 'babes' were indeed—allegedly—only fourteen or fifteen years old.

Elsewhere on *Led Zeppelin I* women are told that their "Time is Gonna Come" (a rather empty threat, as it turns out, since the male speaker is in fact frightened of the dominant female partner); they experience a "Communication Breakdown" with verbally impotent men; and dismiss the male of the species in "How Many More Times." Here "Little Robert Anthony" threateningly—*misogynisti-*

cally—pleads with his beloved to come home, declaring that he has her "in the sights of [his] . . . gun." In fact, it appears that the only track on *Led Zeppelin I* which does not focus on the fraught relationships men and women share is "Black Mountain Side." Fact. (Those of you reading this who are still awake will realize that "Black Mountain Side" is an instrumental. Those of you reading this who are not still awake: HEY! There's drool running out of the corner of your mouth.)

Trampled Underfoot: Consuming the Her-She Car

The misogyny is clear, then, in the lyrics of Zeppelin's first album. At the same time that women are desired, they are rejected. The fetishistic expression of this apparently contradictory state is still in evidence—as we have already suggested—by the time of their sixth album, *Physical Graffiti*. The songs here, on the surface at least, seem to be obsessed with women's bodies. However, those bodies are always displaced so that the focus is significantly *away* from the female form: she *can't* be looked at because—remember Freud—in her castrated form, she's too threatening. Arguably, making music is an act of fetishistic displacement. In other words, for a heterosexual man, it's in itself an attempt to experience an almost sexual release without a woman being present.[4] Jimmy Page summed up his sense of exertion and release in making music in saying: "I came up with that title because of the whole thing of graffiti on the album cover and it being a physical statement rather than a written one, because I feel that an awful lot of physical energy is used in producing an album."[5] It's maybe worth mentioning here that *Physical Graffiti* was the first Zeppelin release on the band's own label, Swan Song, which had been set up the year before, but was originally going to be named either 'Slut' or 'Slag', names that recalled, for Plant at least, their US tours. Wisely, they decided this was not the way to cement their reputation. Nevertheless, the Swan Song launch party, held on

---

[4] See, for example, footage of Jimi Hendrix at Monterey in 1967, where he makes violent love to his amplifier before smashing up and burning all his gear; or consider the tendency of Ritchie Blackmore in Deep Purple days to 'penetrate' his amps with his Stratocaster.

[5] Dave Lewis and Paul Kendall, *Led Zeppelin 'Talking': Led Zeppelin in Their Own Words* (Omnibus, 2004), p. 49.

Halloween 1974 in Chislehurst Caves in south London, featured naked women and strippers dressed as nuns. And, if that's not hard enough to swallow, the final three gigs of the second leg of the *Physical Graffiti* US tour were introduced by Linda Lovelace, star of the infamous porn movie *Deep Throat*. So much for reputation.

Physical Graffiti's "Trampled Underfoot" marked a stylistic departure for the band with its repetitive funk-influenced rhythms and motifs. Its automobile-fetishism, however, marked Zeppelin's continuation of a longstanding musical convention with its origins in Robert Johnson's 1936 "Terraplane Blues." "When I mash down on your little starter," Johnson sang to his beloved, "then your spark plug will give me fire." Whoever said romance was dead? As well as Zeppelin, other classic rock bands of the 1970s engaged with the tradition. In "Highway Star" Deep Purple's Ian Gillan expressed his "love" and "need" and, most worryingly perhaps (and proof of the fact that the most appropriate rhyme in songwriting is not always the first one which suggests itself to you), his desire to "seed" all eight cylinders of his car. Quite. Freddie Mercury made no secret of the fact that he was also "In Love with [his] Car," not least because, presumably unlike human lovers, "Cars don't talk back."

What is it about the *car*, then, that squeezes so many rockstars' lemons? Marc Bolan and Cozy Powell died in theirs; Keith Moon took his swimming; Nick Mason (Pink Floyd) and Jay Kay (Jamiroquai) collect them with a fervour Bonzo would certainly have recognised. ZZ Top pimped theirs to the point where it became synonymous with the band; Status Quo didn't want "Baby" to drive theirs; and the Cars . . . just were. In terms of status symbol, of course, the car provides an immediate shorthand for the observer. The Hummer screams excess (or, some would argue, overcompensation); the red Chevy Corvette suggests middle-aged denial; the Thunderbird *is* the Road Trip; the Volvo implies suburban sobriety; and the Dune Buggy conjures up hazy memories of the excesses of spring break.

The car, then, constructs a public image for the rock star which, psychologically speaking, protects the private individual. That image, or persona, is also, in popular belief at least, the same one which binges on drinks or drugs, throws TVs through hotel windows, or sleeps with numerous women. It's interesting to note that Bonzo, the band's biggest car fanatic, was the member most renowned for his excesses, not only in terms of the booze, but also musically: he used the biggest drumsticks he could find in order to pound out his rhythms. In this formulation, the woman, the drugs and the car are all *objects* which serve the purpose of maintaining the rockstars' public image. To borrow some Marxist terminology for a moment (we promise to give it back as soon as we're done with it), these objects are *commodified*.

Custard Pie: Food for Thought

The step from commodification to fetishism is easy to see: people and things are all . . . things. The recurrent image of the commodification of the female body establishes a narrative theme where the spurned lover focuses his energies by creating a fetish object out of the female. In "Candy Store Rock" for example, the object of desire is seen as sweet and is "good enough to eat" ("got my spoon in your jar"), while in "Custard Pie" the song is not just about the consumption of baked goods, but is, to borrow another term from Freud, about an altogether different kind of 'oral fixation' which requires that the woman "drop down, drop down." "Black Dog" transforms the power of female sexuality into a dangerous, addictive foodstuff (honey) to satisfy male appetites. In "South Bound Suarez" the lovers' congress is referred to as "sweet con carne," while the singer tries to reject all treats in "Boogie with Stu" ("I don't want no tutti-frutti, no lollipop"). Portraying the woman as able to be eaten or consumed is akin to possessing and, therefore, controlling her. In one of his *Essays on the Theory of Sexuality* Freud wrote that children must experience—and in most cases pass through—a period of "cannibalistic pregenital sexual organization. Here sexual activity has not yet been separated from the ingestion of food."[6] Again, there's evidence of this Freudian train of thought materializing as behavior in one of the most notorious episodes of Zeppelin folklore, the incorrectly-named 'Shark episode' of the 1969 US tour. The story goes that there was a hotel in Seattle where you could hire fishing tackle and bait in the lobby and go fishing from your bedroom window, which is precisely what Richard Cole, tour manager at the time, did. When he caught a red snapper fish, there followed a lewd drunken incident involving Cole, Bonzo, a member of Vanilla Fudge, the red snapper and a naked red-headed woman. This unsavory episode also conjures up the myth of the

---

[6] Freud, *Three Essays*, p. 198.

vagina dentata, or vagina with teeth, feared by some men as the means by which they will suffer the castration they associate with women's sexual organs.

Transforming the woman into woman-as-food, woman-as-car, or woman-as-'vixen' ("Ten Years Gone") neutralizes her phallic threat, a threat which looms large in "The Wanton Song" where the predatory Succubus-like woman steals the singer's "seed" from his "shaking frame." The use of the adjective "shaking" here emphasizes that the male is both afraid and orgasmic; he is subject to the desires of a sexually dominant female figure. The image of the earth moving was also key to "Going to California" where the earthquake that caused "the mountains and the canyons [to] start to tremble and shake" was surely not just a geophysical phenomenon. "Houses of the Holy" begins like a conventional-sounding love song, but the tone quickly changes and we're back in those ol' sulphurous pits of female sexuality, here located in an Eden-gone-bad where the Adam figure wants to sow "seeds of love" to fertilize the "garden" not of Eve, but of "Satan's Daughter." Indeed, such seed-sowing does seem to be a prominent theme in the band's lyrics. The female, as we have seen, must be remade as fetish object in order for the male to be able to engage with her—when she is *not* fetishized but instead is in control, the male singularly fails to consummate the relationship: "Squeeze my lemon," begs Plant on *Led Zeppelin II*, in imitation of Robert Johnson, "'til the juice runs down my leg," and the singer's "children" spill onto the "killing floor" in an image of ejaculation. The 'juice' has not 'run' into, or been in any way appropriated by, the potentially castrating woman. In other songs, too, a terror of the castrating vagina is apparent. On *Presence* it's regarded as safer by far to let a woman grab your citrus fruit than your genitals (the threat of castration is thus averted): "You said I was the only, with my lemon in your hand" sings Plant on "For Your Life." In "Whole Lotta Love" the singer proposes being a "backdoor man," that is, engaging in anal sex with his partner, and oral sex seems to be the preoccupation both in the 'going south' image of "South Bound Suarez" and in the gold-lined mouth of the later "Travelling Riverside Blues" (another substitute object to be found in this song, of course, is a "brown-skinned sugar plum").[7]

---

[7] Heterosexual fellatio might be understood to be a substitutive act in itself: the oral focus allows the man to deny the fearful presence of the vagina.

My Woman Left Home: Cock Rock and Doomed Relationships

We've already discussed how, in Freud's formulation, it's virtually impossible for a man and a woman to have a healthy relationship of equals. Men's deep-seated fear of castration leads them to demonize women. It also enables them to cope with what they would regard as inevitable betrayal in a heterosexual relationship—if sexual desire has been focussed not on the woman herself but on a fetishistic substitute for her, she can leave but the substitute remains (a pot of honey or an automobile cannot up and leave of their own will. Unless you're Stephen King and the car's called Christine. But that's unlikely). The inevitability of this betrayal is repeatedly expressed in the band's lyrics, as we've seen in "You Shook Me." On *Led Zeppelin III* the woman has either "gone and left me" ("Friends"); or she is "1000 years" away ("Tangerine"); the singer is thwarted by a disapproving mother ("That's the Way"); or the beloved must be shot to be controlled ("Hats off to Roy Harper").

The only real hint of fidelity comes in the "Bron-y-aur-Stomp," but the song turns out to be about a Welsh sheepdog (and that's a whole other chapter right there). On *Houses of the Holy* the optimism of "Rain Song" is somewhat washed out; the lover of "Over the Hills and Far Away" laments that "Many have I loved, many times been bitten"; pleads to his woman not to leave him in "D'yer Mak'er"; and only finds any kind of peace in the upbeat "Dancing Days" and the meditative "Ocean"—this latter written for an *entirely* unthreatening female: a three-year old daughter. (A similarly affirmative sentiment had appeared on "Thank You" on *Led Zeppelin II*.) On *Physical Graffiti*, the most sadistic punishments are visited on the singer's body: in the course of one song, "Black Country Woman," he moves from having beer thrown in his face to being "crucified" by his lover (his revenge in this case is, one might venture, somewhat dastardly— he sleeps with his ex's sister). By the time of *In Through the Out Door* the sense of abandonment has scarcely abated—the singer's jilted in the cautionary "In the Evening"; he's a "Fool in the Rain" because he's been stood up; and a hard-hearted Texan woman left him in "Hot Dog." *Coda* provides a satisfactory coda to the pattern, as the singer is cuckolded in "Poor Tom" and is almost destroyed by jealous, lustful feelings in "Darlene."

In live performance Plant's particularly flamboyant variety of Cock Rock relied heavily on sexual suggestiveness and on fetishism. Otherwise it would have been 'Castrated Rock' (which does not have quite the same commercial appeal). In Cock Rock, "music is loud, rhythmically insistent, built around techniques of arousal and release."[8] As anyone who has ever watched *The Song Remains the Same* will tell you, the camera angles in the movie often unapologetically center on Plant's improbably bulging crotch as he sings (*Spinal Tap* armadillos, anyone?). Early on, Plant expressed some surprise that he should be seen as a sex symbol, saying "maybe if the audience can see a cock through a pair of trousers, then that must make you a sex symbol. Since I'm the only one of us who doesn't have a guitar or drums in front of mine, I suppose I started out with a bit more chance than anybody else in the band."[9] Despite this false modesty, by the time of the shooting of *The Song Remains the Same* in the summer of '73, Plant seemed to have adjusted to the label of sex symbol as he brought together a whole mess of the concepts we've been discussing here. In his own segment of the movie, which he insisted on writing, he portrays himself as a romanticised medieval Welsh soldier-monarch who overcomes his enemies using a sword (phallic image) given to him by a fair maiden (actually played by his wife), to whom he returns the weapon (a symbol of his virility, remember) to be rewarded with gold (the woman is controlling his sexuality, even commodifying him; the gold might also function as fetish-object), before he then leaves her and is on his own again (men and women are fundamentally incompatible, after all).

I'm Gonna Crawl

Contradictory sexualized symbols surround Led Zeppelin, the men and the music. The image on the cover of *Led Zeppelin I* shows the Hindenburg airship in flames; the potent male symbol has, literally, crashed and burned. On *Remasters* the blimp's shadow overlays a Yoni-shaped crop circle in a suggestively penetrative image. On *Led Zeppelin II* the image is potentially more macho. The dirigible is reprised, but this time as a vast blank in front of which is a sepia photo of world war one flying aces onto whose bodies the faces of the band are superimposed. The cover of *Houses of the Holy* con-

---

[8] Simon Frith, *Sound Effects: Youth, Leisure, and the Politics of Rock* (Pantheon, 1981), p. 227.

[9] Yorke, *Led Zeppelin*, p. 110.

tinues to attract controversy today because of the naked pre-pubescent children on the Giant's Causeway in Northern Ireland crawling across its cover; and the creepily nuclear family stare fixedly at the mysterious phallic object on their table on the sleeve of *Presence*. (The album was originally going to go by the even more suggestive title of *Obelisk*.) Onstage, too, there is a phallic forest of mic stands, guitar necks, and drumsticks, emphasising erect male agency and overcompensating in the face of the threat of castration. Plant promised—and delivered—every inch of his love to his audience.

Images of domination and control in Zeppelin's songs result in the active female body being both demonized and neutralized. The process of substituting an inanimate object as the object of desire allows the hero (in this case Plant) to conquer the enduring and horrific fear of castration. Exactly who is 'trampled underfoot' has become key—a symbolic relationship with a car ("Guaranteed to run for hours, mama it's a perfect size") is considerably less threatening for the male singer than one with a human female, and it is one that still delivers an almost orgasmic satisfaction: "Gun down on my gasoline, I believe I'm gonna crack a head." This chapter should, at the very least, offer a possible explanation for the band's repeated—almost compulsive—return to the impossibility of an unproblematic relationship between men and women. This theme was dramatised in their albums in new and innovative ways but also had at its heart age-old psychological and musical impulses and traditions. Human relationships transcend time and place, and, to use one last metaphor, whether it's the Sacher-Torte of early twentieth-century Vienna, or the Custard Pie of the English Midlands in the 1970s, the pie remains the same.

6

The Enviable Lives of Led Zeppelin?

SCOTT CALEF

We were buccaneer musicians, ready to try anything.

—ROBERT PLANT

Although Led Zeppelin had an image, and were zealous to cultivate it carefully, talk of the band's image fails to capture something
important, indefinable, and transcendent. More like a presence or
evocation of feeling than an image, it wasn't the kind of thing that
could be concocted by marketing mavens at Atlantic. Nor was it an
artificially created hype. In a lot of ways, Zeppelin's marketing
decisions and deliberately limited self-disclosures flew in the face
of conventional record-selling wisdom, and the band seemed quite
proud of that. Bound up with and reinforced by their music, Zep's
"image" nevertheless went way beyond the music (just as the music
itself transcended simple formulas like "acid blues", "progressive
rock," or "heavy metal"). The fact is, the band and its music were
cloaked in myth and mystery.

It's difficult to explain to anyone who hasn't felt it what I mean
by this aura or presence[1] surrounding the band, but to millions of
adolescent males like me, it was—and still is—deeply intoxicating.
Undoubtedly the Tolkien and the tarot, the black magic and dark
glamour, the runes and albums without writing all contributed. So
did the band's inaccessibility, anonymity, and refusals to grant

---

[1] According to Storm Thorgerson, who designed the cover art for *Presence*, the
album title "Presence" was meant to capture this feeling or aura that surrounded
the band.

75

interviews, release singles or appear on television. But it was more than all this, too.

Paradoxically—and paradoxes are quintessentially mysterious—despite being shrouded in secrecy and impenetrable, ancient magic, Led Zeppelin embodied what has now become a virtual cliché—they were rock stars.[2] More than any other band I can think of, they oozed it. They lived it. They taught me personally what it means to be a rock star and made me and tens of millions of others want to *be* rock stars. Hell, I still wish I was a rock star! On some level, even though I'm not a kid anymore, I have a hard time understanding how anyone could *not* want to be a rock star. My wife has no interest in rock stars, and being a rock star hasn't the slightest appeal for her. I think she might be from another planet, though.[3]

A huge part of being a rock star is, of course, being cool, and nobody was cooler than Led Zeppelin. They *looked* cool. You don't have to be good looking to look cool, and a lot of cool rock stars are, quite frankly, pretty ugly.[4] Looking like a god definitely doesn't hurt though, and the members of Led Zeppelin had that look. Even their *name* was cool. One day Peter Grant was doodling in his office and dropped the "a" from "Lead" and decided to go with "Led" because it looked better. And he was right. It does. By losing the second vowel, the name became mysterious (as well as pronounceable by the colonials).

But in addition to all of this, Zep and the rock-god lifestyle they embodied represented an ideal of freedom, at least to my teenaged mind. Led Zeppelin could seemingly do what they wanted, when they wanted, where they wanted, with anyone they wanted (especially—and this is important, people—*with women*). Their incredible wealth, combined with the exemption from the ordinary rules that their celebrity allowed (and perhaps encouraged), meant the band lived privileged lives exemplifying uninhibited and unabashed liberty.

---

[2] Andy Fyfe puts it well: "This was the conundrum: gods to their legion of fans, yet outside of that devoted army they were virtually unknown." Being a Led Zeppelin fan was like belonging to a secret society with millions of members!

[3] Needless to say, we don't really understand each other. In her defense, though, she claims that rock stars never seem to be very happy. She may have a point, and I want to come back to this in a bit.

[4] For some reason there're a lot of bad teeth in the rock biz. (I love you though, Keefe.) And Rick Ocasek? Gene Simmons without his makeup? Pretty scary. Zep were frickin' super models compared to these guys.

Sure, other rock bands were debauched and rowdy. The Who come to mind, and groups like the Stones more than lived up to their "bad boy" reputations. But Zeppelin kicked all their asses. For one thing, they were not only free to slash their rooms to shreds with samurai swords or toss the furniture off the balcony or piss on their airline seats mid-flight;[5] they were free *professionally*. Jimmy Page learned a valuable lesson from Mickey Most's imbecilic production of the Yardbird's *Little Games*. He insisted that Peter Grant secure the group a nearly unprecedented level of artistic independence.

Led Zeppelin maintained total control of their music, the manner of its release—for example, no singles in the UK—and the artwork that contained it. The Who, the Stones, Alice Cooper and AC/DC certainly were able to get away with things I couldn't get away with, but without diminishing the awesome music they created, few could match Zep's originality, eclecticism and breadth of imagination. Zep's raw talent and freedom to control all aspects of their musical output, combined with Jimmy Page's pioneering vision as a producer, resulted in one of the most stunningly original bands of their era, or any. There. I've said it, and I'll stand behind it.

Now I want to get philosophical. In fact, I am already. The freedom that was such a part of Zep's allure is, like the band itself, fundamentally mysterious. Everybody wants to be free. That's partly why we envy rock stars, and Zep in particular.[6] Their *work* is actually *fun*! They don't do it because they *have* to; they do it because they *want* to. And again, if they want to holiday in Martinique or take off in a Jeep through the Atlas Mountains or scribble on the paintings in a gallery with a magic marker, they can! They did! Now, here's the thing. We (at least many of us) tend to think that if you can do what you want, you're free and happy. Led Zeppelin could do what they wanted, so it stands to reason that they were happy and free. Happy and free lives are, all other things being

---

[5] Bonzo also pissed over a balcony at Tokyo's Byblos disco onto a DJ whose taste in music obviously differed from Bonham's.

[6] Also, because we know we're not that cool and wish we were. Being a fan identified with a band like Zeppelin and living vicariously through them provides an antidote to low self esteem and a way to get revenge on the kids in school who teased us because they were members of the "in" group and we weren't. That wasn't just me, was it?

equal, better than lives which are less happy or less free. Therefore, Zep's lives were better than the lives of most people. (Duh!) It's just not that complicated. But philosophers—frustrated non-rock-stars, all—can't leave things well enough alone, and ask "How reliable are these inferences?" Should the rest of us envy Led Zeppelin (at least, in their prime, circa. 1969–1975) for the fantasy lives they led, lives we can only pine for from afar?

Although I feel a certain temptation to try to disprove the idea to assuage my superego and the University administration (who may not groove on faculty running around wishing they could cut loose like Bonzo), in all honesty, I'm not so sure. Part of me thinks Zep basically had the right idea. It's easy for lesser mortals to try to diminish their Idols, whether out of resentment or a pathetic effort to redeem their own less-than-exciting lives. That's one reason we eventually needed the Punks. So we could spit on our heroes. What I'm going to try to do is be honest, and look at the philosophical arguments to see where they take us. When all is said and done, we may or may not wind up envying Zep. But the place to start is with the concept of freedom itself. What is freedom?

Tell Me that I'm Free to Ride

Since the time of John Locke (the philosopher, not the guy on *Lost*) it's been customary to distinguish two types of freedom, "strong" and "weak." Locke (1632–1704) illustrates as follows: Jimmy Page is in his suite at the Continental Hyatt House in LA with his latest pubescent paramour. Unbeknownst to him, Peter Grant has ordered that the door to his suite be sealed shut so Jimmy can't get out.[7] If anyone catches wind of the fact that Page is, uh, friends with a four-teen-year-old, nobody but Michael Jackson will understand. And having your guitar player in prison makes it hard to get to your gigs on time. Jimmy, however, doesn't know his door is locked, and couldn't care less, because he just wants some down time with Lori Lightning, and they've got all the room service they need for awhile.

---

[7] It seems something like this really happened. Nigel Williamson reports that "Grant insisted that she [Lori Maddox] was kept locked in a hotel room with a security guard on the door, fearing that if Page was caught with her, he may have difficulty gaining any further US work permits." *The Rough Guide to Led Zeppelin* (Rough Guides, 2007), p. 254.

Jimmy wants to stay in his room, and gets to do what he wants. Locke would say he's free in the "weak" sense. Weak freedom is being able to do what you want. For the sake of argument, assume that Jimmy wants to have sex with Lori and be left alone, and that's exactly what he gets. On the other hand, because the door is barred, he can't do otherwise. I don't mean they couldn't play backgammon or just cuddle instead. I mean he couldn't leave his suite, even if, contrary to fact, he wanted to. Locke would say Pagey lacks "strong" freedom (at least with respect to staying or leaving), because strong freedom is the ability to do otherwise than as we do and Page pretty much has to stay put.

Now, we might think Page is free as long as he doesn't try to leave and is ignorant of the fact that he's essentially caged.[8] Maybe Pagey only becomes unfree when he discovers he has no option but to stay. If we think this, we're making freedom a matter of psychology. It doesn't matter whether you're bolted in or not, it only matters whether you *know* that you are, and what you know is in part a matter of having beliefs, and beliefs are things in your head. (Well, maybe.) Locke takes a different view. Consider, he says, two scenarios, one where Page is happy to be confined to his room, and one where he wishes he could leave but can't. The difference, according to Locke, isn't that Page is free in the one scenario and unfree in the other; it's that in the first case Page is fortunate and in the second he's unfortunate. The happily imprisoned Page is lucky because the very thing he must do is exactly what he wants to do. The frustrated Page is unlucky because he doesn't want to do what he has to do. They're equally lacking in freedom, but in the one case that's experienced as an inconvenient hindrance and in the other it isn't.

Okay, well and good. There are these two types of freedom, strong and weak. What has this to do with whether rock stars, and especially Zeppelin, are free? We might agree that they have weak freedom, in the sense that they can generally do what they want. At least, they enjoy more weak freedom than most of their fans do because they're rich, adored, extremely creative, and so forth. Locke, and many others following his lead, think that it's strong

---

[8] It would be strange if the difference between a free man and an unfree one is that the free man is ignorant; we usually think of knowledge as liberating. But I suppose it's possible.

freedom that really matters, however; only strong freedom is "real" freedom. According to Locke, just being able to do what you want doesn't make you free; you have to be able to do otherwise. This line is plausible for several reasons.

For one, our interest in freedom is all tied up with ethics; we intuitively recognize that it makes no sense to praise or blame someone unless they could have done otherwise. Ethics, at least since Kant, doesn't mean doing what you want, but doing the right thing, even if you don't especially want to do it. On at least one occasion Led Zeppelin were scheduled to headline a gig for which another band was the opening act. LZ refused to play unless they could switch the order of the bill right before the concert and go on first. They did this because opening the show would leave more time later in the evening to jet off to their favorite club in New York and party.

Most people would probably blame the group for a shocking lack of professionalism, because they didn't have to do what they did. There was no necessity to it. If, on the other hand, they insist on playing first because Page has a mild case of food poisoning which they fear will worsen, we don't blame them. If Page is sick, they can't perform, and we don't hold people responsible for things they have no control over. Better the band plays first than not at all. Here the band has no choice; they have to go on first or risk disappointing the fans even more. They can't really do otherwise, and so aren't culpable for last-minute changes to the program.

This explains why it's useful to have a concept of strong freedom[9] but doesn't answer the question whether Zep are free. So consider the following: Suppose I'm at a Led Zeppelin concert, on the floor near the front, close to the stage. (I was: Seattle Kingdome, 1977!) The crowd surges at the first familiar notes of "Whole Lotta Love," and I get pushed in the back. This makes me bump you, and you spill your beer. You give me a glare and I yell into your ear, "SORRY MATE! COULDN'T HELP IT! I WAS SHOVED!" If you're a reasonable person, you might still be pissed

---

[9] Assuming we think ethics matters. Zep, however, seemed largely unconcerned about right and wrong—except when it came to bootleggers or promoters trying to steal from them. And where's the evidence that LZ suffered for their amorality? If ethics is a kind of scam, and if strong freedom is important only because ethics requires it, perhaps we shouldn't worry much about strong freedom. More on this below.

(in the American sense) but you won't blame me for the mishap. I didn't jostle you of my own free will; I was caused to do so by the surging crowd, and couldn't help it. To put it in a somewhat philosophical way, we might say that being *caused* to do something is excuse-providing. Because I was caused to bump you, I didn't do it freely, and therefore I'm not to blame. I have an excuse. Now consider a second scenario. Once again, we're at the concert and once again I bump you and make you spill your beer. You're about to punch me when I explain, "SORRY MATE! I MADE YOU SPILL YOUR BEER BECAUSE I THOUGHT IT'D BE FUNNY AND WANTED TO HUMILIATE YOU IN FRONT OF YOUR GIRL-FRIEND!" You, being a reasonable person, hit me. The fact that I *wanted* to make you spill your beer doesn't provide me with an excuse.

One way to interpret this scenario is to say that because I wanted to do it, I did it freely, and if I did it freely, I didn't have to do it, and therefore, I'm without excuse. But this assumes that if I have weak freedom I have strong freedom too, and earlier (when Pagey was locked in his suite at the Riot House) we noticed that this can be false. Besides, even if I want to do something and do it, that doesn't mean I do it freely. Maybe I really did want to make you spill your beer because I thought it'd be funny, but I bump into you not for that reason, but because someone shoves me into you. I had the desire, but that doesn't make my bumping into you a voluntary act. I still have an excuse because bumping you was caused by the crowd surge and not by my desire.

Another way to interpret the situation is: If I explain my action in terms of causes, I have an excuse. If I explain my action in terms of my reasons (for example, "I did it because I wanted to"), I don't have an excuse. Therefore, reasons are not causes of behavior! And if my desires don't cause my behavior, how can they account for my freedom? They could do so only if being free has nothing to do with how I act! This is very strange.

This can be put in terms of a logically valid syllogism: All Causes are Excuse-Providing-Events; No Reasons are Excuse-Providing-Events; Therefore, No Reasons are Causes. By the way, this suggests another argument that reasons are not causes of behavior. For causes are generally thought to be events—a cause occurs when something *happens*—and reasons are not events but states—psychological states of persons. A desire, for example, which might be a reason for doing something, is not an event, but a *condition* of the desiring agent. We might put it this way: desires are not "things" that happen to people but things that people *have*.

Ultimately, though, this is all beside the point. Everyone will agree that Zep had weak freedom. They could pretty much do what they wanted, and if doing what they wanted wasn't caused by their wanting it, who cares? For if their reasons didn't cause their behavior, neither do ours. It isn't as if they're worse off or less free than the rest of us. They're still the ones with the groupies, after all.

The other main reason philosophers think strong freedom is what we normally mean by freedom is that we don't usually choose our wants and desires. You either like "Tea for One" or you don't; nobody *decides* they're going to like a song. If we could do that, I'd choose to like the songs on *Presence* and *In Through the Out Door* more than I do. But I can't help it. Those albums have great moments, but they'll never appeal to me the way the first six do. But if we can't choose what we like or dislike, our desires and aversions, then how can the freedom to act on our desires constitute genuine freedom?

Maybe it can't. But this is a problem for both strong and weak freedom, and so strong freedom doesn't necessarily come out on top. Or at least, that's the situation if we think our reasons and desires affect our behavior. It's easy to see why. If what I do is *caused* by my desires, then given those desires I can't do otherwise! Granted, if I don't choose my desires it's hard to see why acting on them should make me free, as the advocate of weak freedom holds. But if I can't do otherwise given that I have them, I'm not free in the strong sense either. The result then seems to be that we're not really significantly free in either the strong or weak sense. If that's so, Zep aren't any more free than the rest of us, but neither are they less free. We're all in the same boat (except their boat probably has champagne and groupies).

But then, why is it so natural to think they have more freedom than I do? Maybe because I associate freedom with happiness, and I think they're likely to be happier than I am. Perhaps we're happy if our desires are satisfied, regardless of whether or not we choose those desires. Since, judging from afar, it certainly looks like rock stars get to satisfy their desires, they seem to be happy. If we say this, though, we'll also have to allow that my wife is happy if her desire to listen to Norah Jones is satisfied, even if she can't help liking Norah. (Can't help liking *Norah*? A funny kind of happiness in my book, but okay.)

Let's assume what seems plain enough—that the members of Led Zeppelin could for the most part do what they wanted. I'm not saying they never had to do anything they didn't want. Bonzo hated flying, but he had to fly. He sometimes hated being on the road and away from home, but tours happen. Plant may be sick to death of singing Stairway, but find it impossible to disappoint the fans. (And Wayne may want to *play* Stairway in a music shop, but be forbidden. "Stairway, denied!") Still, compared to you and me, Bonham, Jones, Page and Plant enjoyed a high level of weak freedom. If someone wants to disparage the rock'n'roll life by arguing that bands like Zep weren't free—that they were somehow victims of their own success, say—presumably it's strong freedom which is denied them. But why think the band lacked strong freedom? Or at any rate, that they lacked it more than the rest of us? And is strong freedom really as important as Locke and his followers make out?

There are reasons to be skeptical. First of all, strong freedom— the only freedom worth worrying about according to Lockeans— is purely hypothetical. Someone's free in the strong sense if they could've done otherwise than as they did. But in the whole history of the universe, *no one has ever done something different than what they did*! The advocate of strong freedom says free people have the ability not to do what they do. What kind of ability is that? How can I not do what I do? Ask yourself honestly: when was the last time you didn't do what you did? It's crazy! If Page is improvising during a solo, there are any number of note combinations he might select. But no matter how many solos he plays over the course of a concert, he'll never play a solo other than the one he played. So what does it mean to say that he's free if he can do this?

This actually seems to me important for the moral argument mentioned earlier. Remember how it goes: A link between strong freedom and morality is said to exist because it isn't our moral practice to blame or praise people when they couldn't have done anything else. But maybe morality is based on deeply confused notions about freedom, and maybe common thinking about morality is misguided. (Rock bands like Zep, in particular, might make this argument!) For if conventional moral reasoning rests upon Locke's idea of strong freedom, and if strong freedom is purely hypothetical and something for which we have no empirical evidence—because no one has ever observed anyone doing something other than they in fact did—then morality would seem to sit upon pretty flimsy foundations. Better would be to construct a moral theory based on something more solid.

If I make you spill your beer because I wanted to amuse myself, that's enough right there to make it wrong; whether or not I had to do it (whether, for example, given my desires, my jostling you was unpreventable) is irrelevant. Suppose Bonzo is sloppy drunk and out of control. If he punches someone for requesting an autograph, we don't say, "Well, he couldn't help it; he was wasted; he's not to blame."[10] We hold him accountable. That he couldn't help it, even if true, doesn't exonerate him. To the contrary, it's one of the things that makes the act so distasteful. For we wonder, what sort of foultempered chap can't help smashing an enthusiastic admirer and fan in the mouth?

The State of Nature Is in LA

Since a big part of Zep's libertinism manifests as a disregard for the usual rules of decorum, let's talk about what society gives and what it takes away from citizens in general. Jean-Jacques Rousseau (1712–1778) invites us to contrast society with a hypothetical, presocial condition he calls the "state of nature." In the state of nature, humans live as isolated individuals without social bonds or norms in a condition without law, religion, morality, technology, culture, communication, or even family. There are no economies, private property or concepts of ownership. According to Rousseau, people in the state of nature are relatively equal and free because the only inequalities that exist are physical—differences of strength, health, age, sensory acuity, height, and so on. The impact of these sorts of inequalities is minimal, however, because they don't result in social inequalities of wealth, education, political influence or in hierarchical structures like those in the military or business. Humans in the state of nature are free because prior to society there are no coercive social structures and no peer pressures or expectations. There are no police, priests, prying parents or copy-

---

[10] Actually, people do sometimes make these excuses, but they're almost always pretty lame. The proverbial "Oh, man, sorry I slept with your girlfriend last night. We were really drunk and it just kinda happened. Once we got goin' I just couldn't stop!" has never struck me as particularly genuine. Bastards!

right infringement attorneys. So, you can pretty much do what you want.

But what would we want to do? Since there's no society or culture to influence us, our choices and responses to our environment might be thought due to "human nature". One of Rousseau's predecessors, Thomas Hobbes (1588–1679), thought that humans were inherently selfish; consequently, in the state of nature people would be violent, greedy, and vain. Life without society, he argued, would be "solitary, poor, nasty, brutish and short."

Rousseau, however, astutely asks: What if there *is* no such thing as human nature? What if the very *idea* of "human nature" is itself a social or philosophical invention? To constitute human nature, a characteristic would have to be true of all humans in whatsoever condition we find them. It would be the "essence" of humanity, an immutable and invariant quality. But Rousseau doubts that unchanging qualities define us, arguing instead that humans are fundamentally altered when they enter society. We aren't static and unalterable beings; our "nature" is dynamic, evolving, and malleable.

Rousseau relents a little, and shows us something paradoxical in the process. He considers two promising candidates for human nature, construed as something that differentiates our species from other, non-human species. These candidates are freedom, and perfectibility.[11] Since Zep, and especially Page, were relentless in the pursuit of perfection, and since, as we discussed above, they at least seem to typify an ideal of freedom, Rousseau might be able to tell us something important about them.[12]

---

[11] It's common to think humans are unique by virtue of their rationality, but Rousseau disagrees. Animals, he argues, can reason since they can connect up ideas. Plant's dog Strider can infer it's dinner time when he hears the familiar sound of the can opener, and some believe even a hound can perform what logicians call a "disjunctive syllogism": It comes to a fork in the road, sniffs the first fork, then pursues its prey down the second. The thought process is: The fox either went this way or that way. It didn't go this way. Therefore, it must have gone that way!

[12] We can't really go into perfectibility here, but suffice to say that Rousseau thinks humans are constantly striving to improve themselves, and that this manifests not only in individual lives but culture as a whole. The problem with the relentless pursuit of perfection, though, is that it means we're always "becoming" and never "being." By trying to transcend and surpass our current level of talent, skill or perfection, we are striving to *be* what we *are not*. This amounts to self-negation, and is a symptom of our individual and collective dissatisfaction. The same factors are at play in Rousseau's account of freedom, which follows.

If freedom is human nature, freedom is what all humans have in common which makes them human. Animals, according to Rousseau, act purely according to instinct. They feel certain promptings of nature, and have no choice but to yield. Humans feel the same impulses, but unlike the brutes are able to acquiesce or resist. (Well, maybe not Bonzo, but most of us.) For example, if Robert Plant is aroused and wants to bed a groupie, he can refuse to act on this inclination out of respect for his wife. If Bonzo is in the middle of playing "Moby Dick" at Madison Square Garden and fancies a cold, frosty beer, he can resist the urge to stop playing, walk off stage, and quaff a cold one until after his (probably abbreviated!) solo. If Page, a vegetarian, is hungry but there's nothing around except a platter full of Slim Jims, he can choose not to eat until room service delivers his smoothie (well, actually a banana daiquiri with powered vitamins and protein). And if Jonesy is tired, he can force himself to stay awake to keep working on a string arrangement. Because humans can resist these instinctual urges for things like food, drink, sex and repose, we are free.

According to Rousseau, then, freedom is the capacity to oppose the promptings of nature, and thereby cancel or neutralize that which is natural. Because we can do this, we can assert our independence from nature and its causal control.

As Rousseau also points out, however, the freedom characteristic of humans carries with it certain risks; in particular, it makes possible self-destructive behavior. (The self-preservation instinct is our most powerful natural urge, and freedom, which can nullify that which is natural, enables us to act contrary to our best interests, and even our survival.) Let's look at some examples.

On the one hand, Rousseau argues, promiscuity is natural and monogamy unnatural. Since it is unnatural, marriage represents a kind of slavery, and particularly, the entrapment of men by women. Married people have surrendered their freedom. Though, with the exception of Page, the members of LZ were married, they didn't act like it. The rock life is a sexually unfettered one, and Led Zeppelin were nothing if not promiscuous. In this sense, they were liberated. Of course, this is only part of the story. The band sometimes went to epic lengths to deceive their wives and girlfriends, to the extent of producing fake itineraries for their partners with no LA dates and not subscribing to music weeklies that carried pictures of them in compromising situations. And though Page was "free" to seduce fourteen-year-old Lori Maddox, they had to hide in Pagey's hotel room and couldn't enjoy an ordinary social life together.[13] Beyond these limitations, though, Rousseau also argues that from the male perspective, in the state of nature, any woman is as good as any other. This is because, prior to society, aesthetic preferences and hierarchical standards of beauty didn't exist. Consequently, intercourse was a purely sexual act innocent of considerations of status. Certainly the band was not free of these sorts of desires. They wanted the hot chicks, and instructed road manager Richard Cole to let only attractive women backstage!

Alas, as Rousseau suggested, freedom can be our undoing. Consider drugs. The "natural" state of humans is a sober one. We take drugs, if we do, to alter our natural state and consciousness. Since freedom is displayed through our opposition to that which is natural, the ability to alter our natural state with drugs is the expression of freedom. But at the same time, since freedom which leads us away from the natural is most often detrimental to our wellbeing and happiness, this freedom is a freedom to destroy ourselves.[14] Though worshipped from afar, rock stars—or at least those heavily into drugs—are not so much to be envied as the popular imagination assumes.

Looked at another way, in abandoning that which is natural— a lifestyle dedicated to sobriety—we abandon our freedom. There's a paradox here. The ability to act unnaturally is a sign of freedom. But using our freedom to take drugs can result in a loss of freedom, since many drugs, after all, are addictive. As Dave Dickson notes, "Crowley discovered [heroin] is eventually going to destroy you, because you become its slave. The heroin stops working for you and you start working for it."[15] Drug use by rock bands has the appearance of freedom because the copious and obvious use of hard drugs by musicians amounts to a flagrant violation of the law. Since the law is an unnatural imposition on

---

[13] Whether Maddox was free is another matter. According to some accounts, she was virtually kidnapped by Zeppelin road manager Richard Cole who, absconding with her, presented her to Page.

[14] Rousseau argues that humans in the state of nature are generally healthier, stronger, more robust, and more content. Their few needs for food, drink, shelter and rest are easily satisfied. Most of social humans' infirmities, he argues, result from society itself, which gives us more ailments than cures.

[15] Quoted in Mick Wall, *When Giants Walked the Earth: A Biography of Led Zeppelin* (Orion, 2008), p. 371.

human behavior, to disregard it is to act "naturally" and outside of society's artificial constraints and coercive impositions. But insofar as the drugged person is in an unnatural state, the person is, on Rousseau's account, unfree. That's because, according to Rousseau, freedom is human *nature*, and therefore what is *natural* for humans. The drugged person is in an unnatural—and therefore unfree—state.

The paradox of freedom is that, because we have it, we can use it to enslave ourselves. One way we do this is by forming societies and entering into a social contract which obliges us not to act like Bonzo. Another way is to freely abandon our natural consciousness for a drug-induced and artificial substitute. But this unnatural state is, if persisted in, self-destructive. Sadly, we see this in the band, and not only in Bonzo's untimely death from alcohol poisoning. After *Physical Graffitti*—much of which was written and recorded several years earlier—as the group's heroin consumption increased, there was a marked drop-off in the quality of the group's music. Not that there weren't brilliant moments—"Achilles' Last Stand" is one of their greatest songs ever. But overall, the music, and the band itself, lost its joy. By the time Zeppelin got around to recording *Presence*, a lot of the magic had gone. The fantasy scenes filmed for *The Song Remains the Same* were half-hearted. Knebworth notwithstanding, the band was clearly in decline.

The notorious and deeply disturbing violence surrounding the band and its entourage can be analyzed in terms of Rousseau's account of freedom too. We tend to consider violence natural and law a necessary antidote to our inherent inclination to fight. Thomas Hobbes and Sigmund Freud certainly held this view, but in our culture it's come to seem almost common sense. If you think humans are given to spontaneous outbursts of fury or that we're evolutionarily hard-wired to beat the shit out of people we don't like, Led Zeppelin are acting in a completely natural way. We may not like it, but that's probably because we play by the rules and they make their own, and while we admire to a certain extent the liberty to do that, at the same time it seems unfair.

What's interesting, though, is that Rousseau actually doesn't think we're violent by nature. Rousseau's view is that in the state of nature we have an "innate repugnance to see any sensitive being suffer, and particularly other members of our own species." Like most other animals we have a kind of natural pity or compassion.

We have an aversion to suffering, even when the suffering isn't our own. Society, however, is based on private property, and property introduces inequality, envy, competition, pride, ambition and a callous willingness to put business interests ahead of human needs. Consequently, Rousseau thinks that when people leave the state of nature and enter into society, their natural pity is squelched or suppressed. This loss of compassion, coupled with the rise of vanity and the egoistic enjoyment in dominating others, actually results in an *increase* in the incidence of violence. Since violence is bad for business, and the wealthy can't very well have too many bandits running around without a conscience, religion, morality and law are created to compensate. That is to say, we construct an artificial and external social substitute for the natural pity that has been subordinated to the desire for profit. The main point is, in the state of nature compassion and sympathy flow spontaneously from our very being and are the natural expression of human nature. In the bosom of society, human nature is altered, and in consequence we need to construct a replacement for the sensitivity which has become attenuated. That's what the norms of religion, morality, and the law are. But since these purely conventional and external devices can't possibly have the force of the original and natural sentiments they replace, humans in society behave less humanely than in their original and pure, pre-societal state.

Now apply these lessons to Led Zeppelin. Bonzo smashes someone in the face without provocation and simply drops a handful of bills on the man's prone body as he walks away. Bonzo, Richard Cole, Peter Grant, and security goon John Bindon beat to a pulp an employee of Bill Graham's who reprimanded Grant's son for removing a sign from Zep's dressing room door in Oakland. Bonzo apparently attempts to rape Ellen Sanders, a journalist for *Life* magazine traveling with the band, on board the group's hired plane. Bonzo offers Benoit Gautier, a French employee of Atlantic records, heroin to snort while pretending to offer cocaine, a "joke" that clearly could have killed the man had he not discovered the ruse in time.

What are we to make of such "we are your overlords" conduct? On the one hand, we might think "boys will be boys" and that this sort of thing is only natural and to be expected. Rousseau, on the other hand, would say it's unnatural and symptomatic of an important impoverishment of the human psyche. Bonham's oft-times barbarous behavior shows he'd lost all sympathy. Unfortunately, the "rules" society has enacted to compensate fail miserably. The group's wealth, security detail, and well-practiced knack for making a quick getaway enabled them largely to avoid the consequences of such lawlessness. Although one of Bonzo's nicknames was "the Beast," for Rousseau, he was anything but. No animal would be so cruel without purpose.

Singing of the Good Things

For Rousseau, then, freedom is a mixed blessing. It makes us human and allows us to rise above the animals, and yet by offering the option of behaving unnaturally, it allows us to override our self-preservation instinct. That is, freedom permits us to act contrary to our own best interests. Socrates (469–399 B.C.E.) claims something similar. For Socrates, there's a big difference between doing as we please and doing what we really want. What we truly want, he thinks, is always something good, because no one wants to be harmed. What we please to do, on the other hand, is what seems good to us at the moment. But when what *seems* good to us at the time is not *really* beneficial but harmful, we're not doing what we want even though we're doing as we please. The point is, some pleasures are counterproductive if they don't further our true good, and determining whether they do or don't requires wisdom and discernment.[16]

If we're enamored of the Zeppelin lifestyle, we probably think Socrates was a buzz-kill busybody out to harsh everybody's mellow. Socrates would argue that he's keeping us from bondage. Living for pleasure, Socrates argues, is slavish, for we come to be ruled by our appetites when we should be master of them. Only through self-control can we achieve our long-range best interests instead of sacrificing them in the moment before the idol of instant gratification. Only the temperate person is free. The rest, in the words from "Nobody's Fault but Mine," have a monkey on their back.

Until now, I've been assuming that Zeppelin have weak freedom because they can do what they want. Socrates challenges this

---

[16] Of the four, John Paul Jones best exemplified the Socratic ideal of prudent forethought and good judgment. As Richard Cole observed, "Perhaps Jonesy was smarter than any of us, keeping his distance while the rest of us were gradually sinking into the quicksand . . .". Quoted in *When Giants Walked the Earth*, p. 335.

assumption. Admittedly, Zeppelin can do what they please, but for Socrates, that's not the same thing as doing what they want. If, as we defined it at the outset, being free in the weak sense is a matter of doing what we want—what we *really* want, that is—Zep, like most of us, may fall short. Just listen afresh to "For Your Life." If Zep, or any of us, do falter as we seek what is truly to be desired, Socrates would say the solution is philosophy. That alone can provide the wisdom to really get from life what we want. Philosophy liberates the soul. In short—loath as I am to admit it, especially in print—maybe my wife has a point. She thinks a lot of rock stars look miserable most of the time. If Zeppelin's hedonistic lifestyle didn't ultimately work to their advantage, only a fool would envy the life they led. Indeed, Socrates suggests, such are to be pitied. The enjoyment of pleasure in and of itself isn't enough to give life meaning. It can actually make life less meaningful if it detracts from, interferes with, or works against our having a good life.

Is there any evidence that Led Zeppelin's pursuit of pleasure did in fact interfere with their ability to lead a good life? Who am I to pass judgment? I don't know. But, somewhat reluctantly, I have to admit it's possible. Whether or not it was caused by the pursuit of pleasure, their superstardom came at a price. It made them tax-exiles from the homes they loved. Drugs and drink undoubtedly took their toll. I do know I'm not as envious now of their wealth, drugs, and women as when I was in high school. I do envy their musical talent and achievements. Now, when I still sometimes think I'd like to be a rock star, it isn't because I want to party like a rock star. It's because I want to make music. That was true of Zeppelin too, I'm sure. It's what brought them together. The rest—the excess—came later, and at least for the less-experienced Midlanders, somewhat as a surprise. Plant mused, "I've all this wonder of earthly plunder / will it leave us anything to show?" It's a fair question. Socrates thought, what we *really* want is always something good, and Zep's music is way beyond good, beyond transcendent. It's sublime. Wanting that is hard to fault. To quote Socrates again, whether the rest of it is worth pursuing at all is probably "known to no one, except the gods."

7
With Flames from the Dragon of Darkness

THEODORE SCHICK

> I was living it. That's all there is to it. It was my life—that fusion of magick and music.
>
> — JIMMY PAGE

Like the blues out of which it grew, rock'n'roll is considered by some to be the "devil's music"—a raucous, unbridled cacophony that incites its listeners to engage in lewd and lascivious acts. As further evidence for this appellation, they often cite the high regard with which rock's elite hold Aleister Crowley, the writer, occultist, and mountebank whom the British press dubbed, "the wickedest man in the world." Crowley, for example, appears on the cover of the Beatles' *Sergeant Pepper* album (which portrays a rogues gallery of the Beatles' heroes), Ozzy Osbourne pays homage to him in the song "Mr. Crowley" which appears on his *Blizzard of Ozz* album, and Led Zeppelin guitarist Jimmy Page says of Crowley: "I feel Aleister Crowley is a misunderstood genius of the twentieth century."[1] Page was so enamored of Crowley that he named the occult bookstore he owned—"The Equinox"—after one of Crowley's publications, he purchased one of Crowley's former residences— Boleskin Manor—located on the banks of Loch Ness in Scotland, and he amassed the largest known private collection of Crowley memorabilia. Crowley had a profound influence on Page and his music. To better understand this influence, let's see if we can clear

---

[1] Jimmy Page, quoted in John Ingham, "Technological Gypsy," *Sounds* (March 1976).

away some of the misunderstanding that surrounds Crowley and his philosophy.

The Great Beast 666

Born in 1875 to a wealthy English brewing family, Edward Alexander Crowley was raised by members of a conservative evangelical Christian sect known as the Plymouth Brethren. Like many fundamentalists, the Brethren practiced strict discipline and self-denial. The child Crowley was not allowed to play with anyone outside of the sect, and was required to study the Bible every day. His father, who became a preacher after retiring from the brewing business, died when he was twelve. Following the death of his father, Crowley became increasingly skeptical of the stories he read in the Bible and impatient with the code of conduct expected of him. He ultimately became so rebellious that his mother took to calling him "the Great Beast 666" (after the monster in the Book of Revelation), a name he later took for himself.

In 1895, Crowley enrolled at Trinity College, Cambridge. He had planned to pursue a degree in English literature, but in December 1896, he had a mystical experience and devoted himself instead to the study of the occult. In 1897 he left Cambridge after having changed his first name to Aleister—the Gaelic form of Alexander.

Crowley's interest in the occult led to his becoming a member of the Hermetic Order of the Golden Dawn—the pre-eminent occult organization of Victorian England—which counted among its members such notables as the poet William Butler Yeats, the writer Arthur Machen, and the pacifist Evelyn Underhill. There Crowley met Samuel Liddell MacGregor Mathers—the leader of the organization—who introduced him to the Western magical tradition.

Mathers had recently translated *The Book of the Sacred Magic of Abramelin the Mage*, a "grimoire" or book of magical spells written in the fifteenth century by a shadowy figure known as "Abraham the Jew." The book describes in detail a number of ceremonies or rituals that supposedly can invoke and control various spirits. By properly performing these rituals, one can allegedly fly, become invisible, open locks, find hidden treasure, and so on. It's all very Harry Potter, but for the members of the Golden Dawn—and for Crowley—it was all very real.

Many of the spells described use a talisman or symbol to bring about the desired effect. The assumption behind this practice is that

Magick: the science and art of causing change to occur in conformity w/ the will. [handwritten annotation]

the universe contains hidden forces that can be manipulated by using the appropriate implements. In this regard, the theory behind talismanic magic is similar to that which underlies modern science. Both seek to predict and control the world. Where it differs is in its belief that the forces controlling the world are spiritual rather than material in nature.

The products of stage magic are illusions, for they are brought about by deception and sleight of hand. The products of talismanic magic, however, are supposedly real, for they are said to be brought about by cause and effect. To distinguish real magic from stage magic, Crowley coined the term "magick," pronounced mage-ick.

In his *Magick in Theory and Practice*, Crowley defines magick as "the science and art of causing change to occur in conformity with the will." He fleshes this notion out as follows:

> What is a Magickal Operation? It may be defined as any event in nature which is brought to pass by Will. We must not exclude potato-growing or banking from our definition. Let us take a very simple example of a Magickal Act: that of a man blowing his nose.[2]

On this conception, we all practice magick. How can this be? William Burroughs, in an interview with Jimmy Page for *Crawdaddy*, explains:

> The underlying assumption of magic is the assertion of 'will' as the primary moving force in this universe—the deep conviction that nothing happens unless somebody or some being wills it to happen. To me this has always seemed self-evident. A chair does not move unless someone moves it. Neither does your physical body, which is composed of much the same materials, move unless you will it to move. Walking across the room is a magical operation. From the viewpoint of magic, no death, no illness, no misfortune, accident, war or riot is accidental. There are no accidents in the world of magic. And will is another word for animate energy. Rock stars are juggling fissionable material that could blow up at any time . . .[3]

According to the magical conception of the world, changes are caused by acts of will. Magick is simply a method of strengthening

---

[2] Aleister Crowley, *Magick in Theory and Practice* (Castle, 1991), p. 107.

[3] William Burroughs, "Rock Magic," *Crawdaddy* (June 1975).

and focusing one's will. By practicing magick, we supposedly can come to control bodies other than our own.

Page the Mage

Jimmy Page became acquainted with Crowley's theory of magick at a very young age. In an interview in *Melody Maker*, he reveals:

> My interest in the occult started when I was fifteen. I do not worship the devil but Magick does intrigue me. Magick of all kinds. I read *Magick in Theory and Practice* when I was about eleven years old but it wasn't for some years that I understood what it was all about.[4]

Eventually he started collecting Crowley's writings and works of art. His occult bookstore, "The Equinox," located at 4 Kensington St. in London, supposedly housed a number of books signed by Crowley.

The depth of Page's knowledge of the occult tradition became apparent with the release of the fourth Led Zeppelin album. People had criticized *Led Zeppelin III* because it hadn't been a direct continuation of the second. To indicate that the fourth album should be judged on its own merits, Led Zeppelin decided not to give it a name. But they wanted to put something on the inner bag, so Page suggested that each member choose a magical symbol to represent themselves.[5]

Robert Plant chose this symbol:

Known as the feather of Ma'at, the Egyptian Goddess of justice and fairness, it is used to represent writers because of the association between quills and writing.

John Bonham chose this symbol:

---

[4] Jimmy Page quoted in Michael Watts, *Melody Maker* (September 1974), http://victorian.fortunecity.com/updike/723/page.html (accessed March 18th, 2009).

[5] "Zoso—Jimmy Page's symbol from the *Led Zeppelin IV* album," www.inthe-light.co.nz/ledzep/zososymbol.htm (accessed March 18th, 2009).

The three interlocking circles normally represent a trinity: man, wife, child; Father, Son, Holy Ghost; Isis, Osiris, Horus; Brahma, Vishnu, Shiva. In Bonham's case, however, they may represent drums (or Ballantine beer).

John Paul Jones chose this symbol:

Known as the triquetta, it is used to symbolize someone of confidence and competence.

Page chose this symbol:

It's an ancient symbol of Saturn, the planet that rules the astrological sign under which Page was born: Capricorn. It can be found in the grimoire *The Red Dragon and The Black Hen* published in 1521 and reprinted in 1850. The Red Dragon (Dragon Rouge) is an ancient occult symbol and the name of a society based in Sweden. According to the society,

> The Red Dragon is a mythological entity which exists in all times and cultures. The Dragon can be viewed as a winged serpent. From the perspective of the history of religions the serpent is a symbol of the earth and the underworld. The eagle (and birds in general) are symbols of the heavens. The dragon is a unity of these two fundamental principles. The Dragon is a picture of the Hermetic principle "That which is below is like that which is above and that which is above is like that which is below." In China the dragon is a symbol of Tao, that which is beyond all terms and all polarities (Yin and Yang) but also is the force behind all. The Dragon represents the unknown and the hidden energy in man and in nature.[6]

During the 1973 tour, Page wore a suit that had a red dragon embroidered on its back.

Page also often wore these signs on his trousers:

---

[6] "What Does the Red Dragon Represent?" www.dragonrouge.net/english/general .htm (accessed March 18th, 2009).

The top symbol is another sign for Capricorn, the middle symbol is a sign for Scorpio, Page's ascendant sign, and the bottom sign is a sign for Cancer, Page's moon sign. (Page was born on January 9th, 1944 at 03:00 GMT in Heston, Middlesex.)

In an interview with *Guitar World*, Page comments on his use of symbols.

> GUITAR WORLD: Your use of symbols was very advanced. The sigil [symbols of occult powers] on *Led Zeppelin IV* and the embroidery on your stage clothes from that time period are good examples on how you left your mark on popular culture. It's something that major corporations are aggressively pursuing these days: using symbols as a form of branding.
>
> JIMMY PAGE: You mean talismanic magick? Yes, I knew what I was doing. There's no point in saying anything about it, because the more you discuss it, the more eccentric you appear to be. But the fact is—as far as I was concerned—it was working, so I used it. But it's really no different than people who wear ribbons around their wrists: it's a talismanic approach to something. Well let me amend that: it's not exactly the same thing, but it is in the same realm. I'll leave this subject by saying the four musical elements of Led Zeppelin making a fifth is magick into itself. That's the alchemical process.[7]

Alchemy is the occult precursor to modern chemistry which sought to turn base metals into gold or silver and to discover the elixir of life (which would grant one immortality). Succeeding in either of

---

[7] Jimmy Page, quoted in *Guitar World* (January 2008).

these goals requires producing something that is greater than the sum of its parts. Led Zeppelin, Page intimates, did just that.

The ultimate goal of magick isn't just to predict and control things. It's to understand the universe and one's place in it. Central to this quest is the belief that the universe at large—the macrocosm—is reflected in each individual thing—the microcosm. In the words of Hermes Trismegistus, one of the founders of the Hermetic or occult tradition in the West: "As above, so below." According to this tradition, by coming to know one's true self, one can come to know the true nature of reality.

Page considered himself to be a seeker of truth in the Hermetic tradition. This aspect of his character is reflected in the persona of the hermit which he adopts in the movie *The Song Remains the Same* and in the image of the hermit which appears on the inside cover of *Led Zeppelin IV*.

Page elucidates:

> **GUITAR WORLD:** Could we talk a little about the meaning behind your sequence [in *The Song Remains the Same* movie]?
>
> **PAGE:** To me, the significance is very clear, isn't it?

GUITAR WORLD: Well, I find it interesting that you were choosing to represent yourself as a hermit at a time when you were really quite a public figure.

PAGE: Well, I was hermetic. I was involved in the hermetic arts, but I wasn't a recluse. Or maybe I was . . . The image of the hermit that was used for the [inside cover] art-work on *Led Zeppelin IV* and in the movie actually has its origins in a painting of Christ called "The Light of the World," by the pre-Raphaelite artist William Holman Hunt. The imagery was later transferred to the Waite tarot deck [the most popular tarot deck in use in the English-speaking world]. My segment was supposed to be the aspirant going to the beacon of truth, which is represented by the hermit and his journey toward it. What I was trying to say through the transformation was that enlightenment can be achieved at any point in time; it just depends on when you want to access it. In other words you can always see the truth, but do you recognize it when you see it or do you have to reflect back on it later?

GUITAR WORLD: There was always a certain amount of speculation about your occult studies. It may have been subtle, but you weren't really hiding it.

PAGE: I was living it. That's all there is to it. It was my life—that fusion of magick and music.[8]

For Page, music was not just an emotional outlet. It was a path toward spiritual enlightenment. The path that he adopted, however, was the one outlined by Crowley.

Do What Thou Wilt

The Book of the Sacred Magic of Abramelin the Mage promises that if one faithfully performs all of the rituals described, one will receive a remarkable reward:

> If thou shalt perfectly observe these rules, all the following Symbols and an infinitude of others will be granted unto thee by thy Holy Guardian Angel; thou thus living for the Honour and Glory of the True and only God, for thine own good, and that of thy neighbour. Let the

---

[8] Jimmy Page quoted in *Guitar World* (January 2008).

Fear of God be ever before the eyes and the heart of him who shall possess this Divine Wisdom and Sacred Magic.

After leaving Cambridge, Crowley set about performing these rituals. In 1904, he reportedly received his reward—his Holy Guardian Angel, Aiwass, dictated to him *The Book of the Law* which became the basis of Crowley's philosophy. Known as Thelema (from the Greek word for will), its central teaching is: "Do what thou wilt shall be the whole of the law."

This phrase appears on the inner groove of the first side of the original pressing of *Led Zeppelin III*. Side 2 contains the phrase "So mote it be," a phrase used in the rituals of the *Ordo Templi Orientis* (*Order of the Temple of the East* or the *Order of Oriental Templars*), a secret society Crowley once headed. It means "So may it be." It has been rumored that Page is a member of this organization, but there seems to be no truth to this rumor.

Crowley borrowed the fundamental principle of his philosophy from the sixteenth-century monk and satirist François Rabelais. In his book *Gargantua and Pantagruel,* which recounts the adventures of two giants, Rabelais describes an abbey known as Theleme whose only rule was "Do what thou wilt." In this fictional abbey, the monks

rose out of their beds when they thought good; they did eat, drink, labour, sleep, when they had a mind to it, and were disposed for it. None did awake them, none did offer to constrain them to eat, drink, nor to do any other thing; for so had Gargantua established it. In all their rule and strictest tie of their order there was but this one clause to be observed, Do What Thou Wilt; because men that are free, well-born, and conversant in honest companies, have naturally an instinct and spur that prompteth them unto virtuous actions, and withdraws them from vice, which is called honour.[9]

Rabelais thought that this rule could form the basis of a utopia. Others, however, consider it to be a recipe for anarchy.

Libertinism

One who satisfies his desires and indulges his senses free of any restraint is known as a *libertine*. *The Book of the Law* seems to

---

[9] François Rabelais, *Gargantua and Pantagruel* (Everyman's Library, 1994).

encourage such behavior. In section 11.22 we read: "To worship me take wine and strange drugs . . . Be strong, O man, lust, enjoy things of sense and rapture, fear not that any God shall deny thee for this." Crowley apparently took this advice seriously. He chronicles his experiences with cocaine in his book *Diary of a Drug Fiend.* He extols the virtues of hashish in his article "The Psychology of Hashish." And he allegedly died a heroin addict. His sexual exploits were equally prodigious and varied. In his *Confessions,* he reveals that he could not go forty-eight hours without having sex, and he laments the amount of time he spent finding suitable partners. "The stupidity of having had to waste uncounted priceless hours in chasing what ought to have been brought to the back door every evening with the milk!" he complains.[10] Crowley was bisexual, and practiced "sex magick" which involves performing occult rituals during sex in an attempt to harness the power of the orgasm.

Crowley's libertine lifestyle is certainly part of what endears him to many rock stars. Rock'n'roll has always been about sex and drugs. On the road, both are hard to avoid and often are available in abundance. The members of Led Zeppelin availed themselves of both. As Jane Fryer notes in *Mail Online*:

> Led Zeppelin rewrote the book on rock'n'roll excess and extremes.
>   Constantly trumping one another with drink, drugs, sexual conquests, and unspeakable acts of debauchery, they made even the likes of Mick Jagger and Keith Richards look like Cliff Richard.[11]

The most legendary act of debauchery with which Led Zeppelin is associated is the famous "mudshark" incident. In a list of the top hundred sleaziest moments of rock, published by *Spin* magazine in 2000, it was rated Number One.

It seems that while staying at the Edgewater Inn in Seattle, where visitors could fish from their rooms, the members of Led Zeppelin tied up a groupie and stuffed pieces of fresh mudshark into her orifices. According to Snopes.com (the website devoted to checking urban legends for veracity), it didn't happen quite that

---

[10] Aleister Crowley, *The Confessions of Aleister Crowley: An Autohagiography* (Penguin, 1989), pp. 1, 12.

[11] Jane Freyer, "Led Zeppelin: "The Real Monsters of Rock," www.dailymail .co.uk/tvshowbiz/article-481880 (accessed March 18th, 2009).

way. Here's Led Zeppelin's manager, Richard Cole's version of the story:

> It wasn't Bonzo, [John Bonham] it was *me*. It wasn't shark parts anyway: It was the nose that got put in. We caught a lot of big sharks, at least two dozen, stuck coat hangers through the gills and left 'em in the closet . . . But the *true* shark story was that it wasn't even a shark. It was a red snapper and the chick happened to be a fucking redheaded broad with a ginger pussy. And that is the truth. Bonzo was in the room, but I did it. Mark Stein [of Vanilla Fudge] filmed the whole thing. And she *loved* it. It was like, "You'd like a bit of fucking, eh? Let's see how *your* red snapper likes *this* red snapper!" That was it. It was the *nose* of the fish, and that girl must have come twenty times. But it was nothing malicious or harmful, no way! No one was *ever* hurt.[12]

Many of the rumors regarding Led Zeppelin's antics may have even less truth to them than the mudshark tale, but there is little doubt that, at least on the road, they lived the life of libertines.

Libertarianism

Libertinism is not the only aspect of Crowley's philosophy that is attractive to rockers, however. His *libertarianism* also has great appeal. "Libertarianism" is a political philosophy that maintains that everyone has a right to do with their lives what they want, as long as they don't violate anyone else's rights. Some see Crowley's "Do what thou wilt shall be the whole of the law" as a laconic expression of this view. Brian Doherty, for example, writing in the libertarian magazine *Reason* says that:

> This credo is boldly libertarian, denying the authority of law to circumscribe individual freedom in any way. (To be sure, it lacks the usual proviso of "as long as you don't directly harm other people or their property.)"[13]

This aspect of Crowley's philosophy resonated with the Beatles. As John Lennon revealed in *Playboy* magazine: "the whole Beatle idea

---

[12] "Shark Tale," www.snopes.com/music/artists/mudshark.asp (accessed March 18th, 2009).

[13] Brian Doherty, "Do What I Wilt: The Individualist Authoritarianism of Aleister Crowley," *Reason* (February 2001), www.reason.com/news/show/27919 .html (accessed March 18th, 2009).

was to do what you want . . . do what thou wilt, as long as it doesn't hurt somebody"[14] The Beatles opposed oppression of all types, and they saw in Crowley one who had succeeded in throwing off the shackles of social convention.

Page, too, found Crowley's philosophy liberating. But the liberation he found was not social or political—it was spiritual. In a *Gig* interview, he explained:

> But what I can relate to is Crowley's system of self-liberation. In which repression is the greatest work of sin. It's like being in a job when you want to be doing something else. That's the area where the true will should come forward. And when you've discovered your true will you should just forge ahead like a steam train. If you put all your energies into it there's no doubt you'll succeed. Because that's your true will. It may take a little while to work out what that is, but when you discover it, it's all there.
>
> You know, when you realize what it is you're supposed to be here for. I mean, everyone's got a talent for something. Not necessarily artistic but whatever you care to say. And it's just a process of self-liberation. I mean, I just find his writings to be twentieth century. As a lot of the others weren't.[15]

Crowley's philosophy is self-liberating because it liberates the Self from the self. That is, it frees one's True Will from one's ego-based desires. Nothing stands in the way of those who have achieved this state. Like a steam train, they sweep away all obstacles in their path. To get a better idea of how this is supposed to work, let's take a look at the world view from which it springs.

The Perennial Philosophy

Thelema is a specific example of a type of philosophy that Aldous Huxley calls: "The Perennial Philosophy"; "perennial" because it has been around for at least 2,500 years. Also known as Hermetic or mystical philosophy, Huxley believed that this philosophy contained the basic beliefs common to all religions. He referred to

---

[14] John Lennon, quoted by David Sheff, *The Playboy Interviews with John Lennon and Yoko Ono* (Putnam, 1981) p. 61.

[15] Jimmy Page quoted in Chris Salewicz, "The Gig Inverview: Jimmy Page," *Gig* (May 1977).

these beliefs as the "Highest Common Factor in all preceding and subsequent theologies."[16] These beliefs include:

> First: the phenomenal world of matter and of individualized consciousness—the world of things and animals and men and even gods—is the manifestation of a Divine Ground within which all partial realities have their being, and apart from which they would be nonexistent.
>
> Second: human beings are capable not merely of knowing *about* the Divine Ground by inference; they can also realize its existence by a direct intuition, superior to discursive reasoning. This immediate knowledge unites the knower with that which is known.
>
> Third: man possesses a double nature, a phenomenal ego and an eternal Self, which is the inner man, the spirit, the spark of divinity within the soul. It is possible for a man, if he so desires, to identify himself with the spirit and therefore with the Divine Ground, which is of the same or like nature with the spirit.
>
> Fourth: man's life on earth has only one end and purpose: to identify himself with his eternal Self and so to come to unitive knowledge of the Divine Ground.[17]

All of these beliefs can be found in Crowley's philosophy of Thelema.

With regard to the dual nature of man, Thelema teaches that each person possesses a "True Will" or "Silent Self" that is distinct from one's conscious self or ego. One's True Will is one's destiny— it's one's ultimate purpose in life. For Crowley, it also represents the "spark of divinity" within each of us that Huxley spoke about. Crowley identifies this divine spark with the Holy Guardian Angel of *The Book of Sacred Magic of Abramelin the Mage*. Like all perennial philosophies, Thelema maintains that the ultimate goal of life is to understand the true nature of reality by understanding the true nature of the self. As Crowley puts it in *Magick in Theory and Practice*:

> There is a single main definition of the object of all magical Ritual. It is the uniting of the Microcosm with the Macrocosm. The Supreme and Complete Ritual is therefore the Invocation of the Holy Guardian Angel; or, in the language of Mysticism, Union with God.

---

[16] Aldous Huxley, *The Perennial Philosophy* (Harper and Row, 1945), p. vii.).

[17] Aldous Huxley, "Introduction," *The Song of God: Bhagavad-Gita* (Signet Classic, 2002), p. 13.

Because the Self (the microcosm) is a reflection of God (the macro-cosm), a complete knowledge of the Self produces a union with God.

One's True Will is supposedly divinely ordained. So following it should not lead to conflict. Just as the stars in the heavens move without colliding with one another, so a society in which everyone was following their true will should also be free from conflict. Page explains:

> I feel Aleister Crowley is a misunderstood genius of the twentieth cen-tury. Because his whole thing was liberation of the person, of the entity, and that restrictions would foul you up, lead to frustration which leads to violence, crime, mental breakdown, depending on what sort of makeup you have underneath. The further this age we're in now gets into technology and alienation, a lot of the points he's made seem to manifest themselves all down the line.[18]

The conflict we see around us is the result of people pursuing false desires created by conventional ways of thinking. If we all followed our True Will, then, like the monks in Rabelais's Abbey of Theleme, we would live in peace and harmony. This may be why Crowley did not include a proviso after "Do what thou wilt." He may have believed that if one follows one's True Will, one will not cause harm to others.

Discovering one's True Will is no easy task. The procedure described in *The Book of the Sacred Magic of Abramelin the Mage* takes months to complete. To speed up the process, Crowley wrote a number of rituals that are less time-consuming. As with the ritu-als practiced in Hinduism and Buddhism, they involve quieting the conscious self or ego. Crowley apparently thought that drug use could achieve the same effect. Thus Crowley's defenders claim that his drug use was less libertine than it seemed. Like Timothy Leary, the Harvard psychologist who experimented with LSD, Crowley, they say, was using drugs to explore inner space and unlock the secrets of the self.

Led Zeppelin's song "Stairway to Heaven" can be seen as allud-ing to many of these themes. The first stanza describes a lady whose only desire is for material goods—"she's sure that all that

---

[18] Jimmy Page, quoted in Jonh Ingham, "Jimmy Page: Technological Gypsy," *Sounds* (March 1976).

glitters is gold." All that matters to her is money, and she believes that money can buy anything, even salvation. She has no inkling of her True Will.

The second stanza suggests that her attitude may be mistaken; that there may be more to reality than just the material world, because "you know, sometimes words have two meanings." Consequently her desires may be misplaced.

The third stanza expresses the awakening of the spiritual side of her being. She has seen glimpses of a reality beyond the material—"rings of smoke through the trees"—and comes to realize that there may be more to life than the fulfillment of her earthly desires. She yearns to know her True Will.

The fourth stanza describes what happens when we come to know our True Will—"the Piper will lead us to reason." Crowley used the word "reason" to mean absolute truth. The "piper," then, would be our True Will (or our Holy Guardian Angel, which comes to the same thing). Once we realize our True Will, a new day will dawn because we will come to see ourselves and the world as they truly are. In such a condition we may indeed laugh at the silliness of our old pursuits.

The fifth stanza suggests that we will encounter obstacles on the path to self-realization—"a bustle in our hedgerow." We may even return to our old habits. But even if we do, we can always get back on the path to enlightenment.

The sixth stanza reminds us of the desire we all have to understand ourselves and our world—"the piper's calling you to join him."

The seventh stanza describes what awaits those who have taken the path to enlightenment and realized their True Will. Like the alchemist, they can turn anything into gold. The knowledge they attain is so complete that they become one with the universe—"all are one and one is all." Such a person is as solid as a rock because their will is unwavering.

True Selves: Found or Made?

What is a reasonable person to make of all this? Are there spiritual forces at work in the world that can be harnessed by casting spells? Do we possess a divinely inspired True Will? If we do, would following it be liberating? Let's consider spells first.

Spells, unlike prayers, do not involve asking divine beings for favors. They supposedly involve a direct manipulation of the spiritual forces that govern the universe. Like the material forces of electromagnetism and gravity, these forces supposedly work according to certain immutable laws. Thus the failure of a spell cannot be blamed on the ineffable will of a supernatural being. Like a scientific experiment, if a spell is done correctly, it should produce the same results every time. But there are no credible reports of a spell's ever working. No one has ever successfully—much less repeatedly—cast a spell under the controlled conditions needed to rule out fraud or deception. No one, for example, has ever successfully used magick to fly or become invisible even though many grimoires claim that this can be done by following the proper procedures.

Page may well have felt that his magick was working. There's no doubt that he and the members of Led Zeppelin became some of the most successful musicians of all time. But from the fact that something happened after the use of magick, it doesn't follow that it happened because of the use of magick. Your cold may go away after you wear a crystal around your neck, but that doesn't mean that it went away because you wore a crystal around your neck. To make such an argument is to commit the fallacy of false cause, also known as *post hoc ergo, propter hoc*—after this, therefore because of this. Page and the other members of Led Zeppelin may have become successful simply because they are remarkably creative and gifted musicians. To determine whether magick had anything to do with it, we'd need successful controlled experiments demonstrating the power of magick—and that we don't have.

There is a less literal and more plausible interpretation of magick, however—one suggested by Crowley himself. In his introduction to *The Goetia*, another grimoire translated by Mather, Crowley claims that "The spirits of the Goetia are portions of the human brain."[19] On this interpretation, the spells described in the grimoire don't call up any spirits that exist independently of the magician. Instead, they produce changes in the magician's brain that create the illusion of having invoked those spirits. In other words, the magician doesn't change anything in the external world. He merely changes his perception of it.

On this view, performing magick is no different than doing drugs. It may create the illusion of doing something, but that's very

---

[19] *The Goetia, The Lesser Key of Solomon the King, Lemegeton, Book I Clacicula Solomonis Regis*, edited and illustrated by Aliester Crowley (Weiser, 1995), p. 15.

different from actually doing it. Physicist Carl Sagan illustrates this point by suggesting that the notion that witches fly on broomsticks comes from the sensations produced by the herbs they used during their rituals:

> there is some evidence that atropine—one of the chief active ingredients in hemlock, foxglove, deadly nightshade, and jimson weed—induces the illusion of flying; and indeed such plants seem to have been the principal constituents of unguents self-administered to the genital mucosa by witches in the Middle Ages—who, rather than actually flying as they boasted, were in fact atropine-tripping.[20]

After they applied the atropine-laced unguent to their genitals, it's not difficult to imagine what the witches might have done with their broomsticks.

Altering your perception of the world can be an effective way of dealing with it, as anyone who's received a prescription from a psychiatrist can tell you. But if it impairs your ability to distinguish fantasy from reality, it can lead to ruin. Every action you take is based on beliefs about the nature of reality. If those beliefs are false, your actions are not likely to succeed. Crowley himself may have been the victim of his altered perception—he died a penniless heroin addict. Apparently he didn't master the spells leading to hidden treasure.

But what about the notion of True Will? Does each of us have a destiny that's written in the stars? Page remarked to Chris Welch that "There are powerful astrological forces at work within the band. I'm sure they had a lot to do with our success."[21] Are we part of some cosmic plan that was laid out before we were born? Not according to existentialism, one of the most influential philosophical movements of the twentieth century. Existentialists explicitly repudiate the idea that our lives were planned out by some supernatural force before we came into existence. Instead, they believe that we come into existence and then decide for ourselves how we are going to live our lives. This view is summed up in their slogan: existence precedes essence. Philosopher and Nobel prize-winning author, Jean-Paul Sartre, explains:

---

[20] Carl Sagan, *The Dragons of Eden* (Random House, 1977), p. 214.

[21] Quoted in Mick Wall, *When Giants Walked the Earth: A Biography of Led Zeppelin* (Orion Books, 2008), p. 263.

Atheistic existentialism, of which I am a representative, declares . . . that if God does not exist there is at least one being whose existence comes before its essence, a being which exists before it can be defined by any conception of it. That being is man or, as Heidegger has it, the human reality. What do we mean by saying that existence precedes essence? We mean that man first of all exists, encounters himself, surges up in the world and defines himself afterwards. If man as the existentialist sees him is not definable, it is because to begin with he is nothing. He will not be anything until later, and then he will be what he makes of himself. Thus, there is no human nature, because there is no God to have a conception of it. Man simply is. . . .Man is nothing else but that which he makes of himself. That is the first principle of existentialism.[22]

In Sartre's view, then, we have no True Will because there is no divine purpose that we are designed to serve. We have not been put here to do anyone's bidding. Consequently, each of us is responsible for our own fate.

But what if Sartre is wrong and we are part of a divine plan? Would following that plan be liberating? Not necessarily. Einstein explains:

I do not believe in freedom of will. Schopenhauer's words, "Man can indeed do what he wants, but he cannot want what he wants," accompany me in all life situations and console me in my dealings with people, even those that are really painful to me. This recognition of the unfreedom of the will protects me from taking myself and my fellow men too seriously as acting and judging individuals and losing good humor.[23]

According to Einstein, doing what you want does not make you free. Only if you want what you want—only if your wants are your own—can you act freely. But, like Schopenhauer, Einstein doesn't believe that we have the power to want what we want. In his view, we're unable to alter our programming. Consequently, he doesn't believe that we have free will.

Many disagree with this assessment. Known as metaphysical libertarians (to distinguish them from political libertarians), they

---

[22] Jean-Paul Sartre, "Existentialism and Humanism," *The Humanities in Contemporary Life* (Holt, Rinehart, 1960), p. 425.

[23] "Einstein on Freedom of the Will," *Harper's Magazine* (June 7th, 2007), http://harpers.org/archive/2007/06/hbi-einstein-quote.

believe that because we are self-conscious, we can be self-programming. Our self-consciousness not only allows us to be aware of what motivates us, but it gives us the power to decide whether we want to be motivated by those things. If we exercise that power, then—and only then—are we acting autonomously. (The word "autonomy" comes from the Greek words *autos* which means self and *nomos* which means rule or law. A Greek city state was said to be autonomous if they made their own laws. Similarly persons are autonomous if they are self-governing.)

All of us have desires for certain objects and states of affairs. Like Bonzo, for example, we may desire to smoke cigarettes, drink beer, or have sex as well as to be healthy, wealthy, or wise. These desires are often the product of nature or nurture. They may be hard-wired into our genetic code or they may have been acquired during the process of growing up. Regardless of where they came from, such desires are known as "first-order desires." Self-conscious creatures, like ourselves, however, have a remarkable ability: not only can we be aware of our first order desires, but we can decide whether we want to be motivated by them. That is, we can formulate second-order desires—desires about our first order desires. For example, we can formulate the desire *not* to have the desire to smoke. Such second-order desires indicate the sort of person we would like to be. According to Gerald Dworkin, as long as those desires are arrived at independently—as long as they aren't forced upon us by some sort of brain washing, for example—and as long as they accurately reflect the kind of person we aspire to become— the actions that flow from them are autonomous. For Dworkin, then, only those who formulate and act upon second order desires act freely, for only they are truly doing their own thing.[24]

The notion that we possess a True Will, then, is problematic. It suggests that there is a program we're designed to follow, and that following it would make us free. Existentialists suggest, on the contrary, that no such program exists and that even if it did, following it would not be liberating. If we had no hand in writing that program, following it would simply turn us into "loyal plastic robots," to borrow a line from Frank Zappa.

The most serious problem facing the notion of True Will, however, is that of identifying it. How can we tell whether we've found

---

[24] Gerald Dworkin, "Autonomy and Behavior Control," *Hastings Center Report* 6 (February 1976), pp. 23–28.

our True Will? If there's no way to distinguish our True Will from our ordinary will, then the claim that we should find it is vacuous, because we would have no way of knowing whether we've succeeded. Consider, for example, the fact that in 1958 Jimmy Page told Huw Wheldon on his BBC television program "All Your Own" that he wanted to go into biological research.[25] How do we know that biological research is not Jimmy Page's True Will? You might reply that his success as a musician indicates that's what he was destined to do. But how do we know that he wouldn't have been more successful as a biological researcher? Maybe he would have discovered the cure for cancer. The point is, if there's no way to identify your True Will, then the claim that it exists is no more plausible than the claim that there's an invisible, undetectable diamond buried in your back yard—not the sort of thing you want to spend your time digging for.

The mistake behind the belief in True Will is the belief that selves are found, not made. Our selves are not something we're born with, they're something we create. Who we are is determined by the kinds of choices we make. Our choices shape our characters which in turn influence the actions we perform. If we had no hand in shaping our characters, we cannot be held responsible for the actions that flow from them. Only if our actions are our own—only if we do our own thing—can our actions be free. Contrary to what Crowley and Page would have us believe, then, True Will cannot be imposed from without—it must come from within.

---

[25] "Jimmy Page the Research Biologist?" http://cf.q107.com/station/blog_ion_tech.cfm?bid=25507&m=11&y=2008 (accessed March 18th, 2009).

8
Magic Pages and Mythic Plants

RANDALL E. AUXIER

The occult dabbling of Jimmy Page is well known, if not very well understood. Since Jimmy doesn't tell *me* (or anyone else) what's up with all that, it leaves us guessing—and oh how we *love* to guess. He doesn't talk about this stuff any more, so it is hard to know whether his much publicized dalliance with the devil was just a phase he went through, or whether it has more permanent meaning for him.

During Zeppelin's heyday, these dark doings were very much the engine of gossip. I was attracted to it (the gossip, not the occult) as a teenager, and yes, also disturbed—one of oh-so-many things that vexed the not-quite-children we all were. Like many of you, I played my copy of "Stairway to Heaven" backwards and yes, I heard "Here's to my sweet Satan." It's there. Mr. Plant can deny it 'til the cows get sacrificed, but I know what I'm hearing.

Maybe the whole point was to get us wondering and keep us talking, you know? Thinking back on it, maybe it was just a brilliant marketing ploy. Zep was horrified of being perceived as a "pop" band and they were intent on staying on the shadowy side of rock celebrity. I mean, these are the guys who compared the Rolling Stones to Bobby Goldsboro, since they were competing for time on the same airwaves, after all. This brings a groan from the real rockers. If ever a band had sympathy for the devil himself, it was the Stones, and here we have Robert Plant saying they're just namby-pamby. I don't think so, fellas. But that was pure posturing, and Plant knew it even at the time. We have enough historical distance now to know the difference between neighborhood trash talking and genuine judgment. Really, you can't diss a band, or a human being, more profoundly than with a comparison to Bobby Goldsboro. And besides, the Stones were "borrowing" from the Mississippi Delta well before Zeppelin had any similar notions.

It Makes Me Wonder

But, back to the deal at the crossroads (see "Nobody's Fault but Mine"): Was Page's self presentation as a Devotee of the Dark just more marketing? If so, then it makes sense why Plant and Jones were always saying they didn't know much about what Page was doing—which was believable for Jones, but not so much for Plant. If Page was holding black mass (or some such) Plant would have known it—and *Plant* knew that *we* knew that *he* would *know*, which makes his disclaimers seem feigned. All a game? Let's entertain that idea for a moment.

By all accounts Jimmy Page was very much in control of the "idea of the band." He knew exactly what he wanted Zep to be, from the start, and Page was a brilliant strategist when it came to shaping the public perception of the band. So the cynical interpretation of Page's dealings in black magic is that it was nothing at all. He just muddied the waters around himself (and the band) to make them appear deep. (The true adept in this technique is Sting—toss in a couple of literary references and suddenly people think you're a genius.) Maybe Page aimed to attract rebellious, hedonistic teens to the image he was crafting, to set Zeppelin apart from the Stones, The Who, and their other "competitors." Being "bad boys" wasn't enough by 1970. Zeppelin was plenty bad, but that had all been done. They needed to be *devilishly* bad in order to get the upper hand on their bad boy competition. So they conjured an image of mystery and black magic (to go with the usual sex and drugs) and we bought it. Or at least, that's how the cynical story would go.

But I don't believe it. Even if Page understood that he could accomplish certain goals in publicity by making himself a man of mystery, using Plant to deflect and dismiss, and thereby intensify the intrigue, I also think that the *reason* the black magic strategy occurred to Page has to do with a certain path he was already following. Page and Plant were genuinely curious (in different ways), very smart and quite creative. They wanted to know things and understand things. In different ways, they valued the past and all that lay in the grit and the dust of history. If I'm wrong, Page should feel free to contradict me, when he reads this (in my dreams). I think the more reasonable story is that Page and Plant together went on parallel quests for their roots, and I have a theory about how and why it happened. I think that Page's predilections were magical while Plant's were mythical. Myth and magic are related but very different, as we shall see.

The Magic Runes Are Writ in Gold

Here 's what I want to do, boys and girls (mainly boys, I'm sure; Zeppelin is something of an acquired taste for girls—at least if my long-ago girlfriends and long-time espoused are any barometer). I want to tell the tale of Page and Plant in a general way, using what *everyone* learns about myth and magic when we start looking into it, when we get beyond the particular version of myth and magic that drew us in. As we learn more, we move into a more general understanding of what magic really is and why myth is so pervasive in human history and in our present experience. When we've had a general look at myth and magic, it becomes clearer how and why Page moved toward, into, and through (black?) magic. But this is not an exposition on Aleister Crowley (1875–1947). Page found Crowley and became a fan, but it wasn't just a fascination with the life and views of a single practitioner. Rather, Page and Crowley had some things in common, like a fascination with magic, but more importantly, they shared a fascination with "will."

Not many philosophers write about magic. It doesn't often appear because most philosophers regard belief in magic as a quaint superstition that has been replaced by a more rational understanding of cause and effect. And philosophers have always been more concerned about present and future knowledge than about our ill-informed past. The past is the record of error, they think, but the future holds the prospect of progress in knowledge and wisdom. So one could say that there is a fairly stark difference between philosophy, as a *practice*, and the *history* of philosophy, which is the written record of what practicing philosophers have thought about over the millennia. Studying the history of philosophy is important for learning the practice, just as it is in art or religion or poetry or science, but the *practice* is not just the repetition of the history. No one would say that a historian of poetry is a poet, and so it is with philosophy, generally speaking. So most philosophers learn their history and then take stock of the present and future and set themselves to thinking. Other *fans* of philosophy may spend their lives studying, say, Plato or Aristotle, but these are simply scholars, unless they do *more* than explain to us what Plato or Aristotle thought, and when and why.

The Beads of Time Pass Slow

In the last two centuries, however, *some* philosophers (not just scholars) have become increasingly convinced that understanding our past is more crucial to understanding our present than we had previously suspected. These philosophers are called "historicists," and their numbers are ever on the rise. Some of the historicists are infamous, like Karl Marx, but most historicists work in the shadow (if not the shade) of the greater project of elaborating the triumph of science and scientific reasoning. Sometimes historicists *like* science and sometimes they don't, but all of them are interested in questions about roots and origins of ideas and culture. If science gives us knowledge, it's because *we* invented science, and long before we had science, we had a desire to *control* nature. The story of how we become better and better at controlling nature is the story of science, and before science there was, you guessed it, magic. Before there was history there was myth—the stories we tell ourselves about how we came to be the way we are. So, these two kinds of thinking, scientific and historical, are themselves the end results of magic and myth. The story of how magic *becomes* science and how myth becomes history is not just a tale of correcting our errors; it's about how we take a basic mode of human thinking and refine it until it becomes a more reliable tool for manipulating nature and understanding time.

Among the historicists, most do not worry about our distant past, the part that is shrouded in myth. But a few historicists have become interested in those questions and have expounded philosophies that take myth and magic into account. The most *successful* and famous of these philosophers was a fellow named Ernst Cassirer (1874–1945). Yes, those life dates make him Crowley's close contemporary. There were a lot of people interested in myth and magic belonging to that generation. It isn't an accident. You could well think of Cassirer as Dr. Jekyll to Crowley's Mr. Hyde. When I say "successful," what I mean is that Cassirer talked about magic and myth seriously and managed to remain *respectable* in the estimation of, well, everyone. Almost every other philosopher who has attempted to include myth and magic in his philosophy as something important, something that contributes in a positive way to our progress, has been bounced out of the company of respectable inquirers. The reason Cassirer has remained "legitimate" is that he wrote so many renowned books on science and math and history that no one was quite willing to dismiss him when he went on about myth and magic. But very few philosophers still study all that stuff. I'm not going to quote Cassirer much in what follows, or even explicitly mention him, but I want you to be alerted that most of what I have to say about magic and myth came from his books.[1]

Your Head Is Humming, and It Won't Go

I will get to Cassirer's theories in a few minutes, but first I want to visit a few points about music and philosophy. Page and Plant never were philosophers, of course, nothing of the kind. A musician is a kind of practicing artist, as we all know. A musician who only plays and perfects music written by *others* is sort of like a scholar who only studies and explains the ideas of other people. It preserves culture, having many people who basically re-enact the past before our eyes—whether it's a string quartet playing Beethoven or a Zeppelin tribute band (or a philosophy teacher yacking on about Plato). All musicians begin this way—playing what others have written, training their bodies to do what has been done before, and then awaiting an experience of the *thoughts* that gave rise to that music, or accompany the playing of it, or which followed it. A part of understanding how a musician got the "idea" for this or that piece of music depends on enacting the music oneself. That's what makes your head hum. A music critic who cannot play or sing will never really "get it."

If you want to understand the blues, for example, you have to sit down and learn how to play them, and then think about how it feels to play that way, and then ask yourself how that kind of bodily expression symbolizes *other* experiences in life that a person might have. If re-enactment is all you ever do, you don't really

---

[1] Cassirer is pretty difficult to read, and his books are pretty long, but if you are dead set upon finding out more, the shorter book is *An Essay on Man* (Yale University Press, 1944). But the coolest stuff on magic comes from a much longer work, *The Philosophy of Symbolic Forms*, four volumes (Yale University Press, 1955–1996), especially Volume 2.

"have the blues," but if you play well enough there's a genuine experience that you and your audience will share, sort of a remembrance of the *possibility* of the blues. It's an *appreciation*, not the true blues, but appreciation is very important. Another way to put it is that such a performance isn't *magic*, but it *reminds* us of the magic, or to put it in overly precise words, it is magic*al* but not actual magic. Remember this point!

If You Listen Very Hard

I choose the example of blues for a reason, of course. Obviously, Page and Plant collaborated on an "appreciation" of this sort (and this is the kindest word one can employ for the practice of borrowing so liberally from one's colleagues). As Page said in *Guitar World* in 1998, "As a musician, I'm only a product of my influences." There's a John Lee Hooker–Willie Dixon–Howlin' Wolf–Lead Belly–Albert King–Blind Willie Johnson–Robert Johnson–Sonny Boy Williamson–Memphis Minnie thing going on here. We all know that Zep had to settle out of court more than once (most notoriously for "Whole Lotta Love" taken from Willie Dixon, without credit). Their cheery "appreciations" were regularly offered without credit or compensation to those who were being so richly "appreciated." Page said that "bluesmen borrowed from each other constantly and it's the same with jazz." The singer/songwriter Danny Dolinger put the point a little more acutely when he said "any songwriter who doesn't admit to being a thief is *also* a liar." So listen hard and you'll be able to call the tune.

There's the sense both of history and of re-enactment in Zeppelin's blues tributes, but it's a new plant that grows from old roots, the rhizome theory of musical originality. This is what makes Led Zeppelin a roots band, but it is a radical re-invention of the old plant that pops up into the sunlight here—or perhaps the plant is really a nightshade. In any case, the fruit has been desirable, and it doesn't taste like the blues. In the same way, a Plato scholar enacts an appreciation of Plato, along with his readers or the hearers of his lecture. If he sticks to explaining Plato, putting as little of himself into it as possible, it is philosophic*al* but not quite philosophy. There's always a vital connection, but also a difference between the history of a symbolic form and its original enactment in the present. We can't quite repeat history and no ritual is perfect. Obviously, then, no two concerts are ever the same, and when we drop back in time from the concert to the rehearsals, to the arranging, and regress to the experience of creating the music and the lyrics to begin with, we will approach a widening gap between what *has been* and what *will be*.

Magic, for whatever else it does, arcs across the gap between what has been and what will be, and it does so by employing the means of what *is*, what exists in any present moment—the ideas, the materials, the will power. Magic is an art of bringing the will to bear on what *is* so as to connect what *was* to what *will be*. In short, magic is literally an art of *timing*. To *time*, to temporalize, actively, is to link past, present and future into an experience, and to will is to discern the element in those connections that is both causal in its power and not fully necessitated by the combination of circumstances. Where more than one thing *can* happen, "will" is a name we give to the cause of the thing that actually *does* happen.

If We All Call the Tune

In a very real sense, all serious musicians believe in magic. That's because they believe in the power of the *will* (whatever it is), when added to technique and repetition, to cause the future in ways that can amaze even the one who is doing the willing. It's not re-enactment. Speaking as a musician, and others will bear this out, countless times I have found myself playing things I have never heard before, never thought about, and upon realizing that such a moment was unfolding, I always try to *stay out of the way* so it will last. I'm *willing* what is happening (my part of it at least, since most often it happens with the whole band), and the willing is *causing* it, in some weird way, but it's not something I can fully understand with my intellect.

Everyone has experiences like this, but in musicians it becomes patterned, noticeable, and sought after. What musicians discover is that the will can be *generalized*, as can its power, its *efficacy*. In ordinary life we get accustomed to using our wills in very specific ways—I will that I should type the next word, and I do. It doesn't seem like magic because it's so mundane. Everyone expects his own will to have at least enough causal power to pull off simple, direct tasks, and to use present means to join past to future. If I will something a little less immediate—say, I decide to get myself a cup of coffee—a bunch of intervening acts lie between me and that end goal. I have to use my will to execute a whole series of equally mundane acts, all of which I understand pretty well, and in the end, I should succeed in getting my coffee. Hold on a second, I'm going to try it out. It's 6:30 in the morning, this essay is overdue, and I need a cup of coffee. I'll let you know whether this works. . . . . Okay, I'm back. It *did* work. No one would call it magic these days, but what I just did is pretty difficult to explain completely. Ask any philosopher or neuroscientist or physicist.

The example of stringing individual acts together, willing each act individually, so as to bring about a specific end is *not* the "generalizing of will" musicians experience. What I just did was fairly mechanical, without much spontaneity or creativity. I also didn't create any *symbols* in doing it, and as a result, there isn't a patterned energy left behind by my actions that can be re-used in the future. If I had left a symbol, there would be something surviving the process that could be used again by anyone who knows how to *read* the symbol.[2] Remember *that* point too, if you would. A symbol is a repository of energy left behind from an activity of willing.

So the goal of getting coffee is general in the sense that it depends on a combination of intermediate actions, but as each action is done, the goal becomes more and more concrete, more within my mundane powers. It only seems magical when I lack the means to attain the end. On the other hand, if I sit here and attempt to will world peace, the means, the intermediate actions, are not within my power, and so my will fails to cause it. For all I know, there might be one thing I could do that would start a chain of events resulting in world peace, but I sort of doubt it. I would probably need a *miracle*—a suspension of natural order—to get *that*, not magic, which works with the natural order of things.

Sometimes All of Our Thoughts Are Misgiven

But what *can* my will cause? How powerful is it? Are some people's wills more powerful than others? Surely they are. Are there things we can learn that will enhance the causal power of our personal wills? Of course there are. That's why we learned to read and write. The command of language we have is proportional to the

---

[2] I know that the emptier coffee pot is a symbol I left behind, and my wife can read that symbol, and I am well aware that having now written down the entire episode, I actually left behind a bunch of symbols that you are reading. Humor me here, okay? Pretend that I didn't write about it and that I live alone.

efficacy of our wills in social situations. And yet, even this doesn't strike us as "magic," right? Agreed. But it's still a source of some mystery as to how all this happens. If I should ever come to the (unwarranted) conclusion that scientific ideas of cause and effect can explain everything that occurs, including the workings of will, I will have ceased entirely to believe in magic. Let's hope that we never come to that point. Magic becomes science, increasingly, but as it does, it opens up larger questions about the efficacy of will that science does not explain.

Magic is safe for the foreseeable future, especially among musicians. The sort of experience that leads serious musicians to believe in magic is *not* the increased efficacy of the personal will that comes from learning, from practicing, from watching and hearing others play and repeating or varying their licks. That is "technique" and more like a practical science. In the case of Jimmy Page (and Clapton, and Beck, and so many others), Bert Weedon's *Play in a Day* guitar instruction book was *not* the source of the magic. Nor did the magic come from repeating and mastering Robert Johnson's licks. No, it's something bigger.

The magic happens when a musician is playing, under control, normally enough, and something in the moment detaches from his conscious intentions, he lets go, and no one thinks out or intends the combinations and movements that then occur—and no one *could*—but what happens also *isn't* an accident. Notes and finger movements start reeling out, almost of their own accord, but not quite. A musician hits a zone, a level in which what is happening is beyond his own understanding, and beyond his ordinary abilities, but not quite beyond his will. This can happen when he's playing alone, but it also happens when musicians are playing in groups, and, more astonishingly, sometimes it happens to two or three or *all* of them at the same time. Experienced musicians know what to do when this occurs: (1) get your mind out of the way and let it happen; (2) stay in the zone as long as you can; and (3) enjoy it because it won't last forever, but it *might* last for the rest of the evening.

The experience isn't magic*al*, it is actual magic, in a sense to be explained. The difference is that the techniques involved *co-operate* with the present patterns and energies of existence (including the moods of audience and musicians, lighting, and acoustics), and all this *co-operates* with the past in ways that go beyond the mundane efficacy of the individual will (or even the "group will").

Forces and powers are co-operating that normally resist our wills, or are at least are normally unavailable for our use, but in these instances of "magic," the will has been generalized in ways that tap into those forces. It happens. Ask any musician. And that is the experience that makes music so addictive.

The Voices of Those Who Stand Looking

When magic happens, the musical instrument (including the voice) becomes a channel for *generalizing* will, extending its influence beyond the normal range. When groups of instruments are wielded by the right prestidigitators, in true concert, their efficacy grows beyond what any mechanical combination of wills can consciously intend or even understand. Chanting is a good, primitive example of the compounding of will that occurs in groups, but so is singing hymns in church. In the same way that three violins played slightly out of tune will tend to draw one another into proper tune as an effect (in individual reality, each remains out of tune), the combination of many voices brings about efficacious effects that are not reducible to the individual, isolated events that compose the general pattern. This "experience" (of the whole being greater than the sum of the parts) occurs in all kinds of group settings, but the point is that it is not mere ritual, not simple re-enactment, not magic*al*, but actual magic.

It isn't hard to understand how Jimmy Page got addicted to this experience of magic, along with so many other things—back then, his was an addiction-prone personality. The predilections of musicians for drugs are fairly well documented, and indeed, one can see how altering the state of one's consciousness might make it easier to get one's *thinking* out of the way so that the larger forces can take over. Thinking, reflection, and conscious willing all get in the way of this experience. Drugs work, sometimes and for some people. So does alcohol. Anything that tends to unweave and loosen the edges of consciousness may create avenues by which peripheral possibilities for action come into greater efficacy. We begin to act without the mediation of thought. And we may like it too.

Musicians come in all kinds, just like normal people, and Jimmy Page is a recognizable type—a Type A musician. He's smart, creative, talented, and very much *in control*. Every successful rock band has at least one musician of this type, sometimes more. But Page knows that control of the "small" variety is the enemy of big magic, so, like all Type A's who also want to experience magic, he is at war within himself: the part that insists upon precision, discipline, exactness (the session player, the middle class Anglican), is against the side that wants magic, the Jimmy Page of Led Zeppelin (most nights). If drugs can get Session Jimmy to take a hiatus and let Zeppelin Jimmy come out and play, then maybe the drugs do the trick. I'm not defending it; I'm just saying it makes sense to me.

The Dark Lord Rides in Force Tonight

Yet, Page is the sort of person who wants to know *why* there is magic sometimes and not other times. Because he's so Type A, he also wants control over it, to be able to *make* it happen, to extend the power of his will until all the obstacles that lie between him and the experience are under his power. It's not surprising that such a person would be drawn to the likes of Aleister Crowley, who had a similar sort of personality. Reading Crowley's ideas about "true will" would resonate with anyone who wanted to know how and why, especially for the purposes of control. We could psychoanalyze Jimmy if we wanted to, but I see no point in that. Everyone has insecurities and unfulfilled desires, and just about everyone is looking to extend his or her will and gain control over things that threaten or please us. Most of us are pretty obsessive when it comes to matters we really care about. And when we reach the limits of our personal influence, nearly all of us begin to strategize about how to get wider circumstances to co-operate with our plans. In short, we'll resort to magic of some sort or another.

And here—I hope my family and colleagues won't be shocked—I will confess that I think the broad philosophical outline of Crowley's thought is probably defensible. We philosophers pay too little attention to those human powers that lie below the level of intellect and understanding, and the will, *whatever it is*, is among those powers. The simple fact of our experience is: the will *has* efficacy in the world, it originates in something like desire, and it is not just a mechanical series of individual actions strung together for the achievement of ends. Will *exists* in a general form that can draw people (and perhaps also other natural forces) into co-operation. In short, if by "magic" we mean "efficacious generalized will operating beyond the reach of intellectual and scientific explanation," then magic *exists*. Page is no more superstitious than you are. He was just more curious than most people about *how* to get this strange phenomenon working and under his control. Whether he *still is* I don't know.

To Bring the Balance Back

There are other types of musicians who just aren't vexed by the issue of *controlling* the magic. In fact, most musicians accept the affordances of magic as gifts, unearned, unmerited, and always to be enjoyed. They don't spend their days wondering how to master the magic or arrange their generalized wills. Instead, they just show up at rehearsal or a gig in a hopeful frame of mind and wait to see if anything happens. If enough time goes by with no magic, they'll find another group of musicians or change the style of music they play, or even quit for a while. But Page isn't like this. He's driven. There is something of Faust in his lust for magical control. Jones and Bonham weren't like this, however. Apparently, everyone knew from the first rehearsal that Zeppelin was going to be magic. The first song they ever played was "Train Kept a-Rollin'." Jones said that Jimmy "counted it out and the room just exploded. There were lots of silly grins and 'oh yeah man, this is it.' It was pretty bloody obvious from the first number that it was going to work."[3] In short, it was magic. Real magic, not just magic*al*.

One last point about magic before we move on to myth: The legends are true. Over time, dabbling with magic will drain you of the life force. It has a (more or less) natural explanation. If you constantly use your own body as the conduit for the organization of efficacious energies that are beyond your ability to understand, the delicate balance is disrupted between your power of understanding (and rational life) and the efficacy of your own desire (which is growing all the time as you indulge it). Your behavior will become erratic because your understanding has been locked in the basement to keep it out of the way of the magic. In time, this disruption of the balance between desire and reflection will affect your judgment, and you will not *know* what is and is *not* within the scope of your will. You will make bad choices. You will begin to lose it. A few years of this and you'll look about like Jimmy Page

---

[3] Most of my factual information about Zeppelin and my quotes come from Nigel Williamson, *The Rough Guide to Led Zeppelin* (Rough Guides, 2007). This was from p. 42. If you haven't read this book, all I can say is, I couldn't put it down.

did in 1977, completely drained of the organized energies that sustain life. I hope you survive, and I am glad he did.

Don't Be Alarmed Now

You wouldn't know it from the way I've been going on about it, but magic isn't very important in the grand scheme of things. It's a collection of techniques for connecting the past to the future by means of resources (including ideas and materials) that exist in the present. But the mechanical ways in which past and future are connected by the present are much more pervasive than the magic. Our wills are not very strong in comparison to natural laws, like gravitation, as you may have noticed. Involving no obvious share of will, natural causes are also easier to predict. Even our magic*al* experience falls short of magic, which is to say that it involves mainly setting our efficacious wills to the task of closely repeating what has existed in the past while largely ignoring whatever novelty and creative possibilities the present situation contains. It is more like mechanism than magic. We play our music not in the moment, but just as we rehearsed it. Magic is rare, and it is also fleeting—*unless it leaves a symbol.*

I said earlier that a symbol concentrates a vital pattern of energy that can be re-used, liberated in any present moment from its physical cocoon and revitalized by the efficacy of the will. That sounds so mystical, but it's quite mundane. Let me prove it. Do something for me, would ya? Just raise your right hand and circle your index finger in the air, like the gesture meaning "whoop-de-doo," or "so what?" I'll wait while you do it. Go ahead.

Okay, are you done? Look, if you actually did it, you just proved my point. I wrote some words on my computer, it was 9:12 A.M., Central Daylight Time, July 7th, 2009. At whatever time and day and year it is where you are (Hell, I might even be dead by now), you released the pattern of energy I created at some point in the past. In the meantime, the energy pattern, and its efficacy, just sort of sat around in various places inside a bunch of copies of *Led Zeppelin and Philosophy*, that don't even exist yet as I'm writing this. There's an extra sort of mystery, beyond magic, that is involved in the way that symbols (like words) can somehow store energies and efficaciousness, and how those symbols actually can preserve and carry forward not only the causal history of their making (in this case, all the printing and distribution processes) but also the concentrated *will* of the symbolizer (in this case, that would be me). Anyone who symbolizes, and that would be all of us, not only believes in magic, practically speaking, but also believes that the past, dead as it may be, remains active in the present and affects the future.

The Piper's Calling You to Join Him

The belief in magic is just one of *thousands* of manifestations of "mythic consciousness," which provided the basis of human civilization. Mythic consciousness is still very much with us, then, and it shows up most tangibly when we "believe" what symbols tell us. In the broad domain of our mythic consciousness, the world is not composed of atoms and chemicals, but of *wills*. Knowing that dead people communicate their wills to us all the time is a pretty clear example. I mean, I get a clear picture of what Bonzo's *will* was (what he wanted all of us to *hear* and feel) every time I put on a recording (which is a symbol) of his solo on "Moby Dick."

When we recognize that we can re-vitalize the will of the dead, we also realize that we cannot be certain that the natural features of our world are *not* symbols too, living manifestations of the will of some other being whose language and symbols are difficult for us to recognize. If you have even the least doubt that there may exist, right now, in the present, symbols created by a will or a power that is non-human, then mythic consciousness is operative in your life and self-understanding. Myth does not mean "falsehood," it means that the past is connected to the present *for us* by a symbolizing power we don't fully understand. That power is somehow concentrated in certain kinds of physical existences that can be ordered in ways that make it possible for others to release some of their efficacy at later times.

Sometimes Words Have Two Meanings

Robert Plant works at the level of myth in a much more conscious way than most people. That's because he's a lyricist who likes to emphasize that mysterious symbolic vitality in some of the lyrics he writes. Plant has a marked tendency to draw upon archetypal images. These are symbols that take in, concentrate, and intensify the causal efficacy of many less powerful symbols. Just as a collection of *wills* can create magic that is beyond the power of an individual will, some *symbols* can concentrate the meaning and vitality of many unconnected symbols. Plant did this with poetry, but it is well worth remarking that Jimmy Page was a talented visual artist (he didn't spend eighteen months in art school for nothing), and those amazing covers to the LZ albums were usually his design concepts.

The point is that Page was no simple magician, he is himself a fine creator of powerful, archetypal symbols. I'm pretty happy to have the original "functioning" covers for *Led Zeppelin III* and *Physical Graffiti*. Yet, the driving force behind the use of poetic lyrical symbols was really Plant. The manipulation of words is a gentler magic than the manipulation of current public perception (Page's Faustian need). But lyrics have a magic all their own that can complement the more aggressive living magic of concert and recording and press.

It was Plant who brought the bucolic Welsh countryside into the creative process of the group. Literally, Plant supplied the plants, the herbs and roots, for Page's magic spells. These came in the form of setting, of the connection to nature, and the affection for simplicity and health, and the poetry of light over darkness. Plant has often been described as a hippie, a sort of "Summer of Love" refugee, a bit of sunshine to complement Page's nighttime prowlings. One sometimes wishes that Pink Floyd had a member like Plant. The "hippie" thing may be more image than reality, but I think it's got a basis in fact because I can discern its results. The music is almost always darker than the lyrics. It is surprising how much peace, love and understanding, even anti-war sentiment, is present in the lyrics themselves. There's an especially heavy dose of "love," as we all know—all kinds of love, done in every conceivable way with almost any candidate. Here's a point where Page and Plant seem to agree: eros. On the other hand, any male who has ever been between twenty and twenty-nine years old can see how likely this point of agreement is.

I have to confess here that I hardly ever paid attention to the lyrics of Led Zeppelin's songs before I began writing this chapter. There are a few exceptions, like "Stairway to Heaven," but mainly, I did what most people do. I would pick up a few lines here and there, as they emerged from the music into articulateness, but I had no idea what Plant was on about, really. I knew there were lots of archetypes in the lyrics, but I also knew that he was more intent upon making his voice the fourth instrument in the band. It wasn't about the lyrics, it was about the way the whole thing sounded and felt, and Plant knew that very well. In other words, even in studio recordings, the mythic had to be subordinate to the magic. And yet, the lyrics still had to be good. There needed to be depth and organization and concentrated power in the symbols, and there *was*.

Plant's lyrics are not great poetry by any stretch, but they're pretty good symbolizations. What I mean is that when the lyrics are read, and considered in relation to the musical feelings, they usually enhance one's overall sense of the whole. Knowing the lyrics does not disappoint the listener. The group all contributed to the lyrics, but I think it's fair to say that, since Plant was in charge of their final delivery, he was also in charge of their final form. Once in a while the group would indulge its love of archetypes. We see it in songs like "The Battle of Evermore," and "Kashmir," and "Achilles' Last Stand." Even a pop song (sorry fellows, you were a pop band too, and you know it[4]) like "All My Love" was almost entirely written in archetypes. Even in the bluesy tunes, images and archetypes from Celtic, Indian, Nordic, and even Christian mythology would surface.

Our mythic consciousness, for whatever else it is, leads us to *expect* our symbols to bear meaning. It's nothing short of the physical graffiti we leave behind, knowing it is a time capsule. To organize the physical world into symbols represents a commitment to the transmission of meaning across eons of time, and that is why the ones who do it with a sense of purpose, like Plant does, can rightly claim "this is a song of hope," in introducing "Stairway to Heaven." Another way of putting the point is that there is no science without magic and there is no history without myth. "Science" is a word we use when we are *ignoring* our own faith in the greater meaning of the natural world and seeking, like a bunch of sadists, its unconditional submission to our all-encompassing wills. "Magic" is a word we might use when we are being a little more humble and less domineering. Similarly, "history" is a word we employ when we are pretending to know the past *as* past, and ignoring the mediation and power of the symbols by which it is

---

[4] It's not so bad, really. Some pop symbols are pretty cool. As my friend Ryan Hesketh says, "the shoes of pop stars dance like the spoons of a psychopath on a plate of tragedy."

freed into our present understanding. "Myth" is a word we might use when we are being a little more conscious of our dependence upon processes we don't fully understand.

As We Wind on Down the Road

So, philosophers emerge from the history of philosophy, scientists from the history of science, and musicians from the history of music. In trying to burst out of the past and into the present and future, a crisis point will always arrive, a place where the artist or thinker will ask what he or she *really* has to say, something that is original, something that hasn't been said before, something that involves great risk. The risk is in creating symbols. It's risky because repeating what the "great ones" have done will always garner praise, when it is performed even marginally well. But to attempt something new is to risk failure, criticism, obscurity, shame, to make oneself vulnerable to derisive laughter, ridicule. So they made up four symbols for Page, Jones, Bonham, and Plant. Some people have laughed at and ridiculed and scoffed when the group said that the name of the album just *is* those four symbols. I am not one of them. I'm no longer a troubled adolescent, but I still think the album is magic.

9
Presence

SCOTT CALEF

For in fact what is man in nature? A Nothing in comparison with the Infinite, an All in comparison with the Nothing, a mean between nothing and everything.

—Pascal, *Pensées*

When Led Zeppelin released *Presence* in 1976, I have to be honest: I wasn't in love with the album art.

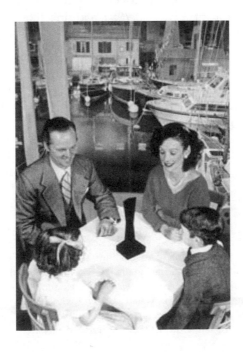

Black obelisk or no, who wanted to look at a bunch of pictures of school teachers, bourgeois families in suits sitting down to dinner, and old guys in factories and banks? I probably thought "THE OBJECT" was supposed to make some kind of profound statement, but the graphics felt more like a deliberate attempt to create an enigma than a natural and genuine expression of the band's undeniable mystique. In other words, it seemed contrived and manipulative. The cover warned that the platter within was likely to be a let down, but that was inconceivable! I'd been utterly enthralled and possessed by everything Zeppelin had done to that point.

When I actually put it on and began listening to "Achilles' Last Stand" for the first time, I was both ecstatic and bewildered. Ecstatic that, judging right from the opening arpeggio, this promised to be as magical an album as any they'd ever done.[1] But what was up with the cover? It bugged me. How could a band so cool be so, well, into photos from old *Look* and *Life* magazines? How hip is that? And what had this rather boring and conservative family on the cover to do with music as epic as "Achilles' Last Stand"? "The Object", which presumably was the key to it all, didn't seem to fit the band's image, at least not like the ruins of *Houses*, the runes and Hermit of *IV*, the sheer novelty of the cover for *III*, or the explosive eruption of *Led Zeppelin I*. I didn't like feeling—for the first time—that my heroes, like Achilles himself, might have a vulnerable heel and be fallible after all.

But hey! I was a junior in high school. What did I know? Now, after years of studying philosophy, the cover art for *Presence* still isn't my favorite aesthetically, but it's a hell of a lot more interesting than I thought when it first came out. Which is good to know, because Zep cared a lot about their album art and, much to the chagrin of execs at Atlantic, were damned inflexible about what did and didn't appear on it.[2] *IV* was held up for months because the

---

[1] Sadly, apart from the guitar solos, after "Achilles" most of the rest of the album didn't hold up. Moral for all you kids out there: Stay off the heroin!

[2] Zep largely were at liberty to call the shots because of their well-nigh unprecedented deal with Atlantic giving the band complete artistic control, not only over their music, but the manner of its release (for example, no singles in the UK) and art design. Page, in particular, was dissatisfied with the cover of *III*, which he decried as "teeny-boppish," and thereafter the band was much more exacting and uncompromising in dictating the look of the finished product.

band and its management wouldn't allow any writing on it. *Houses of the Holy* was delayed for months because the designers *couldn't manage to capture the right shade of orange*! And the release of *Presence*, true to form, was also postponed for months because of problems with the artwork.[3]

Page, in particular, recognized the significance of sleeve design and how it could contribute to or detract from the band's overall image. My experience above is testimony that he was right. It's different now in the age of downloads (nostalgic sigh), but when Zep were recording, public access to the band was largely mediated through their album covers and sleeves. I, being a fanatic, was somewhat the exception because I religiously read music rags like *Creem, Hit Parader*, and *Circus*. But Zep rarely gave interviews, and early on decided not to appear on television. They were thus largely inaccessible when not touring (and largely inaccessible even then if you didn't live near a metropolis or manage to buy tickets the first hour they went on sale).

Though songs like Stairway are hardly self-interpreting, a lot of LZ's music speaks for itself. When it comes to their album covers, however—that aspect of their output that we can actually see and touch—interesting philosophical issues pop up right away. And there's nowhere better to start than *Presence*, as philosophically-titled an album as ever has been.

Didn't Take Too Long 'Fore I Found Out What People Mean by . . . "Presence"!

In everyday use, the word "presence" usually refers to an eerie, felt but unseen spiritual phenomenon, like a ghost or demon. We sense a presence when we feel an uncanny energy or emanation surrounding a person or place. "Presence" can also refer to the company of some person of high or distinguished rank, like a royal or noble, or the space around them. So, one might be ushered into the King's presence. More generally, though, to talk like a dictionary, presence is "the fact or condition of being present."

---

[3] According to *The Rough Guide to Led Zeppelin* "a six-month delay ensued between finishing the record and its release due, once again, in large part to problems with the sleeve design" (p. 182). It's unclear how there could have been a delay of *six* months, though, if recording concluded the day before Thanksgiving, mixing occurred in December, and the album was released at the end of March.

Presence was a great name for Zep's seventh album for at least three reasons. First, it was recorded while Plant was still in a cast and being pushed around in a wheelchair following a near-fatal traffic accident in Rhodes nine months earlier.[4] As he talked about the album with Lisa Robinson he explained, "I've had time to see. Before I was always bowled over with the sheer impetuousness of everything we did, of what we are, and what was created around it. That was knocked off course. . . . [there was] a period of contemplation where I was wondering, 'Christ, is it all through? Is it ended?' And as such the album is full of energy, because of that primal fight within me to get back" (*Rough Guide*, p. 181).

Previously, the band had moved so quickly and "impetuously" they didn't necessarily contemplate where they were going. True, Jimmy Page had in mind a broad musical blueprint for his new band even before he found the personnel to implement it. Still, Zep retained a freshness and spontaneity. Their trajectory was so steep, and their rocket-fueled ascent so quick, that they were swept away and along, acting on impulse and instinct. Plant says he was bowled over by "what we are." What they were is "rampaging rock gods,"[5] and gods are supposed to be immortal. But now Plant wondered "Is it ended?" As Andy Fyfe puts it, "Here was a man weighing up his life."[6] Robert's brush with death aroused, and allowed time for, philosophical contemplation. He was thankful he and his family had survived,[7] that they were all still "pre-

---

[4] The accident occurred on August 4th, 1975. *Presence* was released March 31st 1976 in the US, April 5th in the UK.

[5] Andy Fyfe, *When The Levee Breaks: The Making of Led Zeppelin IV* (A Cappella, 2003), p. 175. A rock god—a god made of stone—is an idol. Zep were certainly that. And arguably, this is the significance of the black obelisk on *Presence*—an "obsessional object" meant to convey the aura and larger-than-life majesty of the band. To see the band or listen to their music is to take darshan.

[6] *When the Levee Breaks*, p. 174. Fyfe goes on to note that the band's "mortality had for the first time been brought very close to their attention" (p. 175). Perhaps, but this isn't obvious. The group nearly perished driving through a blizzard in Washington state in 1969, Robert Plant was badly injured in an earlier auto accident on January 31st, 1970, returning home from a Spirit concert in Birmingham, and John Paul Jones's father, Joe Baldwin, died in August 1970. Significantly, given later events surrounding the death of Robert's son Karak, all four members of the band attended the funeral.

[7] Robert had wanted to call the new album *Thanksgiving*, both because it was completed on the eve of the American holiday, but also because the "presence" of the record gave evidence of how much they had to be thankful for.

sent." That he was alive and able to make a record was itself a present—a gift from on high.

Storm Thorgerson, co-founder of Hipgnosis, and seminal designer of numerous, iconic rock album covers for bands like Pink Floyd, Black Sabbath, and Genesis, had this to say about the album art for *Presence*, which he helped create: the black obsessional object which reappears in various places on the album communicates through its ambiguity "a deep and powerful resonance which was . . . eminently appropriate for the mighty Led Zeppelin."[8] The art directors had always felt that there was a special aura surrounding Zeppelin, and the concept "Presence" conveyed that nicely. Just as "presence" can refer to the company of an august personage like God or the King, it can also refer to rock stars. To see Zeppelin was to be in the presence of greatness.

Third, when the cover scheme had largely been decided upon, there was talk of naming the album "Obelisk," but according to Jimmy Page, "I held out for *Presence*. You think about more than just a symbol that way." Mick Wall goes on to add, "And of course, the acknowledgement of a 'presence' had more occult resonance than a mere 'object'."[9]

Both Plant and Page emphasize, in different ways, that *Presence* is philosophical. Plant's lyrics flowed from the contemplation inspired by his physical trauma and lively experience of mortality. Page, perhaps gesturing back to the "runes" of the fourth album, insisted on the title *"Presence"* because it makes you think, and think about what is real (as opposed to what is "symbolized"). His clearly stated purpose was to provoke thought, and thought about something beyond a mere symbol to what the symbol represents. If the title "Obelisk" would have focused attention on a symbol, *"Presence"* is, by contrast, more than a symbol. Presence is what is; Presence is Being.

Whole Lotta Holes

This is profound, but invites the inevitable question: What's the Obelisk and what does it symbolize? If we know that, Page hints,

---

[8] Storm Thorgerson and Aubrey Powell, *For the Love of Vinyl: The Album Art of Hipgnosis* (Picturebox, 2008), p. 126.

[9] Mick Wall, *When Giants Walked the Earth: A Biography of Led Zeppelin* (Orion, 2008), p. 353

we know something about the nature of reality, a reality with "occult resonance."

Storm Thorgerson offers the following explanation: "There are no shadows nor mouldings on the object, just flat black—hence it is a hole. Not a presence (an object) but an absence (a hole)" (*For the Love of Vinyl*, p. 122). This is philosophically arresting, and all the more so since holes seem to permeate Zep's album art. The most obvious example, of course, is the cover for *III*, where there are *literally* holes in the outer cardboard allowing illustrations and icons from the gyrating wheel to be glimpsed. Turn the wheel and different images come and go, appear and disappear, are present, then absent. A similar concept was used on *Physical Graffiti*, where the windows in the Brownstone buildings were *cut out* and aligned with rectangular pictures on the inner sleeves. This created the illusion of observing through the windows—which were literally *open*—various oddities in the rooms within. The band's self-titled debut features a pointillist representation of the ruptured Hindenburg, smoke and flame hemorrhaging through the hole in its side. Large, circular, cistern-like holes in the rocks of the Giant's Causeway are conspicuous on the front and rear covers of *Houses of the Holy*. Their thematic prominence is emphasized by the suggestion that the nearest child is climbing out of one. On the back of the remastered *Coda* CD, black LPs seem adrift like lily pads on a milky white ether or foggy sea of light. The records themselves look somewhat like round holes, set against their white backdrop, but more significantly, the spindle holes in the records are highlighted graphically by laser-like beams of light radiating from their centers. In addition, the stylized lettering that spells CODA on the front renders the "O" and the "D" virtually indistinguishable, so here we have essentially two circles. Clearly and unambiguously, out of nine studio albums, holes figure prominently in the design of six: the debut, *III*, *Houses of the Holy*, *Physical Graffiti*, *Presence*, and *Coda*. Without too much of a stretch, we can add *IV*, *Remasters* and the *Early Days* compilation too. All four of the symbols which constitute the unpronounceable "name" of the fourth album, for example, contain circles—a total of seven in all. A circle is like a ring, and a ring, like a donut, has a hole. And if we're counting circles, don't forget the crop-circle design for the *Zep Remasters* box set. The box depicts a series of connected circular patches of flattened crops over which the phallic shadow of a zeppelin looms. The shade of the inflated airship graphically "penetrates" a yonilike circle with a ring within its disc. The crop circle design's clear insinuation of the female genitalia is consonant with the hole motif we've seen repeatedly on other releases. (Although, given that, the one woman to appear on *IV*—Sandy Denny—is represented by the only symbol *without* a circle-hole.) Finally, the *Early Days* compilation depicts the band members as astronauts, explorers of the vast, dark, empty nothingness of infinite space—the yawning, cosmic vacuum or hole that comprises most of reality.

Erik Davis agrees that holes feature prominently in the iconography of *IV*'s symbols, although he speaks of discs as well as rings and holes: "the only design element shared by all four sigils . . . is the disc. Page's two rings even have holes in their centers." Thus, he quips, "a sigil is a graven image of energy . . . a lot like a rock record"[10] Indeed, the fact that the first four albums are essentially untitled itself indicates a lack, a void, an absence. The notorious four symbols on the fourth album, "seem to communicate something without saying anything at all" (p. 26). And according to Jimmy Page, even the name Led Zeppelin doesn't mean anything. What matters is the music. If that was good, he insisted, they could have called themselves the Vegetables or Cabbages and it wouldn't have mattered.

In light of all this, the "metaphysical status" of the strange, black, trophy-like monolith from *Presence* is certainly intriguing. On the one hand, it's clearly an object; indeed, Swan Song copyrighted it as "The Object." And it *looks* like an object on the inner bag, where it casts a shadow, reflects light, has edges, and so on. On the defaced photos, which Hipgnosis altered to include this alien entity, as well as on the front and back cover shots specially created for the album, the Object is clearly tangible because the school teacher, the doctor, and the young ladies at the record party and in the field of daffodils all grasp or touch it. On the other hand the art designer, Storm Thorgerson, has told us it's a hole, and he ought to know. In the photos that look like they've come from old *National Geographic* and *Life* magazines, the "object" doesn't cast a shadow. (This is particularly noticeable in the picture of the alpine "scientists" seemingly taking measurements from it. The stool on which the "object" rests casts a distinct shadow, but there's none from the "thing" under investigation.) In these shots the

---

[10] The title of Davis's book is the title is the unpronounceable *four symbols*, and is volume 17 in the $33\frac{1}{3}$ series (Continuum, 2005). The quotation is from p. 44.

"object" is flat, unreflective, and has no seams or edges. A further clue that it's a hole is given in the photo of the golfers on the putting green. The woman is holding the flag as her male companion stoops, apparently to retrieve his ball from the cup. But the spot where the flag once was and the ball should be is occupied by the obelisk. No other hole can be seen.

Holes are fascinating. Because you need them in your head to see, hear, smell or taste anything, without them your encounters with the world—and presumably, with reality—would be extremely limited. Holes are immaterial, in the sense that they're not made of matter. They are, so to speak, pockets of emptiness. But then, our experience of reality is facilitated by nothingness, or, put slightly differently, holes are integrally bound up with awareness of the physical. But they're also metaphysical, since their very presence presents a philosophical conundrum: If holes are regions of nothingness, how can they exist? Can non-being have being? Must we admit the existence of immaterial realities?

Holes provoke many additional interesting questions. For example: Do holes exist or do only the things that surround them exist? If holes have properties, it's hard to see how they could be reduced to things like cheese, donuts, acoustic guitars, rings of smoke through the trees, and burst condoms. For the properties of the hole presumably are wherever the hole is, and it's a wonder if material objects have properties even in regions of empty space where they don't exist. Two objects—microphones or Marshall amps, say—can't occupy the same space at the same time, but could two or more *holes* occupy the same space at the same time? If not, why not? Are holes, like microphones, the kinds of things that prevent or exclude other things from occupying their space? *How* exactly do they do *that*? If holes are just parts of things (like cheese), does Bonzo add a new part to the wall when he punches a hole it it? And if the hotel management repairs the damage by patching the hole, does it thereby remove part of the wall (the part Bonzo contributed when he put his fist through it)? That seems backwards, because we normally think making a hole involves removing something and filling a hole amounts to adding something! According to the causal theory of perception, seeing occurs when reflected light from an object enters the eye and produces in the brain an internal representation of an external reality. But if this is so, how can we see holes? Holes can't reflect anything. Is the causal theory of perception then wrong? Or is it rather that, contrary to what we may think, we've never actually seen a hole? And trust me, these questions are just the tip of the theremin.

Presence of Mind

The somewhat surprising assertion that there are immaterial realities formed the cornerstone of Descartes's system. René Descartes (1596–1650), usually considered the father of modern philosophy, believed that minds or souls exist, but that they're non-physical. Physical things, he believed, were characterized by "extension" or spatiality. Extended things take up space, and therefore have a determinate size, shape, location, number, motion, or rest. These material qualities of a thing can be quantified, and therefore it's possible to have an objective science about them. Physics explains the actions of physical phenomena by subsuming them under laws based on their mathematically describable characteristics. However, because Descartes thought the soul was non-physical, he assumed it lacked the qualities inherent in extended things. The soul has no identifiable size, shape, number, motion, or location. (Ask yourself, for example: How many centimeters in diameter is your mind? What shape is your consciousness? Is it square? Triangular? Circular? How thick or thin is it?) The soul's qualities, Descartes believed, were subjective and qualitative, not objective and quantitative. Despite the aspirations of what would later come to be known as psychology, Descartes thought there could be no authentic science of the soul because science studies the natural world and only material phenomena exist in nature. Since, therefore, non-physical things aren't part of the physical world, unextended minds are non-natural, spiritual entities properly studied by philosophers and theologians, not physicists.

By this kind of maneuver Descartes tried to effect a truce between the church and scientists like Galileo, who had been forced to recant important scientific findings not in accord with ecclesiastical thought. The solution is to allocate to science and religion different domains of inquiry. The church retains authority over non-empirical, non-physical, "spiritual" subjects like God, the soul and morality. Science, on the other hand, has as its proper jurisdiction the material world, and its competence to make findings and rule in this domain should be respected by the church.

But holes, like minds, are also non-physical, and therefore can't exist in the material universe either. Consequently, "nature abhors a vacuum" and seemingly empty space must be filled with an imperceptible ether. Descartes's philosophy thus associates holes and souls.

Unfortunately, because Descartes thought holes non-physical, they pose a problem for his philosophy. That's because they seem to possess properties Descartes reserved for physical bodies. Like extended things, holes have size, shape, location, the possibility of motion,[11] and even a kind of causal potency—they can make things happen.[12] For example, Robert's gonna make you pay because of that great big hole in his heart. The hole in his heart *causes* him to seek a lover's vengeance. Less metaphorically, the small, round hole in your zeppelin can cause the hydrogen to leak, and when you have to *take* a leak, the small round hole in your . . . well, you get the idea! The point is, if holes are non-physical, they clearly possess attributes Descartes denied the soul on account of its incorporeality.

In some respects holes are like music. Music is an immaterial reality.[13] Unlike ordinary objects made of matter, music hasn't any size, shape or physical presence. Music (even Heavy Metal) lacks solidity. Unlike physical embodiments of music such as records or cds, music itself can be "multiply instantiated" in one place. That is to say, more than one tune can exist in the same place at the same time. For example, you can sing "Four Sticks" while "For Your Love" is on the radio, or listen to "The Lemon Song" while strumming "Tangerine". Moreover, like holes, music, though intangible, can set things in motion. A hole in the levee means momma you got to move; "Whole Lotta Love" or "When the Levee Breaks" means momma, I got to play me some air guitar! When you put on

---

[11] Remove the swiss cheese from the fridge or the sock from my drawer and you've not only moved these items, you've moved the holes in them too. This fact, by the way, suggests that holes aren't identical to empty space. Holes can move and space can't. Space is that *in which* things move and therefore it can't itself be mobile. If space were to move it would have to move into someplace where there was no space. But then, *where* would it be moving?

[12] The Object, which is supposed to be a hole, certainly has all of these features. It has size ("a base about six inches square and two inches deep, and the upright column is two inches square, a foot high"), shape ("a single twist like a barley sugar"), location (by the poolside, on the table, in the classroom), the possibility of motion (why else would it be on a dolly outside the vault?), and causal power (the doctor uses it to distract the infant). (Peter Blake, *For the Love of Vinyl*, p. 121).

[13] Although in some ways music is quantifiable—there are decibel levels and frequencies—its *aesthetic* reality *as music* is subjective, emotional, and experiential.

a Led Zeppelin cd, you hear Robert Plant, but Plant isn't there. He's "present" though absent. Same with all of the band. I hear Jimmy soloing, but Jimmy isn't here. In fact, I hear Bonzo playing, and Bonzo *really* isn't here. If holes can exist and yet, as privations of matter, not exist at the same time, are they like Zep's music? Are they, like Zep, there and not there? In through the out door?

There's No Denying You're Incomplete

Back to the ubiquitous black (no)thing on *Presence*. The temptation, of course, is to try to explain it. That's likely to be an exercise in frustration. There can't be any definite interpretation of the Object because *the Object* isn't anything definite! But building on what we already have—that it's both a something and a nothing— Plato would say it's no more mysterious than anything else in the world. Perhaps that's why it makes sense to locate the Object in quaint photos of relatively mundane settings. According to Plato, objects perceived by the senses are only partially real because they partake of both Being and Nonbeing. That which is wholly real is permanent, unchanging, simple, and knowable to the intellect. Plato called these immutable, pure essences "Forms." Numbers are a good example. Consider the difference between the number 'twenty' and a twenty-dollar bill. If (Roy) Harper gave his baby a twenty-dollar bill, he hasn't given her the number twenty. If the number twenty didn't exist, there wouldn't be twenty-dollar bills, but twenty-dollar bills can be created, destroyed, defaced,[14] felt, seen, and spent. But you can't see or spend or destroy the *number* twenty. The number is more like an idea, though an everlasting one. And that II comes before III is an "eternal" or timeless truth. That the number two comes before the number three would be true even if humans had never existed to count and no albums had ever been called "*II*" and "*III*". Mathematical truths and numbers, for Plato, are objects apprehended by means of intelligence (or "pure intellection"), not perception.

Other examples of Forms are what philosophers call "universals." If Robert, Jimmy, Jonesy and Bonzo are all musicians, they must have something in common (or "universal") which *makes*

---

[14] I went through a phase where I drew Kiss makeup on all the presidents on my paper money. If you decide to carry on this grand tradition, you didn't hear about it from me. . . .

them musicians. Moreover, what they have in common must also be shared by the Yardbirds, the Band of Joy, the Jeff Beck Group, Neil Christian and the Crusaders, the Crawling King Snakes, the Honeydrippers—even Hobbstweedle! What all musicians have in common isn't something tangible like a musician, and yet, without this something-in-common, no musicians would exist. Plato would say that what makes someone a musician is the fact that they "participate in" the Form "Musician."

So Plato would insist that the members of Led Zeppelin are "real" insofar as they partake of the Forms (such as the Form "musician"), but unreal insofar as they aren't themselves Forms. They occupy an intermediate status between the real and unreal. And so it is for us all. As Pascal said in the epigram that began this chapter, a human is "A Nothing in comparison with the Infinite, an All in comparison with the Nothing, a mean between nothing and everything."

The Object, then, is a reminder of the Platonic insight that things in the sensory world are but shadows and reflections—indicative of another greater reality upon which they depend, but in themselves unsubstantial. This is particularly so if one takes the view that holes are dependent upon their "hosts" or "surrounds." If the material hosting the hole is thought more substantive, tangible, solid, and concrete than the hole, the surround's relationship to the hole is weakly analogous to the Forms' relationship to the surround.

For Plato, the great task of humanity is to cultivate the philosophical realization of the truth behind the appearances. Plant's feather symbol on *IV* was his iconic tribute to truth. But in a way it illustrates Plato's point. For the feather in the circle on *IV* isn't a *real* feather; it's an artistic depiction of a feather. So it both is, and isn't, a feather; it has a share in both being and non-being.

Big-Legged Woman Ain't Got No Soul

Both Plato and Descartes thought the soul non-physical. Both also thought that physical things are infected with Non-Being and less than wholly real. Descartes embraced the "Great Chain of Being", according to which God has more reality than finite things, and finite things have more reality than their properties. God's existence is absolutely independent of anything else. Hence he is absolutely real. The created order, on the other hand, is dependent upon God for its existence, and is therefore less real. Similarly, the color of Page's guitar is less real than the guitar because the color is dependent on the guitar for its existence, but the guitar isn't dependent on the color. So, for Descartes Being has a hierarchical structure with God at the top, and properties (or perhaps nothingness) at the bottom.

Plato's vision of reality is also hierarchic. The Forms have independent existence, and everything else is dependent upon them. Plato, however, thought souls more akin to the Forms than physical things because both souls and Forms are invisible, intangible and simple.[15] Still, ultimately nothing but the Forms are wholly real, not even persons or their souls.

Much later, David Hume (1711–1776) noted that when he looked within himself, introspection revealed many fleeting impressions, sensations and thoughts but no stable and abiding experiences persisting through the mental life's inner flux. If the self is what *has* impressions and ideas, it should always be present when the impressions and ideas are. Hume's inability (and everyone else's inability) to observe any permanently enduring impressions thus means that, so far as we're able to determine empirically, there *is* no self. The self is an illusion, nothing at all.

Still later philosophers like Hegel (1770–1831) and Sartre (1905–1980) would argue that consciousness and the self are a kind of negation; I'm aware of myself only because I can distinguish between myself and everything else. I exist only because I have the power to interpose a nothingness between myself and what I perceive; therefore, no content attaches to the "I" itself, which is a pure abstraction from all that is Other. Suicide becomes a philosophical issue, and not just a sociological or familial concern, because it demonstrates that the negating power of the self knows no bounds. The suicidal self is self-negating; it can even negate itself.

And So I Say to You that Nothing Really Matters

Which brings us at last to death. If we approach the Object of *Presence* in its aspect as a hole, one message might be that there is,

---

[15] The soul is "simple" in the sense that it's non-composite. Physical things like Caesar's Chariot, double-neck guitars, and human bodies are comprised of a number of separable parts. Plato argued that the soul, in contrast, is an indivisible unity. Because things are typically destroyed through dis-integration or de-composition, a thing without parts has seemed to many philosophers indestructible. The supposed simplicity of the soul has historically played an important role in arguments for immortality.

at the center of our lives and all our everyday activities—at school and at work, at dinner and the doctor's office, in nature and on the green—a nothingness, an abyss. We're aware of this vacuum, if only dimly, and although we seem unconcerned, our cavalier attitudes and carefree enjoyment of life mask a deeper and profound despair. Roy Sorenson notes that, for Kierkegaard—the father of "existential" philosophy—"nothingness wells up into our awareness through moods and emotions. Emotions are . . . directed toward something. If angered, I am angry *at* something. If amused, there is something I find amusing. Free-floating anxiety is often cited as a counterexample. But Kierkegaard says that in this case the emotion is directed at nothingness." Heidegger thinks "we have several motives to shy away from the significance of our emotional encounters with nothingness. They are premonitions of the nothingness of death. They echo the groundlessness of human existence."[16]

Ooh Baby, It's Cryin' Time

These may seem morbid reflections, but *Presence* wasn't produced under very cheery circumstances. Plant was hobbled with crippling injuries and in a highly reflective state of mind following the near-death of his wife and children. The members of the band were unhappily displaced tax exiles. It must have felt at times like an ominous cloud was gathering as the sunny optimism of their early years slowly surrendered to the harsh realities of heroin addiction. Page was becoming more reclusive, Bonzo more erratic, and their life on the road increasingly out-of-control and violent.[17] Excepting the lyrics to "Royal Orleans", much of the music on *Presence* lacks the joy, playfulness and spontaneity that helped make their earlier records so infectious. Heideggerian angst is all over the album. The *Presence* artwork depicts innocent and happy days from a bygone era—lovers swimming, a young woman in a field of daffodils, friends listening to music, a sit-down family dinner—into which an

---

[16] The Stanford Encyclopedia of Philosophy's entry on Nothingness: http://plato.stanford.edu/entries/nothingness/#ExiAspNot, accessed February 14th, 2009. The quotations are of Sorenson's expositions of Kierkegaard and Heidegger. If it seems odd that we might have "emotional encounters with nothingness," consider the facts that fear is typically directed towards the future, which doesn't exist, and that we can fear not only the presence but also the absence of stimuli. People can be afraid of solitude, open spaces, silence, the dark, and death itself.

[17] Culminating in a series of tragedies during their 1977 tour of the States.

alien blight, an indefinable, vaguely sinister shadow intrudes. For Zeppelin, too, things could no longer remain as they were, the halcyon days of their invincibility rocked by uncertainty and their inescapable mortality. Like the ambiguous black object, life refuses to yield its meaning, and no comforting conclusions are possible. If, as Page suggests, the meaning of *Presence* is more than just an Obelisk, which is but a symbol, perhaps the message is that reality is ultimately empty and meaningless. And the universal reality of human existence is death.

Socrates (469–399 B.C.) argued at the conclusion of his trial for impiety that death is one of two things. It's either an eternal, dreamless sleep or a migration of the soul from here to another place. If death is annihilation of the person and the permanent cessation of consciousness, a hole, which is nothing, is an apt metaphor. (Indeed, some philosophers, as we've seen, virtually treat the self as a hole.) A hole marks the limit of its host as death marks the limit of life. A freshly dug grave is a hole, and there's no return. On the other hand, since the Object is a "presence", and presence is the opposite of extinction, perhaps the insinuation is that the second of Socrates's alternatives is correct, and that death is not the end.

Where the Spirits Go Now

But if death is a relocation of the soul, where does it go? In a suggestion worthy of Crowley, not to a luminous realm or celestial heaven, but into the abyss, where "the devil's in his hole" ("Achilles' Last Stand"). On "For Your Life" Plant sings that "In the pits you go no lower / Next stop's underground." The pit is a well-known appellation for the abode of Satan, the "city of the damned" where our cries for mercy will go unheeded and "fate deals a losing hand." When you die, "your stage is empty" so "bring down the curtain" and "fold up your show." You may not have planned it and "could not stand to fry in it" but that's what you get "for your life." Ouch!

So, one possible interpretation of the Obelisk is that it signifies death. Another is that it represents Satan, sometimes referred to as the Lord of this World.[18] The black Object's placement in every scene would then imply that the devil, too, is everywhere—

---

[18] This is the title of a Black Sabbath song on their third album *Master of Reality* (1971), an album which also contains the relevantly-titled songs "Children of the Grave" and "Into the Void."

omnipresent, powerful, influential, and at the center of things. The unnamed "thing" is, like the devil (and Zep themselves?), dark, mysterious, and twisted.

This theory would certainly satisfy Wall's suggestion that the title *Presence* (which clearly relates back to the black idol) has "occult resonance." It's conspicuous that although the album's dark form is to be found in scenes depicting "industry, young love, music, medicine, nature, money, sport, science,"[19] family and education, the one context noticeably absent is conventional religion.[20] Yet I suspect the word "presence" most commonly refers to the Divine presence, and places of worship are where most people hope to find it.[21] If the twisted, lightless Object signifies the Devil, no wonder it's not in church—although the cynical might counter that's where you're most likely to find him! Of course, for Zeppelin the real houses of the holy were the vast auditoriums and great cathedral-like venues where they performed nightly. By replacing God with a chiseled black idol signifying nothingness, the occult subtext may be that God is dead, and with his death, all possibility of finding meaning in a cozy realm of eternal verities vanishes too. And if God does not exist to decree and command, our own highest will must be "the whole of the law."

I Ain't Gonna Tell You One Thing that You Really Ought to Know . . . Ooh!

All this is highly speculative. Once again, because the Object has a dual nature, it's unlikely any single explanation will prove adequate. Other interpretations are certainly possible, including perhaps the two most obvious of all: that it represents the band,[22] or

---

[19] George Hardie in *For the Love of Vinyl*, p. 127.

[20] Maybe. The school teacher is laying hands on her male pupil and the Obelisk in the manner of a Pentecostal healer trying to channel energy from the Source.

[21] God's "name" in the book of *Exodus* (3:14) is revealed to Moses to be "I AM." How's that for Presence?

[22] Recall the view of Hipgnosis, that Zeppelin exuded a presence. The object also suggests the Page-Plant element of androgyny. The Object is a phallus, and yet because simultaneously a hole, it unifies the Yang and the Yin, the male-female duality. On the other hand, the failure of Presence to include any acoustic music— a first in the Zep catalogue—marks a departure from their attempt to achieve a dynamic synthesis of "light and shade, soft and heavy." This album is pretty much all heavy, all lead and no balloon. That, I think, is partly why *Presence* is one of Led Zeppelin's least successful outings.

that *it doesn't represent anything at all!* That's to say, it is what it is, something Present. Zep liked calling things what they are. After all, their second album is called "II", their third album is called "III", the release of their BBC sessions is called "BBC Sessions" and their DVD is *titled* "DVD"! (Jimmy Page also called Jethro Tull "Jethro Dull.") Whatever the Object is, perhaps Wittgenstein (1889–1951), the greatest philosopher of the twentieth century, put it best: "It's not a *something*, but not a *nothing* either!"[23] Or, as he also wrote, "a nothing is as good as a something about which nothing can be said."

---

[23] *Philosophical Investigations*, § 304.

10
Physical Graffiti

SCOTT CALEF

I once saw Steve Marriott clobber a security guard in the head with his mic stand because the hapless bloke was trying to stop a fan in the audience from smoking dope. The applause was deafening.

Without condoning assault (or dope smoking), good rock is aggressive, and rock stars have a knack for turning destruction into art. Hendrix lights his guitar on fire at Monterey and rapes his amplifier. The Who's violent gear-smashing set-closings are the stuff of legend. Alice Cooper beats up Santa and Nixon, guillotines himself, and—as if that weren't enough—has a maniacal dentist work on his teeth! AC-DC have a giant wrecking ball demolish half their set before they even walk onstage. Courtney Love and Amy Winehouse *are* wrecking balls. And then there's Zeppelin.

Scorned by critics as primitive, loud, unoriginal and determined to overwhelm the listener through sheer power and volume, early reviews of Led Zeppelin accused them of using brute force to bludgeon their way into the consciousness of the record-buying public. They were excoriated as bombastic, overbearing, lacking in subtlety, and utterly incapable of self-discipline. And yet, for all the complaints in the media that Zep concerts were excessive, self-indulgent and violent,[1] the band's most notorious acts of destruction

---

[1] Erik Davis nicely summarizes the complaints: "critics explicitly associated the force, heaviness, and sheer volume of Zeppelin's sound with violence. . . . Jon Landau described the band's live demeanor as 'loud, impersonal, exhibitionistic, violent and often insane'" ($33\frac{1}{3}$ series, Volume 17: *Led Zeppelin*, Continuum, 2005), p. 53. These accusations were hardly rebutted by Bonham's Clockwork Orange attire on tour.

happened off-stage. All of the complaints directed at their music seem more appropriately directed to the band after-hours—charges of being crude, loud, excessive, self-indulgent, unrefined and intimidating. In a world where any punk with a can of spray-paint is an artist, Zep's hotel-redecorating brand of physical graffiti knows few rivals.

When I was young and impressionable, I took the stories about the band riding motorcycles down hotel corridors, playing cricket in the hallways, slicing rooms to shreds with samurai swords, having food fights in posh restaurants, hanging sharks in their hotel closets, tossing TVs into pools, and all the other well-documented mayhem with amusement and even a perverse sort of pride. Led Zeppelin were my heroes, and it was practically a badge of loyalty—a sign of true fandom—not only to forgive but defend anything the band did. Not that there were any voices in my circle of friends expressing outrage. It all sounded like a party to us.

Well, if Zep vandalize the rooms they stay in, what does it matter so long as they pay for the damages? The hotel isn't really out of expenses, the band has a roaring great time, sundry carpeting, plastering, and electrical professionals gain lucrative business, and the other guests of the lodge come away with some pretty amazing stories. "Once I was staying at the Continental in LA while Led Zeppelin were in town. Boy, let me tell you . . . !"

What does it matter, indeed?

How you answer that question may partly depend on your ethics, on your theory about what makes something right or wrong. And the previous paragraph suggests thinking about the band's rowdiness in utilitarian terms. This is one of the more important ethical theories, and a real fine way to start.

Don't It Make You Wanna Go and Feel Alright?

There are different versions of Utilitarianism, but I'm going to talk about the most basic, Madison-Square-Garden variety, known as *Classical* Utilitarianism. Basically, utilitarianism says that an action is moral if it maximizes happiness. That's pretty simple, but the theory is a little more complicated than it seems. For one, what do we mean by happiness?

We mean pleasure. Classical utilitarians say we should do the thing that produces the greatest overall balance of pleasure over pain. To this extent, utilitarianism is hedonistic, though the pleasure to be maximized is the pleasure of all affected, not just the doer's own pleasure. In this sense, Utilitarianism is "objective," despite its emphasis on feelings. According to utilitarians, causing pain is okay, but only if it's necessary to produce the greatest amount of pleasure overall; any pain caused must be necessary to get rewards that we couldn't get without the pain. (Did you know Jimmy Page travelled with handcuffs and whips in his luggage?) Of course, according to utilitarianism, if you could get the same or greater pleasure by causing less pain or none at all, that's what you should do.

Here's an example: if you're in the front row at a Zep show, the music might be painfully loud (at least until the quick onset of deafness). But it's necessary for the music to be perhaps painfully loud in the front of the hall to project adequate volume to the back of the arena. All the people further back are totally groovin', the music is nice and loud but not too loud, they can hear great, they're happy. You're happy too. Don't forget, YOU'RE IN THE FRONT ROW AT A LED ZEPPELIN CONCERT! STOP YER BITCHIN'! To avoid causing you sonic discomfort the music would have to be barely audible in the rest of the hall. That's too high a price to pay to avoid causing you some momentary wincing. (You'll adjust quickly enough. I have experience.) You may have a little pain in your ears, but its necessary for the greater good, and so Led Zeppelin are not immoral for inflicting it on you. In fact, for the good of the audience as a whole, they're doing the right thing. If you don't like it, move further back. Trust me, there'll be plenty of greedy people eager to slip into your spot.

Now that we have utilitarianism, what are we to make of the aforementioned boyish antics (and myriad others that could be named)?

First of all, I'm not going to give you all the answers. That's not philosophy; philosophy is thinking for yourself. My role is to help you get a sense of how utilitarianism—and other theories—can help you to do so more thoughtfully. Second, so I don't have to repeat myself endlessly (which is boring, and doesn't maximize pleasure) assume that whenever physical damage is done—to hotel rooms and the like, not your eardrums—the band or its entourage pays for it. (I don't know whether this is in fact entirely true but it seems generally to have been the case.) Cleaning bills, carpet replacement, new TVs and draperies, shark deodorizing, all covered.

The question is, does food-fighting, samurai-slashing, shark-closeting, purse-pooing, TV-tossing, hotel-motorcycle-riding behavior maximize the overall level of happiness in the world?[2]

Probably not. But whether or not it does partly depends on *how much* fun the band had, and *how* annoyed the other affected parties were. If Bonzo's glee at pooing in Jimmy Page's girlfriend's purse outweighed her (and her beau's) horror and indignation, as well as the olfactory discomfort of others in the vicinity, and if no other prank would have produced the same surplus of pleasure, *he did the right thing*! In fact, he may have had a moral obligation to do it! As you can already tell, though, when we try to apply utilitarian moral logic, there are going to be many unknowns. Consider one of the times the band had a food fight in a restaurant filled with other diners. This behavior was probably uproariously funny to the band. It might also have forced the restaurant to cancel a large group reservation—say, your wedding rehearsal dinner—scheduled for the following evening because they have to clean up the gravy stains on everything. That is to say, the band's childish behavior may have been extremely aggravating to a large group of very emotionally invested people out to celebrate one of life's truly significant milestones. The night of the food fight, couples may have been celebrating anniversaries, or their first night out alone after a new baby. A businessman may have been unable to complete a transaction with a critical client vital to his firm because of the mayhem. The clothing of other diners may have been stained irreparably, and the garments impossible or very difficult to replace. Patrons may swear never to return to the establishment, resulting in significant loss of business to the owners. In short, the melee might have caused the other diners and staff more heartbreak and anger than it brought the band pleasure.

Moreover, the riotous joy of the band and its entourage probably could have been achieved in other, less distressing ways. They could have paid everyone in the establishment a thousand dollars each to go to another restaurant, for example. Of course, this would defeat the whole purpose if the point was to watch the reactions of the old gits and see the horrified expressions of folks having an innocent night on the town. But even if just drinking and telling stories instead of chucking Jello wouldn't have been *quite*

---

[2] Who the hell (besides God) could possibly know?!? (That's a problem with Utilitarianism.)

as entertaining, it still would've been a good time, and everyone else could've enjoyed their evenings too. I suspect a utilitarian would have to disapprove.

Damage to hotels caused by samurai swords, the pitching of expensive electronics into pools, and indoor motorcycle wheelies raise similar issues. We've all checked into hotels after a long day's drive or with an important meeting scheduled early the next morning and been enraged by loud and inconsiderate neighbors who just want to party and make a ruckus. That would be nothing compared to staying in a hotel occupied by Led Zep.

The band may pay for new TVs, furniture, cleaning, and so on, but what about your lack of sleep? They don't compensate for that. Besides, it takes time to do all this shopping and repair work. An already overburdened person now has to take on the extra responsibility of organizing contractors and the like. People with reservations may have to endure a room without a TV, or a pool closed until broken glass can definitely be determined not to be on the bottom. If the hotel is booked solid the evening after Zep checks out, a dozen rooms or even an entire floor may be uninhabitable, not yet ready to re-rent, and innocent people with reservations may turn up only to find themselves displaced and with nowhere to stay.

On the other hand, as noted already, sundry professionals—electricians, carpet layers, plumbers—receive lucrative work, which presumably pleases them. Appliance sellers benefit from increased sales in televisions and other expensive electronics. Disturbed guests and the hotel staff have stories to tell, and possibly groupies in elevators to gawk at. Importantly, people like Richard Cole and Stephen Davis have stories to tell too—stories which help them to make a ton of money by writing books which sell well because of their lurid descriptions of life on the road with Zeppelin. And, we who read these lurid books and dig them also experience pleasure. So the hassle to the hotel employees and other guests might be compensated for by the vicarious thrill the rest of us have when we read—and fantasize—about the whole Led Zeppelin tour experience.

Utilitarian considerations also suggest that getting so drunk you urinate all over yourself and your plane seat is inexcusable. The damage may be paid for, but innocent people throughout the cabin have to breathe and smell the consequences. Malevolent thoughts generated by the incident would vastly outnumber any charitable ones. One doubts anyone—including Bonham, the urinator—was made happy by this incident. Although he ended up swapping seats with Mick Hinton, his personal roadie, he had to travel the rest of the flight in coach, not first class. Hinton, of course, now occupying Bonham's newly vacant but rather damp seat in first class, had other concerns. When Bonham took a dump in Jimmy Page's girlfriend's purse, on the other hand, he sickened her, infuriated Page, and managed only to amuse himself.[3] The collective unhappiness of the offended probably outweighed any giggles he got from the short-sighted stunt. So too, hanging sharks in the closet of the Edgewater Inn in Seattle probably didn't cause a great deal of happiness to anyone, and the repulsed maid who discovered them was most probably shocked, frightened, horrified, and incensed all at once. She could be damaged for life. Not to have hung them up would have produced the greatest utility. (And don't forget the pain caused to the unhappy sharks themselves!)

The utilitarian assessment of that most famous of Zeppelin exploits, the "Red Snapper" incident, is rather different. For a utilitarian, sexual issues are likely to be more controversial. Zeppelin road manager Richard Cole, whose accounts are generally relied upon, insists that no one was harmed when a seventeen-year-old Portland, Oregon redhead was tied to a four-poster bed and both vaginally and anally masturbated with freshly caught fish (or fish parts), either Snappers or Mud Sharks. He claims the young woman was an eager participant and enjoyed orgasms. I'm aware of no record indicating she suffered remorse. If that's true, utilitarians would have no reason to object; the incident would seem to have produced more pleasure than pain, if it produced any pain at all. Shocked and outraged moral conservatives may have been pained upon hearing of the incident, but for every offended minister, there were probably a gaggle of teenaged lads high-fiving somewhere. Of course, some think the whole business smells fishy, and argue that such lewd and lascivious conduct demeans or objectifies women. By inciting fifteen-year old boys to high five, it leads to the unhappy social consequence that women are subordinated to male sexual fantasies. But this assertion is as difficult to prove as it is to disprove. All we can do is answer hypothetically that *if* women are

---

[3] This isn't strictly true, as we who hear or read of the incident may be variously outraged or bemused.

demeaned and devalued by such conduct, and to an extent which outweighs the pleasure of the parties affected, *then* it's wrong on utilitarian grounds.

Jimmy Page's reported relationship with fourteen-year-old Lori Maddox similarly seems to have been mutually advantageous. She claims to have loved him; there's no evidence that Page mistreated her; the relationship was, so far as happiness or pleasure are concerned, unobjectionable. The manner of their "breakup" may have caused her young heart to ache, and it may have ached less if they hadn't been involved sexually, but that may only indicate that Page had a utilitarian duty to dissolve the relationship with greater sensitivity. But if pleasure is the standard for determining whether something is right or wrong, that tender Lori was underage is not, in itself, a moral matter. The fact is, some fourteen-year-olds enjoy sex. As a society we have legitimate reasons for protecting them from older predators. But for a classical utilitarian, the only moral justification for interfering would be a determination that the greatest good for the greatest number and an increase in happiness overall would be achieved thereby.

Because utilitarianism assesses the moral rightness or wrongness of an action in terms of its consequences, and because the consequences of actions—especially their long-term or remote effects—are often difficult to determine in advance, some moral philosophers advocate a different approach.[4] So, let's see what else is out there.

I Kant Quit You Babe

Immanuel Kant (1724–1804) thinks the morality of actions can be determined independently of knowing their results because what's important in evaluating someone's actions is an understanding of their motives. This fits with our common-sense belief that people who do the right thing for the wrong reason aren't necessarily praiseworthy. For Kant, the most commendable motive, morally speaking, is acting for the sake of duty. Here we

---

[4] Reflecting on their raucous 1977 US tour, Plant made the following comment, which displays real insight into utilitarian concerns: "I see a lot of craziness around us. Somehow, we generate it and we revile it. This is an aspect . . . which has made me contemplate whether we are doing more harm than we are good." Quoted in Mick Wall, *When Giants Walked the Earth*, p. 374.

see the core difference between Kant and the utilitarians. For Kant, we should do our duty even if it's unpleasant, makes us uncomfortable, and makes other people unhappy or angry. Honesty, for example, may be difficult sometimes, and people might be happier hearing and believing a lie, but according to Kant we should tell the truth anyway. It's the right thing to do; it's our duty.

Kantian ethics gives us guidelines for determining whether or not something is contrary to duty. The most important is the "categorical imperative", or universal command, of morality. At the most basic level, this means we should do unto others as we would have others do unto us. If I treat people otherwise than I want them to treat me, I'm applying a double standard; I'm acting as if it's okay for me to do it, but not okay for other people. Kant thinks the demands of morality are inconsistent with this kind of double standard. Morality is "universal." More specifically, Kant thinks that when we do anything intentionally it's as if we're following rules or instructions. If Robert Plant lies to his suspicious wife, to the point of giving her a fake tour itinerary with no shows in LA,[5] it's as if he's following a rule or maxim which says "I should lie." Whoever stole Page's Les Paul (his "Black Beauty") while he was touring and en route to Canada in 1970 was acting on a rule or maxim which says, "I should steal this guitar." Kant claims that we have a moral duty only to act on maxims which can be willed to be a universal law (hence, "categorical imperative").

Here's how it works. If Plant lies to his wife, he obviously wants her to believe him. Otherwise, what's the point? But if he always lies to his wife (or if men in general always lie to their wives), his wife will stop believing him. This reveals that lying leads to a "contradiction of the will." Plant wants his lie to be believed, but if his "maxim" is universalized, his wife won't believe him. Put differently, if everyone always lied the conditions of trust which make deceit possible would cease to exist. Therefore, the maxim that we should lie is, if universalized, self-defeating. Hence, for Kant, lying is contrary to duty and immoral. We can't practice it without implicitly embracing a double standard. Or suppose I want to steal Jimmy's guitar, and so (simplifying a little) I consider the maxim,

---

[5] It seems members of the band really did something very like this. When Robert's wife Maureen later confronted him with a picture from the *Melody Maker* showing the band in LA with groupies draped all over them, Plant's reply was, "But Mo! You know we don't take the *Maker*!"

"I should steal this Les Paul." My motive is to acquire a guitar I didn't have before. But notice this: if the maxim "I should steal this Les Paul" is universalized, that means everyone would act on the same maxim. But if everyone else did what I'm thinking about doing, the guitar will quickly be stolen from me![6] The point is, if my maxim is universalized, it leads to a contradiction of the will. On the one hand, I want this guitar. On the other hand, universalizing my maxim will result in my not having this guitar. This contradiction reveals that stealing can't be universalized, and so is contrary to duty. Even if stealing the guitar would make me happier than it would make Page unhappy, and so be permissible on utilitarian grounds, Kant would say it's wrong nevertheless.

Without considering all of the many shenanigans mentioned above, it's pretty clear Zep wouldn't want others to treat them the way they treated others! Suppose something like their maxim "I should trash my hotel room" were universalized. How could Zep tour? There'd be no place for them to stay on the road. Indeed, the hotel industry would probably collapse. If everyone always demolished their rental accommodations, the rooms Zep reserved for themselves would be trashed by their previous occupants, and Zep wouldn't be able to hire them. But then, how could they trash them? On the one hand, they want to destroy their rooms. But if everyone did that, there would be no rooms for them to rent and destroy. The maxim is self-defeating. Looked at from a different angle and simplifying a bit, if Zep vandalize their suites, they probably are looking to have a good time. But if everyone does this, when on tour Zep would have to stay in rooms that are uninhabitable, and *that* doesn't make for a very good time!

Or consider the mud shark–red snapper escapade. I suggested earlier that utilitarians might oppose Zep-style hotel demolitions, but would find it harder to object to the snapper episode. Kant provides a different perspective. A good deal of the amusement probably derived from the fact that the band was involved in something outrageous and crazy. It gave them a chance to revel in being rock stars by doing the kind of thing only rock stars do (while raising the bar even for this elite group of miscreants). But if the implied maxim were universalized, the incident wouldn't be outrageous at all, but perfectly ordinary, as commonplace as could be. The goal

---

[6] Assume whoever takes it from me "steals" it from me, even though I don't actually "own" it since I acquired it illegitimately myself.

was, I presume, to entertain themselves, but if everyone did this all the time it wouldn't be interesting in the slightest, but boring as cornflakes. Universalizing the maxim takes all the fun out of it.

Kant's moral philosophy also insists that we should treat others as an end, and never as a means only. This is an alternate version of the categorical imperative. Kant thought that because people are free and rational, they can determine their duties and freely do what duty enjoins. Since all humans can perform acts of moral beauty, they possess inherent dignity and worth. When we treat others as mere means to our own gratification or as tools, we objectify and degrade them. We cease to treat them as ends in themselves, and instead use them as we would unconscious or inanimate beings. Regardless of whether the notorious woman from Portland was a willing participant, the band was using her. Even if everyone had a good time, snappering her failed to show her the respect her status as an autonomous moral agent deserved. Or so a disciple of Kant might argue.

Moving on, consider the noisy ruckus the band often made where they stayed—playing cricket or riding motorcycles in the halls, chucking TVs out the window, pulling down the chandeliers, and generally engaging in physical graffiti. Although the band undoubtedly kept late hours, they have to sleep *sometime*. How's that going to happen, if everyone is always carrying on the way they do? Come sunrise when they're finally ready to retire, VROOM! VROOOOMMMM!!!!!!!!! Down the hallway comes Mr. Smith on a Harley. Or a cricket ball is batted repeatedly into the door to their room by Mrs. Green.[7] The members of Led Zeppelin stay up wrecking havoc until the wee hours because they're too pumped from their gig to go to sleep. But if everyone else is as noisy as they are, they'll be too exhausted to party and gig.

You Didn't "Mean" Me No Good

Aristotle (384–322 B.C.E.) argues that virtue is "the mean between the extremes." What he means by this is best explained through

---

[7] This may not have been such a problem for the band, really. Some of them—especially Jonesy—seem to have been pretty heavy sleepers. When, at the Hilton in Tokyo, Bonham and Cole had finished slicing and dicing their own rooms, they lugged a sleeping Jones into the hallway and proceeded to destroy his room. The ever-so-polite hotel staff, not wishing to disturb the slumbering John Paul, put screens around him for privacy and left him there until morning.

examples. Consider a moral notion like "courage". Aristotle argues that courageous behavior is a "mean" or middle-ground between the extremes of rash, reckless, impetuous conduct on the one hand and timidity or cowardice on the other. If you're too fearless, not respecting things that really should induce caution, you're foolish, and irresponsible fools aren't virtuous. Such overly bold people suffer from an "excess" of courage. Contrariwise, if you fear things that you shouldn't, you're a coward. You have a deficiency of courage. The proper attitude is a "mean" between the rashness of the overly-bold individual and the spinelessness of the over-anxious one. Or consider generosity. The excessively generous are profligate; those deficient in giving are stingy. The right amount of charity falls between that of the miser and the spendthrift.

Aristotle is careful to point out that some things are wrong in themselves and admit of no "compromise." Only a moral moron would reason, "Hmmmm. I wonder what the right amount of adultery is? It must fall somewhere between the extremes of not committing adultery at all, and being continuously unfaithful. I guess I should split the difference and cheat only occasionally. It's the right thing to do." Aristotle also argues that the appropriate amount of courage or generosity or honesty depends on the particular person and circumstances. A professional wrester (like Peter Grant back in the day) might need to eat a certain amount of meat to remain competitive; it doesn't follow that philosophical wimps like me should eat that much. Likewise, the appropriate amount for a rich person to donate to charity and the appropriate amount for a poor person to contribute will differ. And sometimes, Aristotle argues, depending on the situation, the suitable reaction might even be extreme. Sometimes it's right and proper to feel *extremely* angry, and a more measured response wouldn't be appropriate. Developing a sense of what the proper response or emotional intensity should be is largely a product of upbringing and character.

Ultimately, then, for Aristotle, virtue is inculcated through the cultivation of good habits, which are in turn arrived at through emulating citizens who act with integrity, nobility, self-control and restraint. If you take as your role models people who are loud-mouthed, violent, intemperate, selfish, or irascible, you're likely to be maladjusted and your values misaligned. In that case, you're unlikely to grow up with sound moral judgment and sensitivity.

Oops! This doesn't bode well for my rock'n'roll heroes, or for those like me who were, in our youth, strongly influenced by them.

Just as the drunkard is likely to think those who drink moderately are boors who don't know how to party and cowards are apt to think brave people are foolhardy and reckless, so too those infatuated with Zeppelin may regard the lives of ordinary mortals as boring, pedestrian and devoid of adventure. Aristotle, though, would argue that only those of sound judgment have the discrimination, experience, and temperament to perceive these matters rightly. I could be wrong, but I think it's fairly clear that much of Zep's offstage behavior was extreme. I don't blame them for this. They were young, after all, and confronted a cornucopia of temptations few of us are well-practiced at resisting. Still, it's hard to imagine Aristotle arguing that Zep's on-tour debachery was the mean between extremes. If Zep were moderate, who's extreme? Caligula?

Close the Door, Put Out the Lights

Now that I'm an adult the consequences of drunken hooliganism are more difficult to dismiss as high-spirited antics and harmless boyish pranks. When I was a teenager yearning to break free of authority, what was real to me was that the band were having a blast, and weren't letting conventional proprieties get in the way. For that they were to be envied. Other things are real to me now, and instead of identifying with the band exclusively, I can identify with the very real victims of their inconsideration. Even if their suites at the Edgewater were deodorized and the shark pong expunged, what about the traumatized chambermaid who happens upon the gruesome scene and freaks out at the sight of aquatic cadavers pierced through the gills with coat hangers? Uncool, dudes.

None of this has any direct bearing on the group's musical genius. It's a mark of aesthetic maturity to be able to keep distinct our moral evaluation of the band and our appreciation of their art. Someone who thinks "Houses of the Holy" is a crappy song because Plant mentions Satan in a couple of lines hasn't yet learned how art should be appropriated. They make the same kind of mistake as an atheist who dislikes Raphael because his paintings celebrate the Holy Family, or homophobes who can't stand to listen to Queen or Bowie. I love Led Zeppelin and their music—from a safe distance! I *wouldn't* want my family to share a commercial flight with them, and if they ever tour again, before I head to the show I'm gonna lock up my daughters.

11
Let the Son Beat Down

STEVEN GIMBEL

The Black Son. [handwritten annotation]

They were supposed to be the "New Yardbirds." But it quickly became clear to everyone that they weren't. They were something else altogether. The Yardbirds had been a midwife for guitar gods. Eric Clapton, Jeff Beck, and Jimmy Page had all taken a turn as lead guitarist for the band. But this one was different. Sure, there were the blues standards of the Clapton years and the fuzz-tinged psychedelic stuff of the Beck era, but in the end it was a different band. No one would confuse "For Your Love" with "Whole Lotta Love." But what was it that made it a different band?

Different musicians seems the obvious answer, but the Yardbirds had changed membership several times and remained the Yardbirds. The creation of Led Zeppelin, though, was more than just a change in personnel. But what change forced them to change the name to accept a new band identity?

And more interestingly, what would maintain this identity? After the death of John Bonham, the line-up of Led Zeppelin would change again. Yet, the band remained Led Zeppelin. This is not to diminish Bonzo's role in the sound. His heavy hands were not only an essential element of Led Zeppelin, he redefined rock drumming. But when the question of who could possibly sit behind the kit arose, there seemed to be only one option, Jason. The question again is why? Is there something about the father-son relation here that brings a sense of authenticity? Jason is not John, yet there *is* something that makes his selection natural. What could this quality be?

Further, when talk of a Zeppelin reunion tour in 2009 began to surface, fans got very excited. Well . . . that is until word came from

Robert Plant that he wished his old band mates well, but that they would have to do it without him. Singers, some quite famous in their own right and strongly influenced by Plant's work with Zeppelin, were considered. But it was clear to Page and John Paul Jones that the tour could not be billed as a Led Zeppelin reunion without him. What's the difference? Why would it not be the same band without Plant, but would be Zeppelin with the younger Bonham? Other bands replaced singers while remaining the same band: Ronnie James Dio replaced Ozzy Osbourne in Black Sabbath, Brian Johnson for Bon Scott in AC/DC, and Sammy Hagar took David Lee Roth's place in Van Halen.

But the case with Plant seems different and those close to the band agreed. In Mick Wall's *When Giants Walked the Earth: A Biography of Led Zeppelin*, he recounts a time in '73 when Jones was considering leaving the band. The road was hard enough, but the craziness of Led Zeppelin on the road was something else entirely and he confided in band manager Peter Grant his conflicted sense that he might leave. At the same time, Plant was thinking about launching a solo career on the side. When these possibilities reached the ears of Ahmet Ertegun, co-founder of Atlantic Records with whom Zeppelin was recording, Wall writes, "Ertegun was well aware that the bass player might need replacing, but it was a situation that could be managed; losing the band's singer, however remote the possibility, could not be" (p. 301).

Plant, Ertegun believed, could not be replaced and keep Zeppelin, Zeppelin. Why? What is it that makes Plant different from Jones and Bonham? How do we determine when a band keeps its identity and when the change in membership changes the band? What exactly does the name "Led Zeppelin" refer to?

A Traveler of Both Time and Space

When we talk about identity, what it means for something to be the thing that it is, the place to start is always with a challenge posed in ancient Greece by the writer Plutarch. When Greek civilization was rising, the Persians possessed the mightiest military on Earth. Trying to put down Greece, the Persians launched an offensive against them, an attack that was foiled by Theseus, whose naval maneuvers cleverly defeated the stronger Persians.

Out of reverence, Theseus's ship was kept as a monument to the battle, symbolizing Greek strength and freedom. Being made entirely of wood, it was subject to rot. So, each rotting board would be replaced with a new fresh one so that the ship would remain to remind each generation of what happened.

But, Plutarch asked, after each and every piece had been replaced over the course of time, was it still Theseus's ship? Was it a different ship? Let's change the example a little. Suppose there is a captain who fixes part of his own vessel. Surely it is still the same one he had when he bought it. Over the course of many voyages, parts would be replaced, eventually all of them, but when he goes to sail away and leave today, he can truly say that "This ship has been all around the world." It seems like there is a difference between the working vessel and the ship of Theseus. To figure out what, we need to know what makes a thing a thing.

There are three standard approaches to answering this question. The most obvious is that a thing is what it is if it is made of a certain stuff. Comedian Stephen Wright's joke about coming home to find everything in his house had been replaced with an exact replica is funny, but not impossible. There could be exact replicas that are nevertheless still distinct things. If someone claimed to have the guitar Page used in the *Houses of the Holy* sessions, you'd call bullshit. Pictures of the guitar from the sessions, no matter how exacting, would not be convincing evidence. This is, most likely, a replica. The difference between the two guitars is that this is not the actual wood Page had in his hands while recording. It's a question of material identity. To be the same guitar as Page's, it has to be the same actual matter. Of course, the strings, tuning pegs, and pickups may have been changed on the original, maybe even the frets and neck; this is a normal response to wear and tear on a guitar. But at the least there would still have to be the original matter that comprises the body. We can call this the "matter notion of identity" and according to it, Theseus's ship and the replica guitar are different from the originals.

Unfortunately, the matter notion of identity, while plausible, runs into problems when we talk about people. It's true that Alison Krauss recorded with the vocalist of Led Zeppelin. But the Robert Plant of 2008 is not the Robert Plant of 1978. That's not to say he lost his chops over the last thirty years, but rather that the cells and chemicals making up the cells of Robert Plant in 2008 are not the same as those of 1978—not to even begin to consider what chemicals they might have been in 1978! Our cells divide, they die, we eat, we squeeze our lemons, we do what Bonham did in Page's girlfriend's purse; in many different ways the composition of our bodies, the matter that makes us up, changes over time. But surely, we remain the same. "Your honor, that was a different group of cells that were in that hotel room with the fourteen year old Lori Maddox," is not likely to get you off the hook. You are you and you remain you, even if the stuff that makes up you changes. So what could account for identity after such alterations?

One notion comes from Aristotle who argued that there are essential properties that define things. There are qualities that are accidental, that could change without affecting who you are, and then there are some that define your very being. Identity is about maintaining essential characteristics. In this way, the ship of Theseus may be defined by its shape, by its having thirty oars, by its style. As long as these are kept, the ship is the ship of Theseus.

In the same way, we have accidental and essential properties. If Bonzo had shaved off the moustache, he still would have been the same person; but get rid of the intensity and the rhythm and you are talking about someone else entirely. We can call this the essential notion of identity. Different philosophers have cited different things as comprising this set of identifying properties. Some talk about memories, others about characteristics of character or body, but the key here is that there are certain features that make you, you, and without them you would be someone else.

A different approach comes from John Locke who says that what guarantees identity over time is being a continuous thing flowing through time. As people we constantly change: we grow, we learn, we experience, we mature (some of us—others not so much). Though the song remains the same, the singer never does. And yet, despite the fact that our properties are always in flux, there's a path through time that is uniquely ours. We've all had our share of good times and bad times, and it is the continuous history of them that makes us the very person who did those things back in the days of our youth. In this way, the ship of Theseus would still remain the same because at any given time, the ship traces its origin smoothly back to the ship sailed by Theseus. We can call this the continuation notion.

The Band Remains the Same

But things get weird when you talk about groups rather than individuals. Peter French in his book *Collective and Corporate*

Responsibility argues that collections of people arrange themselves in different ways and that there is a difference between what he calls aggregates and conglomerates. An aggregate is a group defined by its membership. It is just some bunch of people and it is therefore defined by the fact that it is those people in the bunch. The people I camped out with for Robert Plant tickets on his first solo tour is just a set of people.

A conglomerate, on the other hand, isn't just some collection of individuals, but rather a group with an internal structure, an organizational arrangement in which different people have well-defined roles and jobs. A conglomerate is therefore not just the people in the group, it is also defined by its particular structure. People in the jobs can change, but the conglomerate still survives. In an aggregate, though, since it is just the people, if you change the composition, you change the aggregate. Substitute someone else in the line, someone who hasn't waited all night, and it's a different set of people—many of whom would have been mighty pissed.

Corporations, on the other hand, are conglomerates. If the receptionist for Swan Song records left and a new hire was made, you do not have a different company. It's the same company with a new member. Mobs, jam sessions, and pick-up basketball games are aggregates; the Supreme Court, colleges and universities, and any other group that maintains an identity when the people making it up come and go are conglomerates. As Aristotle would say, aggregates are just matter, but conglomerates are both matter and form.

Are bands conglomerates or aggregates? It seems clear that a band has to be a conglomerate because we can have Led Zeppelin with Jason instead of John Bonham. Aggregates follow the matter notion of identity, and we can have different matter, different band members and still have the same band.

So, if a rock band is a conglomerate, is it one whose identity is based on its smooth transition from the past or some essential condition? A conglomerate has a structure. What would that structure look like in a band? One part is who is playing what instrument. Page went from being the bass player to co-lead to lead guitar player in the Yardbirds and they kept their identity. Changes in who plays what doesn't seem to necessarily change the identity of the band.

But the move from Plant to another vocalist would force a change in identity. Is it something about Robert Plant? Does he bring something essential that cannot be done without? Something that John Bonham didn't? Or could it be that John Bonham did and Jason just happens to have it too? If so, what is it?

Father of the Four Winds

The place to start seems to be the sound. No one else is Robert Plant. No one else could sound like Robert Plant. What he does within the structure of the band could not be duplicated by anyone else occupying that position. But there are so many rock drummers influenced by Bonzo that it would not be difficult to find one to play in his style. What is it that makes Jason's playing more authentically Zeppelin? If there is an essential property he picked up, surely, it has something to do with being John's son. What could that property be and how did he get it? This leads us to the traditional question of nature versus nurture.

Whenever rumors started about a Beatles reunion, John Lennon's place was always asserted to be filled by his son Julian. The reason, of course, is that Julian sounds just like John. The Beatles were all about the Lennon-McCartney harmonies and the only person who sounded enough like John Lennon to pull it off would be his son. Why did he sound so much like him? Of course, the answer is genetics. Shape of the throat and head, thickness and length of the vocal chords, there are any number of inherited properties that explain why family members sound alike in ways that non-relatives don't.

But Jason Bonham isn't singing, he's playing the drums and there doesn't seem to be a physical component that could be genetically passed along by inheritance that would give a unique family sound on the kit. Could it be a matter of upbringing? It was his father who taught him how to play. Could it be style that could be transferred by environment? Could it be certain tricks, techniques, or habits that someone trying to pick up the Bonzo sound by ear could never replicate?

After Duane Allman's death, one of the people brought in to take his place in the Allman Brothers Band was Derek Trucks, nephew of Allmans drummer Butch Trucks. Derek seemed natural and fit in so well because he was weaned on the Allmans sound and knew the ins and outs of the band's personality and culture. The dual-lead structure of Allman jam style requires a certain sort of sense many players never develop, but one he came to understand as a young guitar phenom. He was a member of the family both metaphorically and literally, and this would have given him a sixth sense necessary to hit the coordinated runs and to play around and through a second soloist.

Could this sort of thing also be what Jason brings to the table? Is his being a part of the family something that would be subtly heard in the music? When the band performed with him for the first time in 1988 at the Atlantic Records Fortieth Anniversary celebration, the band was deeply disappointed with its performance, but John Paul Jones remarked that there were points where he would play a riff, get the response from the drums, look up and be shocked not to see Bonzo. He thought it eerie that something personal that had been developed in the rhythm section, something that came with years of hearing each other, could be picked up by someone who wasn't there. Catch some of the recordings of the O2 show in 2007. Jason certainly drives the music and gives it a sense of life in the way his dad did, something that may not have been the case had there been a fifty-nine-year-old holding the sticks. But isn't it possible that this could also be the case with a non-related drummer who was a complete Zeppelin freak? What is it about the father-son relation that is essential?

To Think of Us Again

Is it possible that it's not a matter of the sound? Maybe it's something else entirely. Consider why Plant is now an essential component of Led Zeppelin. There was serious talk of replacing him after the first album and had that happened the band that recorded *Led Zeppelin II* would have still been Led Zeppelin even without Plant. But now, Page and Jones agree that you can't have Led Zeppelin without him. What's the difference?

Surely David Lee Roth, Bon Scott, and definitely Ozzy were just as much a part of the sound of Van Halen, AC/DC, and Black Sabbath. The bands kept going and made some fine music after their respective departures—in at least two of the three cases not as good, but certainly decent across the board. What is it that makes Plant incapable of being replaced, but not the others?

One big difference is that after the replacement, the other bands did go on to create new music and to make a living playing on the road. Think back to the ship of Theseus question. There does seem to be a difference between the cases of the working ship whose captain has planks replaced to keep the vessel seaworthy, on one hand, and the ship of Theseus that is kept as a monument, on the other. In the first case, the work on the ship is to keep it working or to improve its functionality in doing what it was made to do. The ship was designed with a purpose in mind. It has a function and the change was an act intended to allow it to continue to perform its function or to perform it better. It is getting changed to keep working, to do new things.

In the other case, Theseus's ship is in a sense not still a ship. Now, it is a monument, an object of remembrance, not performing the task it was created for, but given a new meaning, a new purpose. Theseus's ship performs this new job by being a reflection of what it was, heralded not for what it is doing, but what it did. The changes made to it are not changes that make it a better boat, but are alterations designed to save it as a remembrance of what it was when it was used for sailing, for what it was intentionally created to do and what it actually did.

Maybe the context matters here in a similar fashion. We're talking about a Led Zeppelin reunion tour, not the band really going back on the road and into the studio to become a working rock band again. Van Halen, AC/DC, and Black Sabbath all got new vocalists to keep the project alive. They were alive in the same sort of way that John Locke's person was, having new experiences, still growing, still creating oneself, still developing along its trajectory through time. They were like the working ship.

Led Zeppelin, on the other hand, is more like the monument of Theseus's ship. What makes Zeppelin, Zeppelin is not just the talent, not just the image, not just the music. It's that they were a hammer of the rock gods smashing the Abba, Bread, Carpenters sensitive soft rock and the repetitious, flashy disco of their times, taking rock music in new directions, still staying true to its blues-based roots while adding elements never before seen, but soon to become standard. They were trailblazers who made rock'n'roll music what it is today. A Led Zeppelin reunion tour would be a testament to that progress made, to the vision and skill it took to make something new, something both heavy and soulful, raw and smart. The reunion would be a chance to revisit that time for those who were there and to recreate something like it for those who were not yet born. But it would be a recreation, not a revival of the spirit that was Led Zeppelin.

Robert Plant was an inextricable part of the actualization of that spirit. To see Zeppelin was in part to see Plant do his thing, perform his magic. Holding the mic with the cord taut across his mid-section, his improvs, his voice and his presence. That is an element that made Zeppelin, Zeppelin and without it, given its history, it wouldn't be what it is.

Coda

Led Zeppelin was a quartet. Each member had a role and a function. It was what French called a conglomerate. Page was the creative element and guitar god delivering the blistering electric sound that surrounds you. Bonham and Jones were the id and the super-ego of the band; Bonzo's animalistic pounding driving the music forward while Jones' musicianship was the steady, heady intellect that turned metal into art with the adeptness of Alexander Calder. Plant was the face, the sensual and sensuous element that made the music both human and superhuman. It was the melding of these that was Led Zeppelin and any living monument to it must have the four elements. Plant is one of those elements, one of Aristotle's essential characteristics, and with any other front man to stand on stage, it would not be Led Zeppelin.

But what of Jason Bonham? No one would say it was the same, but would it cross the threshold of being Led Zeppelin? The answer certainly seems to be yes, but on what grounds? We all remember him playing along in *The Song Remains the Same*, but it's not like he was really a second drummer up there.

The key here is to remember that Jason Bonham is not being considered for the role of drummer in a new Led Zeppelin or a revived Led Zeppelin, but rather he is being picked to fill the role played by his father in a monument to Led Zeppelin, in a recreation designed to remind us of the greatness of the band. As the son of Bonzo, he not only has the chops and the style, but does two things that another drummer could never do. First, as a matter of family pride, he brings a deep sense of reverence. By taking over the family business, he brings a care and an internal sense of the importance of what he is doing.

Second, for those of us who come to worship at the idol of Zeppelin, it is meaningful that there is a Bonham playing. We can feel as if what we now see is closer to what we would have seen, if we were there back then. The new planks on the ship of Theseus need to be of the same sort of wood. We do not restore George Washington's home at Mount Vernon and install central air; we want the representation to be as close a facsimile as possible. By having Jason Bonham drumming, we may not have been there, but we can come as close as we can to what it would have been like.

The reunion tour, should it ever happen, would be Led Zeppelin only if it has Robert Plant and even if it has Jason Bonham. What is and could maybe be.

12

Celebrating the Agony of Life

ERIN E. FLYNN

> For beauty is nothing but the beginning of terror, which we are still just able to endure, and we are so awed because it serenely disdains to annihilate us. Every angel is terrifying.
>
> —RAINER MARIA RILKE

> [In 1975 we were] more into staying in our rooms and reading Nietzsche.
>
> —ROBERT PLANT

The image most commonly associated with Led Zeppelin is probably the logo of Swan Song Records, the label they launched in 1974. You know the one: a nude, winged male aloft in a blood orange sky above a body of water, head thrown back in a halo of light, arms raised and wings outstretched.

A modification of an 1869–70 painting by the American artist William Rimmer, entitled *Evening, or The Fall of Day*, the figure is ambiguous. Is he exultant or agonized? In the Rimmer original, he is supposed to be Apollo, a Greek god associated with the light and the sun, and who as Apollo Helios came to be identified with Helios, god of the sun. The fall of day is therefore Apollo's fall, the sun's fall into the water, a moment of transition between the clear light of day and the shapeless dark of night. Just as a swan song is sung at death, the image is of anguish or exuberance at the moment of destruction.

Zeppelin's logo mirrors the aesthetic theory Friedrich Nietzsche presents in his first major work, *The Birth of Tragedy out of the*

Spirit of Music. Nietzsche thought there are two fundamental artistic impulses, which in tandem account for the emergence of Greek tragedy. The first is the Apollonian, named after Apollo. Apollonian art is characterized by order and symmetry, by a "measured limitation." It presents individuals as stable, permanent, even eternal. The grace of classical sculpture is probably for Nietzsche its highest accomplishment.

Yet the Apollo of the Swan Song logo is hardly measured or calm. This is perhaps one reason he is not immediately recognizable as Apollo. Indeed, he is sometimes taken to be a different heavenly figure, one also associated with light and one more commonly thought to have endured a great fall, namely, Lucifer. To think of Apollo in this way is to think of the god of light and order falling into chaos, just as Lucifer falls from the order of heaven into the sea of fire and the chaos of hell.

Nietzsche associates Apollonian art with dreams. Nietzsche thought the order of Apollonian art was a kind of mirage, a veil covering over the fact that reality is a chaotic play of force, which creates individuals only to tear them apart again, like so many suites in the Riot House of the cosmos. Apollonian art expresses our faith that we as individuals are real. But when the dream-image flickers and our faith wavers, then we are shaken in horror and in ecstasy, to the point of complete self-forgetting. This might be represented as a fall into the shapeless chaos of a night without dreams. In "Achilles' Last Stand," Plant sings: "the mighty arms of Atlas hold the heavens from the earth," suggesting that the measure and order of the cosmos always threatens to come tumbling down. Only a titanic effort keeps things in their place. But Plant would have known, I think, that the Titans, Atlas among them, were vanquished by the Olympian Zeus, father of Apollo. Hence the burden that Atlas bears is a cost of defeat, as though order is maintained only by turning the titanic forces of nature against themselves. Envisioning the order of the cosmos this way, it is an artificial imposition on the chaotic nature of reality, which is forever bearing down on us.

The other artistic impulse, the Dionysian, named after the Greek god Dionysus, courts this fall into chaos and self-forgetting. It acknowledges that, far from being real, our individuation is a temporary appearance and the source of our suffering. Whereas the Apollonian copes with this knowledge by creating the dream image of a real self, the Dionysian copes with it by creating a pleasurable representation of the self's dissolution, a plunge into the elements, such as Lucifer's descent into fire or Apollo's into water. Later in his career Nietzsche identified Dionysus as an Anti-Christ. For Nietzsche the depth of all Greek art is rooted in Dionysian wisdom: that the very best thing for humans would be not to have been born at all, and the next best thing would be to die as soon as possible. This Dionysian sensitivity to the suffering of individuals at nature's hand is reflected in the anguish of a god of light extinguished by the darkness of the sea.

Yet according to legend, though a swan song is sung at death, it is also achingly beautiful. Alfred Lord Tennyson, for instance, writes of its "awful jubilant voice . . . as when a mighty people rejoice." The swan song is not simply a song of anguish, but a kind of joyous lament. Indeed, perhaps the most significant modification of Rimmer's image seems to reflect this fact. In the original, the figure's left arm is tucked behind his head, as if cradling or clutching it in anguish.

In the logo, the left arm, like the right, is stretched skyward. To my mind, this accentuates the ambiguity of the figure, reinforcing the aspect of exultation.

Nietzsche thinks all good Dionysian art expresses the "jubilation of nature," a strange, even contradictory mixture of agony and ecstasy, cruelty and sexuality. In Dionysian art, pain awakens pleasure, while

joy elicits cries of agony. In songs like "In My Time of Dying" and "When the Levee Breaks," Zeppelin masters this contradictory mixture. Like the best of the blues tradition they appropriate, in such songs the heartrending lament is oddly exultant, while the joy is never without deep mournful yearning, as if over "some irredeemable loss" (*Birth of Tragedy*, §2). This is the core of the aesthetic experience of Dionysian art. Early in *The Birth of Tragedy*, Nietzsche offers an explanation of this Dionysian aesthetic. The yearning lament, he says, is nature's own agony, and nature's irredeemable loss is "its dismemberment into individuals," which creates the conditions of want and strife in the natural world. The same aesthetic experience, and the same wisdom, characterizes the music of Led Zeppelin, helping to explain why the Swan Song logo is so apt.

Kashmir: The Metaphysics of Homesickness

For the young Nietzsche the riddle of the Dionysian mixture of suffering and bliss has a metaphysical solution. Individuation is separation, and separation is pain. The human condition is homesickness. As individuals we are bound to yearn and to strive for what we don't have and can't control. Bonzo's indulgent, violent outbursts, attributed by many to his literal homesickness and longing for his family, reflect this in the extreme. In the face of isolation we long to forget ourselves, even if it means destroying ourselves.

And if reunited, what awaits us? We're still limited, merely temporary manifestations of deeper forces. Returning home should be sweet, but even there we suffer separation. Ultimately, home can't protect us. In "Celebration Day," Plant refers to "new ways to protect the home" which nevertheless prove ineffective when "they break down the door." Perhaps we ache so much being away from home because we know at any moment home itself may suffer, as when a child dies. We then yearn for reunion with nature, so that our strife might cease. But to be reunited with those deeper forces is the end of the individual, our own terrible destruction.

"Kashmir" is a majestic, spectacular song of homelessness. Sung by "a traveler of both time and space" it pictures our condition as perpetual wandering "across the sea of years" and "along the straits of fear." In it Plant imagines being caught in a sandstorm. "All I see turns to brown, as the sun burns the ground / And my eyes fill with sand, as I scan this wasted land / Trying to find, trying to find where I've been." Here the forces of nature, through the wind, sand, and sun, lay waste to everything, obliterating all differentiation and individuation. The traveler himself is engulfed by the storm and is lost. The forces of nature sweep away everything. To reunite with nature is to lose oneself.

The sandstorm is a fitting image of what the young Nietzsche thinks of reality: an eternally suffering, contradictory, primordial unity (*Birth of Tragedy*, §4). Following Schopenhauer, his first great philosophical influence, Nietzsche identifies this underlying unity as the will or drive to manifest itself as the empirical world of individuals. Out of the desert of the real the winds of nature form individuals, separate, yearning, and wandering. But these individuals are bound for destruction by the very winds that formed them. What exists is a driving storm of integration, disintegration, reintegration, and so forth. Musically, "Kashmir" captures this perfectly in the powerful, driving riff which relentlessly ascends and falls in a punishing, pounding cycle, infinitely repeated. Echoing the Greek philosopher Heraclitus, Nietzsche calls this storm of contradiction the father of all things.

For Nietzsche, the artistic impulse is reality's need for release from agonized individuation and redemption in a pleasurable, even ecstatic vision. In Apollonian art the master concept of this redemptive vision is the calm individual, since in remaining one and the same the individual *appears* to resist contradiction. But the Dionysian artist finds a way to take pleasure in the excess of nature, the play of force that overwhelms each individual. Indeed, in spite of its terrible image, listening to "Kashmir" is not terrifying. On the contrary, the song conjures an exhilarating sense of riding along with the forces of nature. Just as on "All My Love," when "the cup is raised, the toast is made yet again" to a force that is forever spinning the cloth of the universe, a force at whose hands we will lose the things most precious to us, so "Kashmir" celebrates "the dust that floats high and clear."[1]

I'm Gonna Crawl: The Eternal Longing of Nature

Because the Dionysian musician speaks from out of this storm of nature, Nietzsche says the "lyric poet needs all the stirrings of

---

[1] Speaking of cups, Dionysus is the god of wine, among other things. I thank Scott Calef for reminding me of that line, as well as for many other observations, embarrassingly many to enumerate.

passion, from the whisper of inclination to the fury of madness . . . he understands the whole of nature, including himself, to be nothing but that which eternally wills, desires, longs" (*Birth of Tragedy*, §6). In blues lyrics, for instance, one of the common images of such longing is walking or traveling. The traveling blues represents the singer as spurred by desire, often sexual or romantic, so that he is forever on the road, sure enough a rolling stone.

Of course, the most explicit traveling blues Zeppelin ever recorded was their exuberant version of Robert Johnson's "Traveling Riverside Blues." Nietzsche says Dionysian artists bring bliss and suffering together in a strange mixture. This is just the kind of thing we experience on "Traveling Riverside Blues." Sometimes the singer laments his condition. "If you see my baby, tell her hurry home / I ain't had no lovin' since my baby been gone." Yet a mood of almost manic joy infuses these very lines. Other times the singer celebrates his satisfaction. "Squeeze my lemon 'til the juice runs down my leg / Squeeze it so hard I fall right out of bed." Plant sings the lines with just a note of pain, which is reflected in the subtle violence of the image. Nature's longing for reunion, manifest in us most explicitly as sexual longing, depends on nature having been dismembered.

Plant's other use of the "squeeze my lemon" lyric occurs on "The Lemon Song," Zeppelin's version of "Killing Floor." That song ends with the ominous line, "I'm gonna leave my children down on this killing floor."[2] Such a declaration, which seems to have many meanings, underscores the violence, futility, and endlessness of sexual longing. First, if the juice runs down his leg, then it yields no progeny, no life. His semen dries on the killing floor. Second, if sexual union is fruitful, it yields children, more mortals to endure life down on this killing floor. Third, in "The Lemon Song" (as in "Killing Floor") the singer is plagued by a lover he should have left a long time ago. Here sexual union is the curse, and so the singer contemplates leaving his family and his children to this despair, this killing floor. On "Traveling Riverside Blues," Plant asks in an aside: "I wonder do you know what I'm talking about?" This at first seems

---

[2] According to PBS's blues glossary, the killing floor is the location in the slaughterhouse where the animals are actually killed, and in the blues the term came to signify a state of intense despair. See www.pbs.org/theblues/classroom/glossary.html.

a not-so-subtle reference to the fact that his "lemon" is not really a lemon. But when you tie the line to the various themes of "Traveling Riverside Blues" and "Killing Floor," it gets to something much deeper about the relentlessness of sexual longing and the ambivalence of sexual union.

This paradox of nature's longing is clarified in another Zeppelin take on the traveling blues: "I'm Gonna Crawl." There, a man has found his true love. He no longer needs to wander, it seems. Yet what's his frame of mind? He dwells on the thought that she might leave. He knows he'll crawl in pursuit of her until he dies, or perhaps worse, has to start again. She might make him a fool and an outlaw, but he doesn't care. He doesn't want to crawl, but knows he will, and he's happy about it! What he tells us about the woman he loves is a fury of madness. The luxurious anguish of the song reveals that even the greatest joy is desperate. If you've been hopelessly in love, you know this undercurrent of misery. Our condition is helpless, yet somehow it makes us feel wonderfully, fully redeemed.

What's at play here isn't the joy of love as opposed to the sorrow of longing. It's rather a release into and redemption of love's longing, a celebration of our helpless, hopeless striving. Even when love works, especially when it works, it's agonizing, tenuous, and doomed, like all our projects. It's doomed by the simple fact that love is a relation between individuals. To be an individual implies that one has limits. The lover's joy depends necessarily on the beloved, who is beyond oneself, out of one's control. Love strives to be one with another, yet true oneness would destroy the very possibility of love since each individual would dissolve in the union. The best we can hope is to die before love ends. So speaks Dionysus.

Some people are so afflicted that they have to restage the drama of seduction all their lives. They separate from one person, so that they may set the stage for coming together with another. But when they find the condition of love remains a paradoxical longing, they separate again to find another. We sometimes scorn, sometimes pity, sometimes envy those people. But the truth is, we too restage the drama of seduction, even if with the same person. The wonderful thing about Zeppelin's staging of this drama is that, like all great Dionysian art, it makes this painful paradox of eternal longing seem exhilarating, so that we celebrate it! *This* is what Nietzsche means by the redemption of our primordial suffering.

In My Time of Dying: Words Bleed into Music

By expressing this eternal longing, Nietzsche would say Zeppelin speak out of the abyss of pure being, the primordial unity of nature. But he wouldn't say they express nature's primordial unity by capturing it in words. On the contrary, Nietzsche thinks lyrics struggle against the limits of language in order to imitate music (*Birth of Tragedy*, §6). Language, after all, defines aspects of the world, including individual things, and distinguishes them from each other. But the spirit of music expresses the primordial unity of things, where such distinctions dissolve. So the Dionysian lyric uses words against their own differentiating tendency, as a mode of the music. Plant, an excellent Dionysian singer, uses his voice as an instrument, and is less concerned to enunciate his words precisely than to use them to pronounce the mood of the song. The lyric serves its melody, as though the melody itself, in strophe after strophe, produces the lyric, and creates language. For the lyricist, as Plant reminds us in "Houses of the Holy," the music is the master.

This helps explain why even great lyricists come off badly as poets, and why words that seem so profound in their musical context often strike us as ridiculous outside it. Lyricists aren't really attempting poetry. They're attempting music. What's remarkable about a good lyric isn't that its meaning translates well to the page or to conversation, but the way its words and meanings fuse with the melody and rhythm. The lyric in isolation can never quite quite convey the Dionysian truth about the original pain of the primordial unity. When we just read the lyrics alone on a page, we often wonder how they managed to move us in the first place.

Plant's lyrics not only "heed the master's call" by serving the melody he sings, they often turn from words into non-words. "In My Time of Dying" is one of many songs in which Page's guitar and Plant's vocal line mimic each other (in particular on the "die easy" part of the refrain). Here the words are bleeding into music. There's also a wonderful vocal moment toward the end of the song (beginning at 10:07), in which Plant seems to slip into a death moan (even though the song begins, "In my time of dying / Don't want nobody to moan") that is itself indistinguishable from a moan of sexual ecstasy. Here the minor death of orgasm stands in for the major death, and death itself induces a kind of ecstasy. The individual's greatest satisfaction is his undoing. So contradictory is our individuation that our most intense pleasure can be confused with our deepest misery. (I leave it to the reader to determine which is which.)

At such moments, even the individual singer slips from view, fusing with the drive of nature, here expressed in the moan of Page's haunting slide. Nature's drive treats all individuals as unreal, temporary manifestations of its own power. To hear this is exhilarating and terrifying. It is to disintegrate just a touch, to feel the seductive pull of oblivion, and to take such pleasure in it that the nagging anxiety of the finite individual is redeemed. The suffering is redeemed not by a myth of happiness or stability, but by embracing the ultimate contradiction: that happiness is underpinned by an abysmal tumult that will undo it.

Whole Lotta Love: The Transgressing Will

For Nietzsche, Greek tragedy expresses this same contradiction of individuation through the strife of the tragic hero. The heroes of Greek tragedy break the norms that set boundaries for individuals and so reveal that the individual is inevitably undone. Transgression defines Oedipus's very existence as an incestuous parricide, for example, and Prometheus not only transgresses against the Olympian gods by stealing fire and giving it to humans, he also teaches them the civilizing arts. Prometheus, the transgressor, humanizes us. Our human origin is marked by transgression and strife. Though heroes such as Oedipus and Prometheus end up miserable, tragedy presents their striving also as a heroic glimmer of light shining out of the dark abyss. The pain of our own strife and separation is redeemed in that heroic image.

Though we don't find full-blown tragic heroes in Zeppelin, in songs like "Whole Lotta Love" we do find the transgressing voice of the will. The opening riff, probably Page's most famous, is as aggressively erotic as anything he wrote. It drives relentlessly through the song, like the surging blood of the will, which Plant's lyrics image as explicitly carnal. "Way down inside, honey you need it / I'm gonna give you my love / Ohhh, wanna whole lotta love." The subject matter is yearning, both the singer's own ("baby, I been yearnin'") and what he insists is the yearning of his would-be lover. Something separates them; they're in need. Sexual desire bids them to cross the borders of the self.

From start to finish "Whole Lotta Love" gives voice to a sexual drive that not only crosses physical boundaries, but normative ones. Plant leaves no room for doubt about what kind of love he's planning to give, a love that can be measured in inches. But it's also a kind of education ("I'm gonna send you back to schoolin'"), a lesson he has to teach his would-be lover, who evidently learns it. This lesson is a kind of taming ("You need coolin', baby I'm not foolin'"). Hence the rule against force is broken. What keeps this transgression from being sinister is the fact that, in learning the lesson, the lover supposedly discovers her own deepest needs.

After the first two verses promise these lessons in sex ed, the song turns to the bridge, which begins like the swirling of libidinal energies. Page's guitars pan severely from channel to channel and Plant's voice mimics breathless sexual arousal. Eventually Page is scratching his strings under such heavy effects that his guitar sounds like the voice of a sexual demon, and Plant simply cries out "love!" By the time Bonham rolls into the break, the rocking thump-thump and the guitar solo, we're back into the heavy pulse of sex.

Just as the song begins with an image of transgression, so it ends with perhaps the most famous of all blues transgressions ("Shake for me girl / I wanna be your backdoor man"). Here the literal boundary, the backdoor, notoriously marks two normative boundaries, against adultery and against anal sex. The lover is shaken, or called upon to shake, as though the transgressing demons of the verse would dissolve in orgasm all her boundaries, normative and otherwise.

For all its cocksure posturing about delivering the goods, "Whole Lotta Love" is a little scary. Much of Page's guitar work lashes us, and Plant's sexual wailing is as tortured as it is insistent. The lead riff is the ride of sexual demons, to which Plant gives voice. The song celebrates their power, but under their influence the singer cries out in need. Even his satisfaction leaves him exposed and vulnerable. As the blues wisdom would have it: "I can't never be satisfied." What keeps the song from egoistic fantasy is that its heroic celebration of sexual ecstasy is coupled with an awareness of this contradiction. The song remains sensitive to the suffering that accompanies our transgressions.

When the Levee Breaks: Excess as Truth

For Nietzsche, Dionysian music reveals excess as the truth of nature: "excess revealed itself as the truth; contradiction, bliss born of pain, spoke of itself from out of the heart of nature" (*Birth of Tragedy*, §4). By nature's excess, Nietzsche means that which, from within or without, bursts the individual's boundaries, overwhelming and consuming the individual. Songs that reveal excess as truth, render our striving heroic, and redeem our suffering are worthy of inclusion in the pantheon of Dionysian art. "When the Levee Breaks" does all this and more.

The opening of "When the Levee Breaks" is Bonham distilled: titanic thunder and sense of song. He's the steady pulsing swell of water against the levee, and to hear him shakes us. He announces the song's twin themes: that the excess of nature will inevitably overwhelm our artificial barriers and scatter us, and that this excess also builds from within, until the dams of the self burst, and in striving we are undone. As with almost everything Led Zeppelin does well, the rhythm is aggressively erotic. "If it keeps on raining," Plant moans, "the levee is going to break." But Bonham reveals the truth: the levee *is* going to break.

Although the wanderer is sometimes presented as a model of freedom, he's also often driven out and compelled to leave, even if by some inner urge he can't understand or master. The line "When the levee breaks, we'll have no place to stay" reminds us that we're transient beings driven beyond our borders by rising rivers, internal and external. The first lines of "When the Levee Breaks" signal the rising of nature, and sexual desire in particular, which like the river can drive us away from home. It declares our struggle for self-control futile. Yet while the song is a vision of our destruction, it's also exhilarating. It celebrates nature's power. Being overcome by it, we also get to try it on, as when we succumb to lust.

As individuals, we're neither stable nor secure behind our borders.[3] Instead, nature pounds relentlessly against them, always threatening to burst through. We reside at these boundaries, just trying to keep it together. "All last night, I sat on the levee and moaned / Thinking 'bout my baby and my happy home." If the

---

[3] In light of the breaking of the levee, compare also *Coda's* "Wearing and Tearing." "Then it grows like thunder / Until it bursts inside of you / Try to hold steady / Wait until you're ready / Any second now will do / Throw the door wide open / Not a word is spoken." Here the storm tears you up inside until you have to open up, not to speak, but to burst, to bleed.

water is the rising of desire, then spending the night on the levee is spending it in the throes of longing, which may be mournful, but also guilty. As Plant later sings, "I'm going to Chicago / Sorry, but I can't take you." The outer excess that overwhelms us parallels the inner excess that drives us away from our happy home. It is, after all, his lover he can't take to Chicago. I invite the reader to consider the many reasons this might be. Nature breaks us up.

It's not incidental that Plant ends the song with "I'm going down / I'm going down now / I'm going down." Down into what, we might ask? Perhaps, as with the Apollo of the Swan Song logo, down into the water. The swirling of the musical elements against Plant's languishing voice suggests a kind of drowning. Or perhaps, as with Lucifer, down into a sea of fire, down into hell, which may be Chicago—an urban den of iniquity—but is likely a more personal descent. In German one can speak of annihilation as "going to the ground." So the singer may just be dying, going down into the earth. Then again, "going down" has a well-known sexual meaning. Water, fire, and earth are elements, so in going down the singer is being dissolved again into nature, returned to the ground of the primordial unity.

While "When the Levee Breaks" is overwhelmingly about the lamentable truth that excess will shatter us, that the home of the self is propped on unstable ground, we take pleasure in the very image. It acts as a promise of ecstatic release and reunion. The song serves as a fantasy of being broken apart, forgetting oneself entirely, and dissolving into the primordial ground. I might go so far as to say that it makes the striving heroic, since it is a levee worker's song, the song of one struggling to erect the very structure that will allow him to live, temporarily, by the river whose rising waters will destroy him. This is the song's lament. Just as the god of nature unifies us all, so we are exhilarated when the levee breaks. This is the song's jubilation.

Our individuation, though it appears so real, is a temporary and excruciating manifestation of forces that outstrip us. Such is the Dionysian wisdom Nietzsche finds expressed in all art. Good Dionysian art redeems this lamentable fate by celebrating our struggle against and ultimate release into the very forces that undo us. Rather than a flight into hedonism, Dionysian art is steeped in the awareness of our painful, contradictory condition.

Led Zeppelin gives ecstatic expression to this wisdom and so something like Nietzsche's Dionysian metaphysics of the self: that we are temporary manifestations of nature's endlessly transformative power.[4]

[4] I'd like to thank Scott Calef, Duane Davis, Sara Eilert, and Martin Hipsky for their helpful comments on earlier versions of this paper. I'm in their debt for its improvements.

13
Bring the Balance Back

EDWARD MACAN

Perhaps no other major rock band of the 1960s and 1970s captured the contradictions of the era as forcefully as Led Zeppelin: the power of their music, so often commented on by fans and critics alike, seems to derive at least in part from their juxtaposition of dualities.

Led Zeppelin were the first band whose music earned the sobriquet "cock rock" from feminist scholars, both for its sledgehammer-like rhythms and overdriven bass and guitar parts, and for the band's macho, swaggering stage posturing and (at times) sexist lyrics. Yet there was an androgynous element to the stage personas of both lead singer Robert Plant and guitarist Jimmy Page, and the same blurring of "masculine" and "feminine" qualities is evident in their music: when Page first met Plant in 1968, he reportedly remarked he wanted the band he was forming to play "a new kind of 'heavy music', with slower and lighter touches, music with dynamics, light and shade, *chiaroscuro*."[1] This contrast is implicit in the name of the band itself: Led (originally "Lead," as in the heavy metal, with the spelling changed so Americans wouldn't mispronounce it), Zeppelin (as in the lighter-than-air dirigible).

Then there's the issue of the seemingly contradictory stylistic sources Led Zeppelin drew from. The early albums are marked by a tension between the band's debt to traditional, earthy "roots" music—above all the blues and other African-American styles, but

---

[1] Stephen Davis, *Hammer of the Gods: The Led Zeppelin Saga* (Ballantine, 1985), p. 52.

187

also British folk music—on the one hand, and their interest in avant-garde sound techniques on the other. There's also the tension, evident throughout their entire output, between their "native" musical heritage (British folk) and their "adopted" musical heritage (American blues and rock'n'roll), and between their grounding in Anglo-American traditions and their interest in Eastern (specifically Arab and Indian) musical traditions. Of their two most pervasive extra-musical influences, one, J.R.R. Tolkien (1892–1973), was a bookish philologist and orthodox Catholic author best known for his fantasy cycle *Lord of the Rings*; the other, Aleister Crowley (1875–1947), was a flamboyant occultist who believed that his controversial *Book of the Law* had engendered a new religion, Thelema.

How does one explain this level of apparently contradictory tendencies in the band's music? This question is especially pertinent because Led Zeppelin's place in rock music history is, while unquestionably seminal, also difficult to categorize. They were far more than just a blues revival band: nonetheless, throughout their entire career, they recorded songs that were not only stylistically indebted to the blues, but which repeated well-established blues tropes (consider, for instance, their frequent celebrations of carnal pleasure from a masculine perspective, "Whole Lotta Love" and "Black Dog" providing just two well-known examples). They were unquestionably an enormous influence on the musical style that came to be known as "heavy metal": for instance, it's hard to overstate the impact of "Dazed and Confused," with its evocation of madness, and "Immigrant Song" with its swords-and-sorcery imagery and storyline, on the future of the genre. Yet considering how much of their material is acoustically based, calling them a proto-metal band is, at best, problematic. Moreover, despite Jimmy Page's ambiguous feelings about progressive rock,[2] a small but crucial part of their output ("Stairway to Heaven," "The Song Remains the Same," "Kashmir," "In the Light," "Achilles' Last Stand," "Carouselambra") fit comfortably within the commonly acknowledged stylistic boundaries of that genre. It's here, incidentally, that the band comes closest to expressing a more or less clearly defined philosophical stance.

---

[2] Susan Fast, *In the Houses of the Holy: Led Zeppelin and the Power of Rock Music* (Oxford University Press, 2001), p. 60.

It's not easy to reconcile the many songs (usually blues-based) that celebrate carnal pleasure, life on the move ("Babe I'm Gonna Leave You," "Ramble On"), relationship issues, and other "non-philosophical" topics with the much smaller body of more ambitious (and inevitably less blues-influenced) songs that address "philosophical" and/or "spiritual" concerns. This particular dichotomy separates Led Zeppelin from contemporaries and near contemporaries such as Pink Floyd, Yes, and Rush, who express a more or less coherent philosophical perspective (and, for that matter, a more or less consistent stylistic approach) in song after song on album after album. Is there a philosophical perspective that would explain how the same band responsible for the breathless carnality of "The Lemon Song" and "Heartbreaker" also achieved the universally acknowledged spirituality of "Stairway to Heaven"?

I believe the answer is "yes"; one can profitably address the apparent contradictions within the music of Led Zeppelin through the philosophy of Georg Wilhelm Friedrich Hegel (1770–1831).

Sing Out Hare Hare: Hegel and the World Spirit

Hegel is best known as a philosopher of history and is, indeed, one of the few major philosophers for whom history has been a central preoccupation. Coming of age in a time of enormous cultural and political change in Europe, he was keenly aware of many tensions and apparent contradictions at work in his society; he came to view these dualities as part of an evolving, underlying unity he called the "World-Spirit," through which the historical process unfolds:

> It is . . . an inference from the history of the World, that its development has been a rational process; that the history in question has constituted the rational necessary course of the World-Spirit . . . which unfolds this its one nature in the phenomena of the World's existence."[3]

Hegel asserts that the intermediaries of the World-Spirit are "great historical men" who "had an insight into the requirements of the time—what was ripe for development" (p. 30).

---

[3] Georg Wilhelm Friedrich Hegel, *The Philosophy of History* (Cosimo Classics, 2007), p. 10. Subsequent references to Hegel in the text are to this edition.

Although Hegel invokes political and military figures such as Julius Caesar and Napoleon as examples of great historical men, had he lived through the upheavals of the late 1960s, he would perhaps have cited the more freedom-conscious, progressively oriented rock musicians of the era such as Bob Dylan, the Beatles, Jimi Hendrix, and Led Zeppelin as mediums of the World-Spirit.

According to Hegel, while nature simply repeats in cycles, human history demonstrates "a real capacity for change, and that for the better—an impulse of perfectibility" (p. 54). History's progress towards freedom involves "dialectical" transformation through inner conflict, resulting from the fact that "Spirit . . . carries within it its own negation" (p. 57):

> Progress appears as an advancing from the imperfect to the more perfect; but the former . . . involves the very opposite of itself—the so-called perfect—as a germ or impulse. (p. 17)

Spirit is transformed the moment it becomes conscious of this contradiction or negation within itself, as its current identity dissolves and it passes on to a new, higher stage in its development. Thus history is a progression in which each successive movement emerges as an ever-more fully realized solution to the contradictions inherent in the preceding movement: "The dialectical nature of the Idea [is] that it assumes successive forms which it successively transcends; and by this very process of transcending its earlier stages, gains . . . a richer and more concrete shape" (p. 63).

One of Hegel's favorite examples of the dialectic process in history is the French Revolution, which first introduced the concept of individual freedom into European politics. Inherent in this movement toward individual freedom was violence, which inevitably turned on itself during the Reign of Terror. Out of this apparent negation, however, emerged the constitutional state.

The three-part process of the Hegelian dialectic is often referred to as thesis-antithesis-synthesis; using this terminology, the French Revolution was the "thesis" that inaugurated this process, the Reign of Terror its "antithesis," and the emergence of the constitutional state the resulting "synthesis." The danger of the thesis-antithesis-synthesis terminology is that it creates the impression that Hegel viewed the historical process as one of unity-from-duality where two countervailing forces collide, and, through the collision, produce a synthesis. To the contrary, though, Hegel stressed that every culture and historical movement contains an inherent contradiction: when that contradiction emerges, the original culture or movement simultaneously dissolves and transforms into a higher-level expression of the contradiction. In other words, Hegel's system is monist, stressing that the underlying unity of a thing is more real than its apparent duality: "Spirit is immortal; with it there is no past, no future, but an essential now. This necessarily implies that the present form of Spirit comprehends within it all earlier steps" (p. 79).[4]

Hegel's influences included "mystic" or "hermetic" writers such as Jakob Böhme (1575–1624) as well as Eastern religious and philosophical thought, just beginning to reach Europe in translation during his lifetime. Given Led Zeppelin's debt to Eastern thought and Western hermeticism (the latter mainly through Crowley), both of which contain a very strong monist element, exploring the dichotomies that characterize their music in the context of Hegel's ideas seems especially appropriate.

An analysis of music on the lines of Hegelian dialectic could take place on several levels. One could make a sweeping analysis of a band's entire output, or, indeed, of an entire style: one could assert, for instance, that the fundamental tension at work in the progressive rock of the 1970s is that of European classical musical forms and techniques being grafted on to an African-American, blues-based musical foundation. In a crude and not very nuanced way, this is true: however, it tells us little about what such a fusion might have meant, or what its cultural significance might have been. I prefer to examine specific songs, teasing out their apparently contradictory elements, paying special attention to how a song's structure reflects its tensions, considering how (or if) these elements are reconciled, and pondering what, on a cultural level, such reconciliation (or lack thereof) portends. Like Hegel himself, Led Zeppelin and other bands that came of age during the late 1960s and early 1970s were aware of many tensions and contradictions in their society, and viewed music as a forum for exploring these tensions. They were, to cite "The Battle of Evermore," involved in the eternal Hegelian struggle to "bring the balance back."

---

[4] Using Hegel's description here, one might usefully visualize Hegelian dialectic as an ascending spiral.

Whole Lotta Love: Balancing Dualities of Gender and Race

"Dazed and Confused," arguably the most influential song from Led Zeppelin's eponymous debut album (January 1969), and "Whole Lotta Love," the even more influential classic from their second album, *II* (October 1969), are rather different in terms of tempo, mood, and subject matter. Nonetheless, the two songs are, in certain important respects, similar. For one, both are widely considered founding texts of the genre that, after 1970, came to be known as heavy metal. More specifically, the two songs share similar structures: intensely physical outer sections dominated by memorable blues-based riffs and powerful vocals, framing middle sections in which Plant's wordless moans become mere strands in shadowy, swirling sound collages that eventually give way to frantic guitar solos. The structural format of the two songs highlights four specific dualities: Primitive/Modern, Physical/Psychological, African-American/European, and Male/Female.

"Dazed and Confused" opens with a descending two-bar bass riff in E minor, played by John Paul Jones with a muffled, almost "dead" tone at a ponderously slow tempo. This riff is quite similar to the chromatically descending ground bass figures of the European baroque, which inevitably had connotations of sorrow and lament, as this one has.[5] A few seconds into the song, Jimmy Page begins to play bursts of reverberating guitar notes, and soon thereafter Robert Plant enters with the first verse. The lyrics develop a common blues trope: the man under the spell of a woman who has bewitched him and he wants to leave, but can't. One is struck by the power of Plant's voice, which is very up-front in the mix, by the irregularity of his phrasing (he consistently begins his verses before the beginning of the riff),[6] and by the spastic, irregular rhythms of his vocal delivery—all consistent with the emotional affect of desperation and confusion.

---

[5] The ground bass figures from Henry Purcell's "Dido's Lament" (from his opera *Dido and Aeneas*) and J.S. Bach's "Crucifixus" (from his *Mass in B minor*) are two well-known ground bass figures of this type, but one could cite many more.

[6] Unlike many "early metal" singers, Plant's vocal lines usually move in counterpoint with Page's guitar riffs. Compare this to Black Sabbath's "Iron Man," for instance, where Ozzy Osbourne's vocal line moves in unison with Tony Iommi's guitar riff.

It's only after the first verse (at 0:35) that the rest of the band kick in full-throttle: Jones and Page with a massive statement of the riff in three different octaves (bass, "grungy" guitar an octave above the bass, "wailing" guitar two octaves above the bass), John Bonham with the song's first full-on drum groove. Plant soon enters with his second verse (the highest guitar part drops out at this point), then at 1:10, for the first time in the song, the riff momentarily drops out, replaced by a short, explosive rising guitar figure which I'll hereafter call the "counter-riff." At 1:20, the original riff re-enters, continuing when Plant commences his third verse at 1:35. A reappearance of the counter-riff at 1:54 transitions us into the middle, B section of the song's A B A format.

The "cushion" that supports the first half of this shadowy section (from 2:02 through 3:23) is a five-note figure (four sixteenths and an eighth) ceaselessly traded back and forth between Jones' bass and Bonham's drums. At first, the exchange between Jones and Bonham is foregrounded, but it is soon overshadowed by Page's and Plant's hazier, more irregular call-and-response: Page plays two- or three-note figures on his guitar with a violin bow, crafting halos of richly vibrating sonorities, to which Plant responds with "ahhs" and "ohhs." From 2:42 the guitar sonorities start to pulsate—eventually the guitar's melodic outlines become so indistinct that Plant can no longer respond to them—and at 2:57 Jones starts to vary the melodic content (although never the rhythmic pattern) of his bass part. A slowly descending guitar glissando gradually overwhelms the pulsating guitar sonorities, eventually even obscuring the sense of beat.

The second half of this section is launched by Bonham at 3:24 with four smartly-struck hi-hat accents; the band suddenly lurch into double time, and, over Jones' driving two-beat bass pattern, Page weaves a frantic guitar solo that seems to struggle to break through the gloom—the madness, if you will—of the preceding section. It almost appears for a moment he will succeed—at 4:42 he suddenly introduces a fanfare-like lick, played three times in all, that appears to move the music towards E major. However, before the transition to major can be consummated, the counter-riff reappears (4:57), followed quickly by the original riff. After Page's desperate solo, the return of the leaden opening riff brings a palpable sense of failing to escape, of sliding down into defeat.

The final A section compresses all the key elements of the song. Plant enters with his fourth and final verse (5:20); we hear the counter-riff at 5:38, and the five-note figure that opened the B section (now without the wordless vocals) at 5:46. The return of this figure suggests that perhaps another "breakout" will be attempted, and indeed, at 5:55, the five-note figure is transformed into a series of pounding D major chords, accompanied by Plant's frenzied "oohs" and "ahhs." But the pounding chords cannot escape the tug of gravity, as it were, and are pulled down (at 6:12) into the E tonic, which reverberates for the final ten seconds.

"Whole Lotta Love" also opens with a memorable riff. Initially occupying two bars in 4/4 time, the riff rolls along at an unhurried pace of 90 and 92 beats per minute, belying the intense sense of energy generated by its rhythmic syncopation: when Plant enters with his first verse, the band compresses the riff from two bars to one, which seems to generate even more energy. In his biography of the band, Stephen Davis asserts that during the Vietnam War "American soldiers and marines bolted eight-track stereos onto their tanks and armored personnel carriers and rode into battle playing the song at top volume."[7] Whether or not that is true, the story highlights the riff's martial nature.

The first part of the song (the A section of the A B A structure) features two verses and choruses; the riff is omnipresent throughout the section. While the music's original, the words are a rearrangement of the lyrics from Willie Dixon's "You Need Love," which Plant apparently encountered through a 1962 single, released by Chess Records, featuring Muddy Waters; Plant excises some lyrics and switches the order of others.[8] As with "Dazed and Confused," the lyrics address an anonymous female, but with a different purpose: here Plant is the experienced man offering his services to a (presumably) less experienced woman, making his goal quite clear: "gonna give you every inch of my love."

"Whole Lotta Love" has often been used as Display #1 by those wishing to convict "cock rock" of sexism: as Charles Shaar Murray puts it, "The woman . . . is here reduced to a mere receptacle; an entirely passive presence whose sole function is to receive the

---

[7] *Hammer of the* Gods, p. 102.

[8] In 1985 Willie Dixon sued Led Zeppelin, successfully, for a songwriting credit. It has been conjectured that Plant may have encountered the song first not through Waters's 1962 single, but through the Small Faces' cover of the song released in 1966, "You Need Loving."

Great Zeppelin"[9]. As with the vocal of "Dazed and Confused," one is struck by the power of Plant's delivery during the verses, his expressive use of vocal distortion, and the intensity of feeling conveyed by his breaking up of rhythms as he extends syllables. His vocals during the chorus ("Wanna whole lot of love"), while equally powerful, are curiously inexpressive and machine-like (no vocal distortion and precise, square rhythms), and perfectly complement Page's descending guitar glissandos, which suggest a train or another large vehicle passing at a high rate of speed and fading into the distance. A convincing argument could certainly be made that this chorus expresses "love" (sex) as a merely mechanical activity.

Like "Dazed and Confused," "Whole Lotta Love" contains a lengthy instrumental middle section that serves as Feminine foil to the intensely Masculine outer sections. As with the middle section of "Dazed," this one is built on a rhythmic cushion supplied by the rhythm section—in this case, Bonham alone, who plays a pattern of straight sixteenth-notes on the hi-hat, which he opens and closes every eighth note. After a few seconds he begins to accompany this pattern with a remarkable "tune" played on the bells of his cymbals; the notes of this "tune" tend to fall on upbeats, undermining the sense of meter and veiling the location of the downbeat. The cymbal "tune" consists mostly of longer note values at first, but he gradually starts to play eighth notes, until finally he is playing a repetitive 3/4 pattern on the cymbals against the unchanging 4/4 pattern of the hi-hat. While Bonham is justly considered rock's premier power drummer, this passage, seldom commented on, shows what a subtle and sophisticated drummer he could be, as he weaves a fluidly polyrhythmic backdrop for the sound collage that slowly takes shape on top. First (1:30) we hear a soft conga (or possibly bongo) counter-rhythm, then a didgeridoo-like sound that resembles a swirling wind storm (1:45); gradually we begin to hear Plant in the background, first muttering (1:56), then panting ("ahh ahh ahh," and so on) while the swirling "wind" (which replicates a circular motion as it moves from left speaker to right and back) grows louder. As Plant's muttering grows more intense, Bonham momentarily gives up his cymbal tune in favor of a snare pattern

---

[9] Charles Shaar Murray, *Crosstown Traffic: Jimi Hendrix and Post-War Pop* (Faber and Faber, 1989), p. 60.

that answers Plant's ecstatic groans. At about 2:23 we hear a sound that's something like a creaky door, which morphs into a reverberating whistle; then, as the circular "wind" pattern again grows more intense, we hear Plant's ejaculation of "Luhv" (2:43) and his more drawn out "Luh uh uh uh ove" (2:52).

Finally, at 3:00 Bonham's dramatic drum break segues into the shorter second part of the middle section. Page launches into an explosive solo, actually a series of passionate ejaculations between sledgehammer-like iterations of two offbeat guitar-bass chords: like "Dazed and Confused," Page's solo introduces a new *persona* to the song, and seems to signify the hero's struggle against the constraints of the previous section. Here, however, the return of the opening riff (3:18) after the solo doesn't feel like sliding into defeat, as it did in "Dazed," but as triumphant affirmation. The song's recapitulation proceeds more or less predictably until 4:00, when the band pauses dramatically, and Plant sings a recitative-like solo passage, accompanied only by a couple of isolated background chords; this proves to be the song's final speed bump, as the opening riff resumes, accompanied by Plant's continuously intense shrieks, moans, and asides. Plant is in the process of emitting one final shriek while the song is fading out.

I've said that "Dazed and Confused" and "Whole Lotta Love" explore four apparent dualities: Primitive/Modern, Physical/Psychological, African-American/European, and Male/Female. The first three are interrelated. During the twentieth century, a school of criticism developed around African-American music—blues, jazz, R & B—that saw its value in its "soul," its "closeness to nature," its "pure feeling," and its "authenticity." In short, much of the critical writing surrounding American popular music in general, and African-American music in particular, is based on a Romantic primitivism that can be traced back to the eighteenth century and Rousseau's "noble savage," if not earlier. According to this ideology, the black bluesman, in particular, is the Noble Savage: in his unselfconscious physicality, he is in touch with a liberating primal energy that the white European has lost touch with, but can recover at least in part through surrendering to the physical power of African-American music.

The danger of saying, in the context of a black-white duality, that black music is "felt" is that white music is, by contrast "thought": that feeling is a "black" characteristic, but thought a "white" one. Here is where Hegelian synthesis becomes such a valuable conceptual tool (and such a compelling way of viewing the historical process): it rises above mutually-exclusive categories, and allows one to view Primitive/Modern, Physical/Psychological, and African-American/European as poles of a single continuum that are subject to interpenetration and ultimately, transcendence. Hegelian synthesis offers a monist perspective in which apparent dualities are just that: apparent.

How, specifically, does the process of Hegelian synthesis work in the two Zeppelin songs under consideration? In both "Dazed and Confused" and "Whole Lotta Love," the outer sections are blues-based and powerfully physical; thus, "Physical" and "African-American" are linked.[10] Clearly, for many white people of Led Zeppelin's generation, the appeal of blues and other African-American musical styles was their unabashed physicality: by putting them in touch with their own bodies, it met a need they felt their "own" music (music of European or white North American provenance) did not. Furthermore, by juxtaposing the "earthy" blues-based outer sections with the "modernistic" avant-garde sound collages of the middle sections, the band creates an implicit Primitive-Modern dichotomy, thus linking "Primitive" with "Physical" and "African-American."

If the blues-based sections of these two songs fulfill one strongly felt need (recovery of one's physicality), then the avant-garde sound collages of these songs fulfill a different need that was at the time equally strongly felt: the opportunity to explore the psychological recesses of inner space. Because they are usually considered a "Seventies band," it is often forgotten that Led Zeppelin came of age during the psychedelic rock era. The desire to enter the sanctum of "inner space" was almost universal among the cutting-edge rock bands (especially British rock bands) active during 1968–69, and musical entrance into inner space was achieved largely through the new techniques and technology introduced by

---

[10] Granted, "Dazed and Confused" is not a traditional blues; Jimmy Page borrowed ("stole" might be a more accurate term) the song from American folksinger Jake Holmes, whom Page heard while touring with the Yardbirds. (The song appears on Holmes's debut album of 1967, *The Above Ground Sound of Jake Holmes*). However, Zeppelin impart a blues ethos to the song both through the stylistic character of the arrangement, and by its placement on the band's debut album: it comes immediately after their cover of Willie Dixon's "You Shook Me," with which it shares both a key and a tempo.

the European avant-garde during the 1950s.[11] Therefore, for the musicians who were active in these bands, the categories of "Modern," "European," and "Psychological" are linked.

Finally, we must address the Male/Female dichotomy as it is developed in these two songs. In both songs, the outer sections are dominated by powerful rhythms and distorted timbres, while the middle sections are characterized by less assertive rhythms and (usually) less strident timbres; it's significant that the middle sections of both songs prominently feature Plant's "feminine" moans and shrieks, but not his actual singing (in the sense of coherent melodic lines). In short, the middle sections of both songs play the role of Feminine foil to the Masculine outer sections. There are three points of interest here. First, "Female" is linked with the categories "Modern," "European," and "Psychological." The last is perhaps less surprising, in the context of Western culture's long-enduring Mind/Body duality; but it is interesting that "Female" is linked with "Modern," specifically with modern musical technology (usually perceived to be a male domain), and with the "European," rather than "African-American," side of the musical equation. (Given that the black bluesman, the "Noble Savage," is implicitly viewed as child-like in primitivist ideology, it is perhaps surprising that he, rather than the white musical technocrat, is assigned the "Male" identity).

Second, note that in the middle section of both of these songs, "Female" is constructed not as soft, pliable, and reassuring, but rather as mysterious, frightening, and potentially dangerous. I believe that the reason the guitar solos at the end of both sections have such a desperate energy, a feeling of trying to break through a powerful constraint, is that they are all about recovering a sense of masculine identity after communion with the Feminine Other. In "Dazed and Confused," this recovery is ultimately unsatisfying, but in "Whole Lotta Love," we experience the recovery of masculine musical identity (the return of the opening riff after Page's orgasmic solo) as a moment of triumphant affirmation. Given that adolescent males were among Zeppelin's largest and most loyal fan demographic during the 1970s, one can easily understand the appeal of this musical gesture to the band's audience.

---

[11] Specifically the electronic music of the 1950s: the *musique concrète* of Pierre Henry and Pierre Schaeffer, Edgard Varèse's *Poème électronique*, and Karlheinz Stockhausen's *Gesang der Jünglinge*.

Notice, too, that in "Whole Lotta Love," while orgasm is *sung about* from a masculine perspective in the outer sections, it's musically *evoked* from a feminine perspective in the middle section, with Bonham's soft, subtle rhythmic cushion and the circular motion of the sound collage evoking not only the Feminine, but the womb. Therefore, Charles Shaar Murray is incorrect in alleging that "Whole Lotta Love" reduces the woman to passive receptacle. Like too many popular music critics, Murray fails to take the music itself into account: Plant's metaphoric partner during the middle section is the sound collage. This point was made explicit in the band's live performances of the song, where, in a call-and-response with Plant, Jimmy Page recreated the studio recording's sound collage via his Theremin. While Zeppelin certainly didn't subvert all the expected constructions of masculinity and femininity in these two songs, their constructions of Male/Female are quite nuanced and, in some ways at least (especially in linking femininity with technology), do represent a genuine interpenetration and synthesis.[12]

The strength of Led Zeppelin's musical vision during 1968–69 is that they bring apparently dualistic categories into a mutually enriching dialogue. In "Dazed and Confused," the middle section is used to explore the feelings of confusion and madness that the protagonist laments (in a more overtly physical, dramatic way) in the outer section. In "Whole Lotta Love," the middle section evokes the sexual experience referenced in the outer sections not just as a physical, but also a psychological experience. In short, during 1968-69 Zeppelin were feeling their way towards a music that transcended the perceived limitations of both their African-American blues and European avant-garde sources: a music that combined physicality with the possibility of psychological depth (through the exploration of inner space), that made the power of the past and of the future available in the present, that experimented with new constructions of "masculine" and (particularly) "feminine," and that brought together "black" and "white" approaches to music-making in a single discourse.

This new music came to be known as heavy metal, although few metal bands achieved Zeppelin's nuance and subtlety. And the formation of this new musical style was in turn emblematic of, and

---

[12] For more on the issue of gender construction in "Whole Lotta Love," see *In the Houses of the Holy*, pp. 189–201. Fast points out that during the middle section, it's hard to tell who is supposed to be representing the "female"—Plant, with his moans and shrieks, or Page, with his swirling sheets of sound.

driven by, tensions—concerning changing racial and gender identities, new modes of consciousness, growing anxieties about the relationship of the present to the past—that operated at the deepest levels of society. That is to say, the Hegelian synthesis at work in the band's music reflects a Hegelian synthesis at work within contemporaneous society.

Although neither "Dazed and Confused" or "Whole Lotta Love" is "philosophical," at their deepest structural levels, both songs reveal a philosophical base that is essentially monist. Apparent dichotomies like "Primitive" and "Modern," "African-American" and "European," "Physical" and "Psychological," and even "Male" and "Female" are merely spectrums along a continuum of experiences and identities. This monist perspective becomes even more evident in the band's later music.

Stairway to Heaven: Balancing Past and Present

In 1970, Led Zeppelin released *III*. As anyone who is even a casual fan of the band knows, side one of the LP is largely dominated by the hard rock/proto-metal manner of the two previous albums, although one track, "Friends," foreshadows the band's growing interest in Eastern music. Side two of the LP shows the band taking a deeper interest in softer, more acoustic-oriented music than they had before, and even includes a cover of a grim old English ballad, "Gallows Pole," that features Jimmy Page picking banjo in his best Earl Scruggs imitation. "Immigrant Song" was the album's only song to achieve the status of a Zeppelin classic, and not surprisingly, many critics, even many fans, considered the album something of a failure. Time has tempered this verdict: while few would argue it is one of the band's stronger albums, its crucial transitional role is now widely recognized. Its juxtaposition of electric- and acoustic-based music (already prefigured by early classics like "Babe, I'm going to Leave You" and "Ramble On") foreshadows the more thoroughgoing synthesis that was about to follow on the fourth album; it also marks the end of the band's experimentation with electronic sound collages.[13] From this point on, Zeppelin (like

---

[13] One exception: the passage of eerily reverberating droning guitars that opens the late-period classic "In the Evening." This passage was lifted from Page's abandoned film score for Kenneth Anger's *Lucifer Rising*, which he fitfully worked on through the mid-1970s.

many of their seventies rock colleagues) became less interested in opening new sonic worlds, more concerned with thoroughly synthesizing the principal elements of their music.

Zeppelin's fourth, untitled album is usually referred to either as "*IV*," "*Zoso*" (for the quasi-runic inscription from its liner sleeve), or "*The Runes Album*." Demonstrating considerable advances in production (especially in finally capturing the full power of John Bonham's drum sound), in arranging sophistication (here Page perfects his multi-layered guitar arrangements, or "guitar army"), and in its magisterial drawing together of the band's primary stylistic sources, it was quickly recognized as the band's finest album yet. Indeed, a sizable contingent of critics and fans continue to rate it the band's greatest album of all. It contains "Stairway to Heaven," arguably the band's greatest achievement, and unarguably one of rock's greatest songs. The band seemed to realize the importance of "Stairway" almost immediately: it became the first Led Zeppelin song for which the lyrics were included in the album, and the artwork for both the outer cover of the album and the inner gatefold are clearly intended to tie in thematically with the song. It's the first song in which Led Zeppelin more or less explicitly reveal a coherent philosophical perspective: but to unravel this perspective, we must coordinate our readings of cover art, lyrics, and music.

First, let's consider the artwork. The front of the album features a photo of an old peasant carrying sticks on his back; the photo is in a rough frame set against old wallpaper. The back of the album features a slum tenement in a grimy urban landscape that suggests the industrial Midlands; the fact a bit of the peeling wallpaper from the front bleeds over into the back suggests that perhaps the photo is to be found in one of the tenements. When you open the album, the inner gatefold shows a night-time scene from the top of a very steep hill, with a sleepy English village far below in the distance. On top of the mountain stands a formidable bearded old man in robe and hood, holding a lantern; far below, strenuously clambering up the side of the mountain, is a young, earnest pilgrim seeking wisdom, which looks a bit like Jimmy Page during the period that he grew a beard.[14] There's not really any need to debate the intended meaning of this artwork, as Page himself has expounded on it:

---

[14] During the "Dazed and Confused" sequence of *The Song Remains the Same* movie, this scene is reprised, with Jimmy Page playing the earnest young pilgrim;

The old man carrying the wood is in harmony with nature. He takes from nature and he gives back to the land. It's a natural cycle . . . His old cottage gets pulled down and they put him in these urban slums . . . The Hermit is holding out the light of truth and enlightenment to a young man at the foot of a hill. If you know the tarot cards, you'll know what the Hermit means."[15]

In the tarot, the Hermit has two complementary meanings: he symbolizes both contemplative withdrawal in search of wisdom, and the guardian and transmitter of such wisdom once gained. In short, the artwork introduces several dualities that will be musically developed in "Stairway"—rural-urban, past-present, tradition-modernity—and the ideal of both natural renewal (represented by the peasant), and of spiritual renewal and transformation (represented by the Hermit figure).

Robert Plant has stated that the lyrics of "Stairway to Heaven" were influenced by *Magic Arts in Celtic Britain*, by Scottish antiquarian and occultist Lewis Spence (*Hammer of the Gods*, p. 132). Another source is J.R.R. Tolkien's *Lord of the Rings*. In "Stairway" what Plant borrows from Tolkien is imagery, and more specifically, perhaps, the very Celtic image of the "lost straight road" and the idea of the spiritual quest involving a journey through the forest.[16] Keep in mind that while the lyrics certainly are about a spiritual quest, one should avoid giving any specific image too rigid of an interpretation: a variety of readings are possible, and what follows is just one. There are two main characters: the Lady, who Stephen Davis describes as a synthesis of "Spenser's Faerie Queen, Robert

---

at the moment when he reaches the top of the hill and touches the Hermit's staff, the Hermit is revealed as an older, more grizzled Jimmy Page.

[15] Quoted in *Hammer of the Gods*, p. 142.

[16] The authors of two of the earliest (and still among the most influential) studies of *Lord of the Rings*, Jared Lobdell and Tom Shippey, both cite Tolkien's interest in the old Saint Brendan legend, which in turn is based on the pre-Christian Celtic legend of "the lost straight road," a hidden path to a land of promise. Both authors see the sea route that ships take from the Gray Havens to the Undying Lands in *Lord of the Rings* as Tolkien's specific adaptation of the "lost straight road." See Shippey, *The Road to Middle-Earth* (Houghton Mifflin, 2003), pp. 287–88, and Lobdell, *The World of the Rings: Language, Religion, and Adventure in Tolkien* (Open Court, 2004), pp. 85-86. Lobdell suggests that the journey into the forested world may be symbolically important to the quest narrative of *Lord of the Rings* because forests "are part of the Jungian memory." For more on the forest as an archetypal symbol in Tolkien, see *The World of the Rings*, 105–06.

Graves's White Goddess, and every other Celtic heroine—the Lady of the Lake, Morgan La Fay, Diana of the Fields Greene, Rhiannon the Nightmare," and the Piper (there is also a fleeting, ambiguous reference to the May Queen). We immediately learn that the Lady believes "all that glitters is gold." This is a direct inversion of a passage in Tolkien's *Fellowship of the Ring* where, during the Council of Elrond, Bilbo Baggins defends Aragorn (at that point in time a rather ragged figure) by saying, "All that is gold does not glitter." Bilbo understands that a thing's worth is not always apparent on the surface: the Lady, on the other hand, advocates shallow, grasping materialism—she wants to buy a stairway to heaven. She appears to be a "dark" anima figure, symbolizing destructive illusion.

As Plant develops his storyline (which he does more through repeated allusions to a common stock of characters and images than through straight narrative), the setting he conjures draws on several Tolkienesque images. Alternating between first, second, and third person viewpoints, Plant describes a journey on a path or a road (each term referenced once) through a forest ("trees" are mentioned twice, "the forest," once), where he finds himself looking anxiously to the West (the sacred direction of both Celtic tradition and *Lord of the Rings*).[17]

We learn that if we will collectively "call the tune," the Piper "will lead us to reason." The Piper, then, symbolizes the transmitter of gnosis (much like the hermit figure of the gatefold art), his melody the call to the spiritual quest,[18] and once he enters the narrative, he and the Lady appear to represent conflicting spiritual values: in fact, we learn "there are two paths you can go by." Soon, our "head is humming" because the Piper is calling us to join him. And although the Lady is told her stairway "lies on the whispering wind" (and therefore is not a commodity to be bought or sold), when we encounter her during the song's climactic section, she again "wants to show how everything still turns to gold"—that is, everything is reducible to material commodity.[19]

---

[17] Lobdell's *The World of the Rings* (pp. 83–87) and Shippey's *The Road to Middle-Earth* (pp. 286–88) both point out Tolkien's symbolic use of "the West" in its sacred Celtic sense.

[18] Consider Jesus's use of the piper symbol in the Gospels: "We have piped unto you, and you have not danced" (Matthew 11:17; Luke 7:32).

[19] When we encounter her in the song's climactic section, "she shines white light and wants to show / how everything still turns to gold." *Contra* my reading

Just before this encounter with her, we are on a road where "our shadows [are] taller than our souls." In Hinduism, "shadow" is often a symbol of Maya—illusion—that which prevents us from seeing the underlying unity of all things. In short, her path (and ours, if we follow it) would appear to be the path of Maya, just as the Piper's appears to be the "lost straight road" that leads to the land of promise. Finally, we're told that if we "listen very hard," the Piper's tune "will come to you at last." And when will it come to us? "When all is one and one is all."

Led Zeppelin went on to pen later epic spiritual quest narratives—among them "Kashmir," "Achilles' Last Stand," and "Carouselambra." However, only "Stairway" explicitly asserts that gnosis begins with the understanding that all is one and one is all; or, put it slightly differently, that (in the words of John Lennon) "I am he as you are he as you are me and we are all together." Thus "Stairway" is the band's great credo to monism: while their entire output is the expression of a monist worldview, "Stairway" is the first, and one of the few, Zeppelin songs that articulates this worldview explicitly.[20]

To comprehend "Stairway to Heaven," taking into account the lyric's implicit storyline is not enough: the music builds its own narrative trajectory, developing a set of dichotomies to create a "message" that both supports and transcends that of the words. With "Stairway," Zeppelin move beyond standard song form, creating the kind of "progressive" or teleological form beloved to contemporary British progressive rock bands like Emerson, Lake and Palmer and Yes. If there is one word that describes the musical dynamic of the song, it's "growth"—of instrumentation, texture, and tempo, but also in the sense of the gradual revelation of new structural components. Another defining feature of the song is its modal harmony and pentatonic melodic outlines, deeply rooted in traditional British song, which give it a different flavor from the band's blues-based songs.

---

above, does her shining white light suggest that she's actually a trickster figure who has understood all along the Piper's process of spiritual refinement, of turning everything to gold? I'm not sure.

[20] I believe the monist worldview is also the basis of the lyrics of "The Song Remains the Same": consider especially "Sing Out Hare Hare / Dance the Hoochie Coo," which has both cross-cultural implications, and a conflation of spirituality and sexuality—which is, after all, something of a hallmark of the Zeppelin experience.

"Stairway to Heaven" falls into three main sections, with Jimmy Page's justly renowned "guitar fanfare" serving as a transitional episode between the second and third. The first section is defined by Page's cleanly picked, smoothly-flowing acoustic guitar arpeggios, John Paul Jones's soothing four-part recorder consort, which in concert he realized on Mellotron, and Robert Plant's relaxed voice, here centered in the lower part of his range. The tempo flows at 76 beats per minute; the tonality is A modal minor, and the melancholy four-bar chord progression that defines the section is built on the guitar's chromatically descending arpeggio which, as I pointed out earlier, traditionally has connotations of lamentation. The section comprises two and a half repetitions of the sixteen bar verse: the first is instrumental, the second vocal (through "two meanings"), and the final half repetition comprises a four-bar vocal segment ("In a tree . . .") followed by a four-bar guitar/recorder continuation. The section evokes both the pastoral (through its use of acoustic instruments) and the archaic (through its use of the sound of the pre-modern recorder and Page's lute-like guitar part).[21]

The second and longest section of the song begins at 2:09, when Page's acoustic guitar suddenly morphs into jangly twelve-string electric guitar, and Jones's recorder consort to the bell-like Rhodes electric piano. One immediately perceives a sense of greater depth (lower frequencies, greater registral range between low and high notes) and greater timbral intensity (the twelve-string electric has a bigger sound that the acoustic six-string, the Rhodes electric piano has a bigger sound than the recorders). The section begins with the song's chorus ("Ooh it makes me wonder"), which

---

[21] As many Zeppelin fans are aware, the first eight bars of Page's guitar part to "Stairway to Heaven" are very similar to the first eight bars of Randy California's guitar part to "Taurus," from Spirit's self-titled debut album (1968). As Zeppelin may have opened for Spirit during their earliest U.S. tour(s), the similarity is probably not coincidental. On the other hand, this is a somewhat different situation than "Dazed and Confused," where Page essentially lifted the entire song's gestalt from Jake Holmes's song of the same name: there is nothing resembling Plant's vocal melody or Jones's recorder consort part in "Taurus." Furthermore, in "Taurus" this eight-bar pattern plays the role of a refrain that simply alternates with other material; it is not developed and expanded. Page's eight-bar phrase, on the other hand, is like an acorn from which the entire song develops and grows. I'm not sure whether Randy California could have won a lawsuit against Zeppelin if he had filed one; my guess is probably not.

we have not heard before: this marks the beginning of a structural practice I call "progressive revelation" that marks later Zeppelin epics ("Kashmir," "In the Light," "Achilles"), wherein key structural elements are not revealed until the song is well underway. The chorus is distinguished from the verse in several ways: it's strummed rather than picked, it's syncopated rather than consisting of even eighth note motion, and consists of just two primary chords, A minor seventh alternating with D major. Because this progression suggests G major just as strongly as A minor (it's a ii7-V progression in G major), it creates a sense of harmonic uncertainty that is only resolved when the verse reappears in a clearly-defined A minor.

At the beginning of the second section, the tempo begins to "move" a bit more: 84 beats per minute at first, increasing to 88 beats per minute by the second statement of the chorus. When the verse returns ("There's a feeling I get"), the vocal melody remains the same, but Page changes the underlying guitar harmonization, eliminating the chromatically descending line on the guitar's lowest strings. The result is that the new harmonization both is simpler (now using four different chords instead of six) and somewhat brighter (it now begins with a C major rather than an A minor chord). The song's lengthy second section is broken into two unequal parts by the entrance of Bonham on drums and Jones on bass guitar at 4:06: besides creating a more powerful bass presence, this entrance also generates more rhythmic energy, and tends yet again to slightly increase the tempo.

At 5:05, just a few seconds beyond the song's structural Golden Mean, Page launches into his famous fanfare passage that ushers the song's climax. Traditionally, fanfares signal particularly solemn and important events: this one is no different. The guitar timbre becomes more distorted, the guitar presence becomes bigger (through the quasi-symphonic layering of guitar lines that dominates the remainder of the song, and, indeed, subsequent Zeppelin epics), the rhythms more jagged and complex. The tempo increases yet again (to 100 beats per minute), and the harmony becomes more dissonant and ambiguous. The two main chords, a D suspended fourth and a C major with an added second, suggest both G major (again, like the chorus) and E minor without confirming either, thereby creating a sense of expectancy.

At 5:23, the fanfare passes on into Page's wonderful solo, regularly cited as one of the greatest in rock's recorded canon. At this point, the tempo increases yet again (to 102–104 beats per minute) and the tonality dramatically returns to A minor, with the harmonic content being reduced to three implied chords—A minor, G major, F major—as a result of Jones' hypnotically-repetitive descending A-G-F ground bass pattern. Throughout the song, chord progressions have become progressively simpler: here harmonic movement is reduced to its essence, and the effect is not unlike a river current that becomes stronger and stronger as it's forced through a narrower and narrower channel. Page's solo seems to introduce a new character into the musical drama. As with his solo in "Dazed and Confused," this solo seems to strive against the straightjacket of the bass pattern: however, it is far less frantic, much more lyrical and deliberate in its expression. It is, in effect, the hero's song, and I think the genius of the solo is that not only does it capture the twin sense of determination and melancholy that characterize the hero's quest, it invites us to experience vicariously the heroic struggle ourselves: the hero's song becomes our song, with Page as its medium.

Finally, at 6:09, we arrive at the third and climactic section of the song. Page takes up Jones' descending ground bass pattern, doubling it in fifths and octaves; the tempo has now increased to between 110 and 112 beats per minute. Plant enters a full octave higher than his opening vocal, singing the hypnotically repetitive two-bar verse with great urgency. His vocal constriction perfectly complements Page's guitar distortion, especially on the two key words that bring the song to its climax, "all" ("one is all") and the sustained "roll" ("not to roll"). Then, the song begins to deconstruct. The repetitive ground bass pattern slows to a halt, with Page playing a thickly distorted line that grows perilously slow before pausing expectantly: then, the song returns to its origins in British folksong, with Plant singing the memorable final "And she's buying a stairway to heaven" (now once again in the low, relaxed part of his range) *a cappella.*

In his seminal study of heavy metal, *Running with the Devil,* Robert Walser states that the music of "Stairway to Heaven" "combines contradictory sensibilities without reconciling them, as do Led Zeppelin's lyrics and cover art."[22] I strongly disagree, and it is here I think one final appeal to Tolkien will be helpful in understanding the unique appeal and power of the song. As Jared

---

[22] Robert Walser, *Running with the Devil: Power, Gender, and Madness in Heavy Metal Music* (Wesleyan University Press, 1993), p. 158.

Lobdell notes, "For the Industrial Revolution and the myth of progress that spawned or was spawned by it, there is a counter-revolution and a myth of anti-progress" (pp. 108–09) and Tolkien's use of this counter-myth is powerful. In expressing anxiety about technology and modernization, the relationship of country to city and of past to present, Tolkien taps into a specifically English ideology that extends back to the dawn of the Industrial Revolution, and was developed by such giants as Blake, Wordsworth, Carlyle, Ruskin, and Arnold. Lobdell notes that one of the underlying assumptions of *Lord of the Rings* is "If we assume that there resides some kind of genius in a land . . . then we could expect, as languages rise and fall within that land that the peoples who speak them will be not unlike each other. There will always—under whatever guise and in whatever time—be an England" (p. 32). He also points out that "Frodo and Bilbo, though hobbits, are Englishmen" (p. 16). Shippey makes a very similar point: "Tolkien wanted to re-create a timeless and idealized England (or rather Britain) in which the place and the people remained the same regardless of politics" (p. 98).

In other words, Tolkien's vision of England is a monist's vision in which past-present dichotomies are only apparent, not real. Hegel agrees, describing the World Spirit as "immortal": "with it there is no past, no future, but an essential now. . . .the present form of Spirit comprehends within it all earlier steps . . . which looked at in one aspect still exist beside each other, and only . . . from another point of view appear as past" (79). One aspect of *Lord of the Rings* that many have found appealing is that it posits an imaginary England of the incredibly remote past that is nevertheless organically connected to the (real) England of the present. It reassures us that even foreign (for instance Norman) conquest, the rise of the machines and rampant urbanization of the Industrial Revolution, and two devastating world wars could not destroy the essential Englishness of England; and conversely, that the magic of this incredibly remote past somehow lingers on. In Tolkien's vision, the past resacralizes the present.

If one understands this, one begins to understand the appeal of "Stairway to Heaven" on a purely musical basis. Robert Walser is mistaken to say that Zeppelin simply juxtapose acoustic and electric, traditional and modern musical discourses in "Stairway," although they did do that to some extent in earlier songs. ("What is and What Should Never Be" comes to mind). Not only does the music of the opening of the song posit an idealized rural England; its recorder consort and lute-like guitar part conjure an idealized "Old England" by referencing a very specific period of English musical history, the late Tudor–early Jacobean period, the Elizabethan "golden age" that plays such an important part in the English national myth. It seems unlikely that John Paul Jones and Jimmy Page were not at least to some extent aware of this. The song's transformation into driving hard rock/proto-metal is so gradual, and so musically logical, that the listener experiences no sense of discontinuity: every part of the musical structure emerges smoothly out of what precedes it, just as every new set of timbres feels as if it emerged logically out of what came before. "Rural" seamlessly flows into "urban," "archaic" smoothly blends into "modern." "Stairway" definitively realizes Jimmy Page's vision of "a new kind of 'heavy music,' with . . . dynamics, light and shade, *chiaroscuro*" (*Hammer of the Gods*, p. 52).

Like Hegel, the members of Led Zeppelin came of age in a time of wrenching cultural transformations: it was inevitable that they would feel anxiety about what appeared to be the increasingly tenuous relationship between the culture of their day and the traditions of the past. As a musical statement, "Stairway to Heaven" almost takes on the force of an aesthetic ideology. British hard rock of the 1970s, which many cultural conservatives of the time saw in anarchic, if not nihilistic, terms, is, in fact, shown to be organically connected to the music of England's golden age, tied together by modal harmony, pentatonic melodic outline, and similarities in figuration and texture. As with Tolkien, the musical past resacralizes the musical present; and, in Hegelian terms, "Stairway" achieves an almost preternaturally perfect reconciliation of past-present, rural-urban, and tradition-modernity, expressing through the song's musical style the same monist vision that its lyrics expressed. Ultimately, like Hegel's philosophy of history, "Stairway to Heaven" presents its dualities as part of an evolving, underlying unity. No wonder Robert Plant introduced "Stairway to Heaven" in *The Song Remains the Same* with perhaps the most profound words of the entire movie: "I think this is a song of hope."

In the Light: Balancing East and West

The fourth album established Zeppelin as the biggest rock band of the new decade; from this point on, both new albums and new tours began to be spaced farther apart. They recorded their eagerly awaited fifth album, *Houses of the Holy*, in 1972, and released it in 1973. Despite its controversial cover, it is in fact one of the band's quieter albums: "The Rain Song" and "Over the Hills and Far Away," in particular, represent the high-water mark of Zeppelin's characteristic approach to expanding the dynamic range of essentially acoustic songs through the discreet use of harder-rocking, electric guitar-centered passages. Among the other songs, the scintillating "The Song Remains the Same" is reminiscent of contemporaneous prog rock (Yes in particular), while "No Quarter" explores a slow, quiet, darkly atmospheric sound reminiscent of Pink Floyd.

Beginning in early 1974, the band recorded eight songs for a new album, and made the decision to release a two-LP album that would also included seven outtakes from *III*, *IV*, and *Houses of the Holy*. *Physical Graffiti*, was released in 1975. Although it does not quite achieve the consistency of *IV* (the fourth side of the LP format, in particular, is relatively weak), the sheer number of first-rate songs have led many Zeppelin aficionados to rank it with *IV* as the band's greatest achievement. While there are still some predominantly or fully acoustic numbers ("Ten Years Gone," Page's beautiful acoustic guitar showpiece "Bron-Yr-Aur"), one senses the band's acoustic muse is beginning to wane. Many of the songs develop the grungy, blues-based hard rock that had always been the foundation of their approach, but now in the context of more sophisticated production and arrangements than in their earlier days. Moreover, it is here that the band's fascination with things Eastern reaches a highpoint in two of their major epics, "Kashmir" and "In the Light."

"Kashmir" is, of course, one of their best and best-known songs: Robert Plant has suggested it is Zeppelin's greatest achievement.[23] It takes as its subject the spiritual quest, which Plant's lyrics express as a trek through Kashmir in search of hidden knowledge. Unfolding at a stately eighty beats per minute, it is characterized especially by the memorable four-bar opening riff, doubled on Page's guitar (left channel) and Jones's Mellotron strings (right channel), with Bonham's stripped down, powerful drum groove generating enormous polyrhythmic energy as he plays a straight-ahead 4/4 rock groove against the riff's 3/4 profile. Although virtually everyone knows that the song is supposed to be "Eastern,"

---

[23] Fast, *In the Houses of the Holy*, p. 88.

fewer are aware that its musical sources are not Indian, but rather Egyptian; furthermore, despite the lyric's supposed setting in Kashmir, Plant's descriptions of the desert-like geography that he passes through on his quest are more representative of North Africa.

The song consists of four slowly alternating musical "blocks." There are Plant's vocal verses which are accompanied by the riff mentioned above; a fanfare-like instrumental refrain (0:54); a bridge section built around a short, syncopated Mellotron "string" figure (2:10); and Plant's "counter-verse" (3:19) accompanied by Jones' "Arabian orchestra" (which he creates via overdubs of florid Mellotron string lines and sporadic blasts of Mellotron brass). In keeping with the song's "Eastern" ethos, Page eschews Western displays of ego. Not only is there no guitar solo, there are few independent guitar parts: none, in fact, outside of the counter-verse, where he strums alternating open fifths on G and A deep in the mix underneath Jones' "orchestra." The stately tempo, Bonham's stripped down, powerful drum grooves, the massively-orchestrated Mellotron and guitar parts moving in unison, and the slowly-shifting musical blocks that come and go in a more or less circular progression all contribute to an impersonal, indeed "timeless," and decidedly monumental musical experience.

"Kashmir" is the last song on the first LP. "In the Light," the first song of the second LP, has some similarities to "Kashmir"—and important differences as well. Like "Kashmir," "In the Light" consists of four distinct musical "blocks": unlike "Kashmir," these four blocks are presented consecutively, then repeated in the same order, but with variations (so the overall form is A B C D A' B' C' D'). Unlike "Kashmir," "In the Light" actually does draw from Indian music: specifically, its opening suggests the opening section of a raga. Using an EMS VSC3 synthesizer, Jones first evokes the drone of a harmonium or a very deep sitar; then, in a higher register, he begins to play lead lines suggestive of the sound of the shenai, a double-reed Indian instrument that sounds like a deep, piercing oboe. These lead lines grow increasingly florid, and Jones uses the synthesizer's joystick to create the pitch bends characteristic to traditional Indian music; however, he renders his raga-like opening "psychedelic" by running the "shenai" lines through an analog delay unit, so that they seem to dematerialize as they blur and blend into each other. The lack of an audible beat and the "melting" of melodic outline create a sense of timelessness and of vast, reverberating space: analogies might include a world without form, the self in the womb, or the depths of the unconscious.

Plant enters at the beginning of the second section (1:43), singing an elemental vocal line (in A-pentatonic minor) four times. Harmonizing with himself in bare intervals, his vocal part suggests an ancient chant: while one might hear it as "Eastern," one might just as easily hear a similarity to medieval European organum, since its most important feature seems to be its sense of the archaic. Jones accompanies with a simple drone, adding a sitar-like melodic figure that rises from the synthesizer's deep registers after each of Plant's vocal stanzas (introducing the musical symbolism of ascent that dominates the remainder of the song). Compared to the song's "formless" opening section, this section suggests a gradual cohesion: there is now a sense of pulse (although weak and implied rather than explicitly sounded) and of melodic outline (although of a very simple, elemental nature).

It is only at the beginning of the third section (2:45) that Page and Bonham enter: Page with a heavily syncopated, descending two-bar guitar riff that suggests both Middle Eastern and blues sources, Bonham with an accompanying groove that momentarily blurs the location of the downbeat. When Plant enters with the verse (3:00), the band switch to another two-bar riff, this one circular and more Arab than Indian; it's a bit reminiscent of the Mellotron "string" figure from the bridge of "Kashmir." Both riffs continue the A-minor tonality of the previous section (the first riff with a blues flatted fifth, the second with alternating raised and lowered sixths); Page's overdubbed off-beat drone G at the end of every other measure creates a mild but continuous dissonance with both the riffs and Plant's vocal melody. The heavy beat, faster tempo (effectively double time from the previous section), and greater bass presence (Jones having switched from synthesizer to bass, on which he doubles Page's line) create a sense of forward motion that the previous sections lacked: one feels that the song has finally achieved a clear sense of beat and melodic profile. The analogy here is time beginning, the world taking on form, the passage from the womb into the world, and from unconsciousness into consciousness.

The first section of "In the Light" is an instrumental prelude, the second a vocal prologue, and the third section the verse. It isn't until 4:09 that we reach the chorus, the song's fourth section. Built around Jones's anthemic Clavinet part, we immediately notice two things: this is the first section that sounds Western rather than

Eastern, and it is only now that we pass from minor to major tonality. Musically, the entire song up to this point has been a metaphor for shadow slowly but inexorably giving way to light, and Page further reinforces the motif of emerging into the light with a new two-bar riff (4:25), an A major scale fragment that climbs two octaves: again, the musical metaphor of ascent. However, the section cuts off suddenly; before Plant ever sings, in fact.

From here, the band recapitulates the four sections of the song, in order, the first three in compressed form: we hear brief restatements of the instrumental prelude (4:55), the vocal prologue (5:26), and the verse (5:52). Finally, at 6:36 the chorus returns, and this time Plant enters immediately, explicitly articulating its meaning in a disarmingly vulnerable grain of voice: "in the light . . . everybody needs the light." This is the moment the entire song has headed towards, and from here on out the band begin to musically develop the chorus: Page layers in reverberating rising fanfare figures, recalling the opening section's sense of vast space, but now with a far greater sense of drive and forward motion. Indeed, Page's leads become increasingly florid and ecstatic as the music begins to fade, recalling Jones's opening synth leads; one feels we have simultaneously come full circle to the opening part, and fulfilled its inherent destiny.

The primary duality explored by Zeppelin in "Kashmir" and "In the Light" is East/West, but the band also engage a number of other dualities subsumable under the East/West polarity: timelessness/time, formlessness/form, unconsciousness/consciousness. These polarities were perceptively and prophetically discussed by Carl Jung (1875–1961) in "The Difference Between Eastern and Western Thinking."[24] Jung begins by asserting the Western mind is primarily extroverted—that is, directed outwards—while the Eastern mind is essentially introverted and focused within. This tendency is most noticeable in the differences between Western and Eastern religious thought. The Judeo-Christian tradition views salvation as coming from without, from a transcendent God upon whose grace all men and women are wholly dependent; Hinduism, however, stresses the imminent God, the God within. In Hinduism, as Jung puts it, "man is God and he redeems himself" (p. 486).

---

[24] Originally published in English in 1939 as part of *Psychology and Religion: West and East*; republished in *The Portable Jung*, ed. Joseph Campbell (Viking Penguin, 1971), pp. 480–502.

The Western habit of outward attention and its "objective" orientation—which, as Jung notes, is responsible both for the West's scientific and technological achievements and its acquisitiveness—is dependent on a highly-developed sense of ego-consciousness; indeed, for a Westerner, "mind" specifically means the conscious mind. Jung points out that this continuous identification with ego-consciousness is "appalling" from the Eastern point of view, since it amounts to complete identification with Maya (illusion). For the Hindu, ego-consciousness is a rather low level of consciousness; in higher forms of consciousness, the ego disappears altogether. For the Westerner, this "higher consciousness" seems identical to the unconscious: it is difficult for us to imagine a conscious mental state without a subject, that is, an ego, to observe it. For the Westerner, samadhi [the highest level of meditation] is liable to be "nothing but a meaningless dream state" (p. 501).

Jung believed he was living through a time in which East and West were interpenetrating: "While we are overpowering the Orient from without, it may be fastening its hold on us from within" (p. 475). More specifically, Jung believed that even as Western influence was profoundly transforming Eastern political, economic, and (as he noted with regret) military institutions, Eastern thought was profoundly influencing Western spirituality. Indeed, Jung saw this development as both inevitable and desirable:

> The two standpoints, however contradictory, each have their psychological justification. Both are one-sided in that they fail to see and take account of those factors which do not fit in with their typical attitude. The one underrates the world of consciousness, the other, the world of the One Mind. The result is that, in their extremism, both lose half of the universe. (p. 501)

Although Jung professed no particular enthusiasm for Hegel, his "Eastern and Western Thinking" presents an unambiguously Hegelian narrative of the convergence of East and West during the first half of the twentieth century; Jung believed the result of this interpenetration would be a new synthesis of Western rationality and Eastern spirituality. Jung specifically criticized the religious movements of the early twentieth century such as Theosophy that believed

> Certain Mahatmas, seated somewhere in the Himalayas or Tibet, inspire and direct every mind in the world . . . the East is at the bot-

tom of the spiritual change we are passing through today. Only, this East is not a Tibetan monastery full of Mahatmas, but lies essentially within us. (p. 476)

For Jung, the Theosophists' belief was another example of the Western habit of looking without for our answer; but, as he saw it, the East-West synthesis would not be genuine until "We . . . get at the Eastern values from within and not from without, seeking them in ourselves, in the unconscious" (p. 490).

Both "Kashmir" and "In the Light" grapple with these issues. While "Kashmir" may be the better of the two songs on a purely musical level, it seems open to the criticisms that Jung leveled against the Theosophists. In creating a metaphor of the spiritual quest, Plant creates a story of himself trekking through Kashmir (in the Himalayas) where a "gentle race" (the Mahatmas, perhaps?) guard a secret wisdom, awaiting the coming spiritual transformation "when all will be revealed." In other words, gnosis is to be found without, in "The East," where we must journey in order to find it, to receive it from the hands of a beneficent Other. "In the Light," on the other hand, invites one to look within for one's answer. And here we will want briefly to consider another of Zeppelin's influences, Aleister Crowley, since "In the Light" is perhaps the Zeppelin song in which his influence is most obvious.

Because of Crowley's profligate, libertine ways, his infamous dictum "Do what thou wilt" is often understood to mean "let it all hang out," and, unfortunately, when his writings went through a vogue of popularity with the hippies during the late 1960s and early 1970s, that is often exactly how they interpreted it. However, Crowley himself said what he really meant was "Let will and action be in harmony," adding, "Will in the higher sense . . . used by Schopenhauer and Fichte."[25] Schopenhauer describes will as the reality that lies behind the world of illusion and appearances that shape ordinary consciousness; Fichte stresses that a man does not become conscious of his freedom until he launches himself into action. For both, will determines consciousness (or at least the state worthy of that name) rather than the other way around.

Crowley concluded that, as Colin Wilson put it, "man possesses a 'controlling ego' which presides over consciousness," and

---

[25] Colin Wilson, *Aleister Crowley: The Nature of the Beast* (Aquarian Press, 1987), p. 166.

believed that through the assertion of one's will, one can access this "controlling ego" and move beyond ordinary consciousness and its illusory appearances into a higher level of consciousness. Thus the importance of magic to Crowley: he saw it as the primary tool for accessing the controlling ego and thus mastering one's own consciousness. Crowley's conception of the will seems to bear some resemblance to the Hindu concept of atman—the innermost core of one's self—and the belief that by becoming fully aware of atman we realize an identity with Brahman, the supreme spirit. Crowley stresses that only when people learn to exercise their will can they fulfill their true destiny. And thus the opening lyric of "In the Light":

> And if you feel that you can't go on
> and your will's sinkin' low,
> Just believe and you can't go wrong
> in the light you will find the road.

"The light" is within; it is one's inner will. Once one has activated "the light" by identifying one's inner will, then one can "find the road" by bringing will and action into harmony. The lyrics of much of the rest of the song are something like an Eastern variant of Paul Simon's "Bridge Over Troubled Waters," with Plant telling an unidentified partner that he will help her bear her burdens on this road, as she will help him bear his.

"Kashmir" places wisdom outside; "In the Light" places it inside, which is, in Jung's view, as it should be. Recalling Jung's exposition of East/West dualities, we can now make more sense of the musical structure of "In the Light" as well. The song begins on a very inward, "Eastern" level; each subsequent section becomes more extroverted, until finally, when the fourth section (the chorus) is reached, the song becomes fully "Western," and shadow gives way to full light. Using Jung's analogy, the song emerges out of the unconscious, and stage by stage becomes more fully conscious until it reaches the full consciousness of the chorus. Of course, one could give this an essentialist reading that sees a progression from undeveloped (Eastern) to fully developed (Western). It's more likely the band meant to depict wisdom (or to use Crowley's term, will) being drawn from the depths of the unconscious and, through stages, being brought into full consciousness; and, during the final chorus, as Page's reverberating fanfare-like leads increasingly come to mirror Jones's reverberating synthesizer leads of the opening, to show "East" flowing into "West," "West" back into "East," in a Hegelian dialectic.

Bring the Balance Back: Led Zeppelin and the Hegelian Dialectic

After *Physical* Graffiti, Zeppelin released two more "official" studio albums. *Presence* (1976), the band's least acoustic album, continued to explore their African-American influences; it produced another classic epic in "Achilles' Last Stand," a touchstone of later prog-metal fusions. *In Through the Out Door* (1979), the album on which John Paul Jones's influence crests, explores two directions: there are yet more tributes to American roots styles, but also two epics, "Carouselambra" and "In the Evening." John Bonham did not long survive the release of this album, and a final album of outtakes, *Coda* (1982) brought the band's career to a close. But by then they were long established as the most influential rock band to come of age during the 1970s; the only band that has seriously challenged them for this title *ex post facto* is Pink Floyd.

Most of the more progressive British rock bands of the 1970s aspired to an "organic" style. They strive to fuse their diverse influences into a unified musical discourse; to thread the various musical elements of their songs (if not entire albums) into a tightly woven tapestry; to reveal unexpected interrelationships between seemingly incompatible musical ideas as a song progresses; and to create a sense of inevitable growth through a series of ever-more transcendent climaxes. These tendencies stem from a utopian impulse, monist in nature, which seeks coherence and underlying unity beneath apparent randomness and meaninglessness, and illustrate Hegel's notion of "the Idea assuming successive forms which it successively transcends, and by this very process of transcending its earlier stages, gaining an affirmative, and in fact, a richer and more concrete shape." One certainly hears this process in Zeppelin's "progressive" masterpieces such as "Stairway to Heaven" and "In the Light."

But Zeppelin's output as a whole forcefully illustrates another of Hegel's assertions that much progressive rock tends to gloss over: every culture and historical movement carries within itself an inherent contradiction—thus Zeppelin's stark juxtaposition of styles and genres, of the sacred and profane, the sublime and the crude. As

Hegel emphasized, there is no point in denying the existence of what we might call "the dark side." Far from being an impediment to the "perfect," the "imperfect" is necessary for its attainment: only through "mighty conflict" with its own negation can Spirit "assume successive forms which it successively transcends." Led Zeppelin's output, through its monist insistence on light *and* shade, rather than light *or* shade, and its juxtaposition and interpenetration of dualities, is engaged in the eternal Hegelian struggle "to bring the balance back."

14
Your Time Is Gonna Come

RALPH SHAIN

It had been quite a weekend for seeing live music. On successive nights, I had seen John Lee Hooker (for the first time), Stevie Ray Vaughn (for the nth time), and now I was sitting in a crowd watching the second ARMs concert, a benefit show which featured Eric Clapton, Joe Cocker, Jeff Beck, and Jimmy Page. The newspaper's review of the show of the previous night had lauded Beck to the skies, but had been scathing toward Clapton and Page. Still, I wasn't worried. Clapton played very well and Beck had justified the review's superlatives, although this was of very little concern. No matter what the critic had said, based on what I now see as no real evidence, I couldn't imagine that Page would play badly. Having never seen Led Zeppelin, I was there for one reason: to see Jimmy Page play guitar. When Page was announced, last after the other stars had finished their sets, he took the stage and said into the microphone, "Now is the time for the critics to leave the auditorium." Hmm, I thought. Even gods care about the critics.

The concept of recognition has played an important role in social philosophy for two hundred years, generating provocative arguments about the nature of the self and our obligations to others. Given the extreme recognition accorded rock stars, and especially Led Zeppelin, they can help us better understand the concept, which itself explains interesting aspects of the band.

Hegel and the Formation of Led Zeppelin

The German philosopher Georg Hegel (1770–1832) first "recognized" the importance of recognition in an argument called "the

221

master-slave dialectic." It's a pretty cool argument, and worth summarizing before we take up Led Zeppelin.

Imagine two individuals (call them "Frank" and "Elvis") meeting in the "state of nature" (a situation outside of society). Since Frank and Elvis are in a state of nature, they have a very rudimentary grasp of their relation to the world. Each considers himself to contain all of the world's meaning and value and both are entirely governed by their desires. Upon meeting, the mere existence of the other constitutes a challenge to the individual: the other doesn't recognize one's claim to contain all of the world's meaning and value. As mutual threats, but without a culture in which to compete, Frank and Elvis fight until one, let's say Elvis, kills the other. However, what seems like a solution fails, since the loser is no longer around to recognize the winner. What Elvis thought he wanted turns out not to be what he wanted after all. Elvis thought he wanted to destroy Frank, but really he wanted to be recognized by Frank.

Hegel concludes that the desire for recognition is a fundamental human desire. This desire isn't satisfied once and for all and left behind, but continues throughout life. Another conclusion Hegel draws, although it doesn't follow from the master-slave dialectic, is that recognition must be "concrete": for someone's attitude to you to count as recognition, it must relate to a characteristic which is specific to you. Hegel is concerned that recognizing someone on the basis of their being "human" will neither satisfy the individual's desire for recognition, nor motivate those who supposedly are recognizing the individual to actually treat them in a decent fashion.

A different sort of example makes the point more clearly. The Grammy award that Milli Vanilli received for musicianship wouldn't count on Hegel's account as recognition, since they didn't perform the music on the album. (Everyone knows the problems that the Grammys have had in being taken seriously as a form of recognition. This is consistent with the same point: if an award is so far off the mark as not to relate to the actual quality of the music which is being produced, then it may cease to be a form of recognition at all.)

Finally, the most important and interesting conclusion that Hegel draws from the argument is that the struggle for recognition is an important component in one's formation as an individual. This means that one becomes an individual through interaction with others, rather than being essentially an isolated individual who later comes into contact with others, as is claimed by leading rationalist philosophers prior to Hegel, such as Descartes, Leibniz, and Kant. Because of the desire for recognition, one's very being as an individual is constituted by one's interactions with others.

Hegel doesn't discuss how this happens, but if we connect his account of recognition with some of his other ideas, we can envision it this way: If someone claimed to be an outstanding songwriter, on the order of Page and Plant, without depending in the least on others, based entirely on his or her own thoughts, his or her own work, we would be fully justified in rejecting the claim as impossible. Any such story is a fantasy. People become songwriters by hearing songs written by others, absorbing them, and then trying to make something like—but also unlike—what has been absorbed. Songwriters inherit and work within traditions, even if they transcend them. Having created, the writer gets feedback and learns through the reactions of others. This was how Page and Plant became songwriters; neither achieved greatness without these sorts of interactions.

The learning takes place within the context of the struggle for recognition; one accepts instruction from those one recognizes as worthy, and one strives to be worthy oneself. The struggle is to reach a point where one's abilities as a songwriter are objectively established, and this can't be done unless one interacts with others in these basic ways. How much recognition is enough may vary from person to person, but the desire for recognition tends to continue thoughout life.

I think Hegel's account applies to the formation of Led Zeppelin in two ways, one pretty straightforward and the other more controversial. Most obviously, Jimmy Page formed Led Zeppelin because the recognition he received from being the top session guitarist in London wasn't enough for him. And John Paul Jones joined for the same reason. They needed more recognition than they could receive in that way. Songwriting and performing have the potential for greater prestige than session work. Of course, their motivations could be stated as a need for creative expression, which is certainly true, but this doesn't negate the role played by recognition. They could have expressed themselves by writing songs on their off time while keeping their day jobs. In other words, the "expressive" explanation fails to account for why they wished to tour as a band and make albums. In short, Jimmy Page wanted to be a rock star.

A complete account of the formation of Led Zeppelin as interactive would consider how the band and each of the musical selves of the members were formed by their interaction with each other. Unfortunately, I don't know enough about this part of the story. However, it's interesting that at their formation Robert Plant was the weakest link. (With the notable exception of "Thank You," it wouldn't be until the third or fourth album that Page would leave him to write lyrics unassisted.) And Plant was the only one to have a substantial solo career after the breakup. Could it be that he felt he still had something to prove?

The Critics and Led Zeppelin

I would consider the career of the band and its relation to rock critics as an example of the interactive formation of a self. Here the "self" is that of the band, rather than that of the individual members. I know that Zeppelin fans have a tendency to see the band as great from the very beginning, that all of their albums were great going back to the first, and that the struggle for recognition was merely a struggle to get the critics to see what was there from the start. However, I see things somewhat differently.

The first two albums are pretty good but not great. They each have a couple of great songs, and some moments on the other songs, but they are bombastic. The first album consists mostly of covers and the second was hastily recorded in bits and pieces. For a band which was supposed to be about albums, not singles, the records are disjointed. Rolling Stone now takes a lot of heat for dissing Zeppelin because the magazine was hung up on some misguided idea of authenticity. But Zeppelin's version of hard rock on their early albums leans very heavily on the blues, so much so that I think it could be called "histrionic blues," and the blues lives on authenticity. The blues has its bragging element, but bragging and bombast are not the same. Neither Plant's histrionics nor Page's virtuosity convey the emotions from which the blues arises. In short, Zeppelin, in spite of its surfeit of musical talent, and Page's highly imaginative production, was no Muddy Waters, nor even an Allman Brothers Band.

From the beginning, Zeppelin was an outstanding live band and was immediately recognized as such by the fans. And fan recognition of the albums was immediate as well. But the reviews of the albums were negative, sometimes harshly so, and this bothered all of the members of the band. (Both Page and Bonham have been quoted as saying that the critics don't understand music—this will be relevant in the next section.) Robert Plant was acutely aware of the band's struggle for recognition at this point in their career, stating in a March 1970 interview, "What we've got to do now is consolidate the position we've arrived at, so that eventually we'll be able to say what we really want to say and people will listen to it because it's us."[1] As I see it, the albums improved in part because of the struggle for critical recognition. *III* is a transitional album; it is perhaps not better than the first two, but it is more cohesive and Plant is writing more lyrics. But it is *IV* where Zeppelin achieves greatness.

The basic elements are the same as on the first three albums, but it's as if a blurry and distorted photograph had suddenly come into sharp focus. All of the songs are very good, and more than half achieve some sort of perfection. The blues is still there—and better than before—but Plant is writing lyrics, not merely appropriating them. The key is not merely that Plant is writing his own songs, but that he is writing hippie songs ("Stairway to Heaven," "Misty Mountain Hop," "Going to California"). This resulted in an improvement because, one, hippie music was more authentic to him than the blues, both as an individual and as a musician—at the time the band was formed, in addition to sharing Page's blues and R&B enthusiasms, Plant was into California bands—and two, hippie music tends to be more self-effacing and this brought the bombast under control.

The Struggle for Recognition

As I said, the musical elements remain the same as on the first three albums, so there can be no thought of Page "selling out" his vision, but his and the band's desire for critical success led them to continually improve, to the point where the individual songs and the album as a whole are stronger. Zeppelin had suffered above all from the critics' claim that from the very start they were nothing but hype. With their fourth album, their substance and seriousness were unassailable. As John Paul Jones said, after *IV*, "no one ever compared us to Black Sabbath again."[2] In other words, with *IV*, Led Zeppelin had won the struggle for recognition.

---

[1] Quoted by Keith Shadwick in *Led Zeppelin: The Story of a Band and their Music 1968–1980* (Hal Leonard, 2005), p. 109.

[2] Mick Wall, *When Giants Walked the Earth*, p. 267.

And the story can be continued. According to Keith Shadwick, circa 1973, "Zeppelin's band members, especially Plant and Page, yearned for wider recognition, not only of their talent but of their increasing sophistication and worldliness" (*Led Zeppelin*, p. 184). After *Houses of the Holy*, another critical flop, Zeppelin produced something which was scarcely believable—an album better than *IV*. *Physical Graffitti* is similar to the previous albums in that it delivers monster, bludgeoning riffs, but due to its different song structures, and the attainment of some genuine sentiment, it sounds unlike every other Zeppelin album. It is notoriously difficult to explain why some music succeeds, and it is especially daunting to criticize Keith Shadwick's approach to the album, given his extraordinary knowledge and abilities as a musician and a music writer. Nevertheless, I will try to articulate the reasons why *Physical Graffiti* is Led Zeppelin's greatest album by responding to his critique of the album.

Shadwick criticizes "Custard Pie" for having "no great distinguishing features." "In My Time of Dying," he says, has "the bloated effect of an overlong performance" (p. 227). "Houses of the Holy" is glowingly described, but after the vocals, Shadwick believes that the song founders because "the contrasting song section that the song cries out for never arrives. . . . the riff starts up again and is here to stay . . ." "Trampled Under Foot" is praised for "some innovative guitar sounds" but Shadwick criticizes its placement after "Houses of the Holy," "with its similar strut rhythm" (p. 229). Plant's vocal on "Black Country Woman" are said to "make for a curiously static performance." "In the Light" is described more positively, but Shadwick again denigrates its length: "Once again the track is very long: close to nine minutes and therefore longer than "Kashmir," which is usually thought of as the epic on *Physical Graffiti*. The introductory section alone of "In the Light" lasts for almost two minutes" (p. 232). In short, Shadwick thinks that the album is tedious. Throughout his book, one can see that he prefers the complex to the simple, variation to repetition. Hence his sneer that the last part of "In My Time of Dying" adds "nothing to the performance apart from time. The joys of repetition, as Prince put it. Or vamp 'til ready."

It is this preference which leads Shadwick to feel that he has to plead on behalf of "Kashmir." He understands the song thoroughly ("a study in repetition and stasis") and his description of it is superb. But he concludes that:

It could be argued that 'Kashmir' ultimately lacks enough variety in its orchestration and dynamics to maintain interest for its nine or so minutes in the way that *Bolero* does. But it is a brave and imaginative shot at a new type of form through repetition taken from Eastern music and applied to rock. Perhaps the imperfections give it a vulnerable charm that *Bolero* doesn't share. (p. 232)

Shadwick is correct that "Kashmir" brings a new type of form to rock, but he fails to see that his criticism—that the song lacks sufficient variety—is thus rendered irrelevant. "Kashmir" is nothing less than riveting for its entire duration. And it's the extended length and repetitiveness of the other songs which gives them a kind of simplicity, different from but just as exhilarating as the simplicity and brevity of punk and early rock. Shadwick's dismissive remarks can easily be turned around and claimed as positives: "the joys of repetition," "the riff . . . is here to stay." The latter can proudly serve as the album's motto. *Physical Graffiti* provides an experience not to be found anywhere else in rock.

While the critics can be faulted for not seeing the good moments on the early albums, I don't think their reactions were entirely unwarranted. And I think that Led Zeppelin was "formed", not as an unfolding of what was already pre-existing, but in the interactive struggle for recognition. As well as critical recognition, there is also recognition by peers. It's clear that Zeppelin felt competitive with the Stones, for example, but it's not clear in what specific ways that affected their music. There were also early negative reactions to Led Zeppelin, from Keith Richards, Eric Clapton, Pete Townshend, and John Lennon (*Rough Guide*, p. 72).

Recognition and Hierarchy

In addition to the conclusions that Hegel drew about the struggle for recognition for self-constitution, he also attempted to draw moral and political lessons from the master-slave dialectic. Returning to that argument, we need to consider its next stage. At the end of the first stage, we saw that killing one's antagonist didn't work out as expected for the victor. Now, however, when two individuals (call them "Page" and "Beck") meet in the state of nature, having no culture in which to compete, they will continue to fight to the death until eventually one of them realizes that being killed is not a desirable outcome either. Only when Page or Beck values his physical life higher than his need for validation, will he give in and recognize the other as master. The winner then has a slave who recognizes him as having all value, which seems to be what he wanted.

Hegel's claim is that this resolution, like the first (death), is not a success for the winner. The master, Hegel says, can't be entirely satisfied with the recognition he receives from the slave, precisely because it's the recognition of a slave. The combatant wants the freely given recognition of a free human being, but receives only the recognition of a lesser being. Hegel draws the conclusion that slavery is self-defeating and thus morally wrong. Whether or not his argument establishes that, his main idea—that the quality of recognition varies with the position in the hierarchy of the one granting recognition—seems indisputable. This is illustrated by the fact that peer and critic recognition still mattered to Zeppelin even after they had achieved fan adulation. And among peer and critic recognition, some counted for more than others.

John Bonham, grumbling about critics, complained, "If Buddy Rich says I'm shit, then I'm shit, but what do these guys know?" Jimmy Page has also claimed that critics don't understand music, but if this were completely true, he would have been entirely unconcerned with their recognition. True, Zep's interest in critical recognition might have been purely strategic, since good reviews help sell records. But they had no need of critical recognition to do that, and it doesn't explain Page's comment at the ARMs concert. The place of critics in determining quality is a bit paradoxical in popular culture—since it is indeed a matter of popular culture. Still, by convention, critics are deemed to be higher in the hierarchy of opinion than the consumer, and Zeppelin recognized this conventional status by desiring and struggling for critical acclaim.

If we think that the value of recognition is relative to position in a hierarchy, then we'll construct a picture of society in which all are constantly struggling to gain the recognition of others, but especially those above them in order to move up or maintain their position. The sociologist Pierre Bourdieu provides a picture of society very close to this. In his terminology, Led Zeppelin was struggling to increase their "symbolic capital" or prestige.[3] Hegel hoped to find a solution which would satisfy the desire of all for recognition,

---

[3] *The Logic of Practice* (Stanford University Press, 1990).

and he believed that it could be found through some sort of "mutual recognition". There are several ways of interpreting and institutionalizing mutual recognition.

Some contemporary philosophers interpret recognition in terms of "human rights," arguing that mutual recognition takes place when all recognize each others' "humanity." One such attempt tries to find a characteristic common to all humans (such as "rationality") which deserves respect and is lacking in other animals. This approach fails because characteristics like rationality come in degrees; some people are more or less rational than others (and some animals, like chimpanzees, are more rational than some humans, like infants or extremely inebriated drummers). This leads us away from the system of equal rights we were aiming for. Are the Bay City Rollers and Led Zeppelin really deserving of equal respect?

Other philosophers, foregoing an attempt to distinguish human beings from animals, think moral equality should be based on sympathy arising from our common ability to feel pain or our shared mortality or "finitude." Since the members of Led Zeppelin and the Bay City Rollers have suffered, they are entitled to treatment as moral equals. Unfortunately, this tack is also problematic. Basing morality and equal political rights on compassion makes sense, but sympathy and recognition seem to be two entirely different things.

Both of these approaches to institutionalizing mutual recognition are based on general concepts of humanity. The one understands humanity in terms of traits like rationality; the other, based on our capacity to suffer. And both ignore Hegel's insight that recognition requires recognition of something specific about the person recognized. Recognizing someone as "human" fails to distinguish them in a positive way from anyone else. Basing our institutions on the concept of human rights is important for many reasons, but it's not going to satisfy anyone's desire for recognition—which was the point of bringing the concept into social philosophy in the first place.

Hegel offers an alternative. He recommends establishing a system of guilds (called "corporations") which will ameliorate the hardships of a free market economy. Sort of a cross between a professional association and a union, these guilds would mediate between the sphere of private individuals and the government. One of the hardships which the guilds would ameliorate is unemployment. Since each worker would be a member of a guild even if unemployed, one would be assured of recognition as a "musician" or "engineer" or "teacher" even without a job. But Hegel doesn't do much to defend the plausibility of his claims. He doesn't address the issue of why the threshold of being a member of a profession or craft is more important than other levels of recognition within the hierarchy. Being a studio musician may be sufficient recognition for some, but others, like Page, are unsatisfied with even being the top session player. Nor does he address the issue of relative prestige of different jobs or professions. Having a guild for insurance brokers may help them with some sort of recognition, but it can hardly be said to equal the recognition of thousands of screaming fans. In order for this sort of mutual recognition to be equally satisfying, it must be equal, and Hegel doesn't establish that a system of guilds could achieve that.

Groupies and Recognition

We have learned of two characteristics of recognition from Hegel: (1) recognition must be concrete, and (2) the value of recognition varies with the position and understanding of the recognizer. In addition, there are three ways recognition is manifested: (3) emulation, (4) association, and (5) gratification. In the rock context, we recognize our favorite groups by wishing to be like them—playing their songs, being influenced by their style or technique, adopting their mannerisms or manner of dress. If I wear a band's T-shirt, I recognize them by associating with them. And if I pay for official Zep merchandise (rather than stealing it or buying a knockoff) I'm recognizing the band by giving something of value, which is what I mean by gratification. On this view, imitation isn't the sincerest form of flattery; imitation, along with association and gratification is more sincere. If we think of Zeppelin's appropriation of blues songs without crediting the writers and thus paying royalties, we can see this as a failure of recognition. Their recognition was deficient because of the lack of association (since they didn't list the songwriter on the album) and lack of gratification (since they didn't give anything of value for their appropriation).

Although it may be true that they were consistent in regard to song appropriation by allowing hip-hop artists to sample their songs, their appropriation of material from older blues artists seems especially heartless given the brutality of their treatment of those attempting to make bootleg recordings of their own shows.

Another aspect of recognition which I would classify under the heading of gratification is generosity in interpreting the actions and merits of the one granted recognition. Those who are admired are given the benefit of the doubt (when there is doubt), and their positive attributes are weighed more heavily than their negatives. Led Zeppelin illustrates this aspect of recognition rather dramatically. People still wanted to associate with them, emulate them, and gratify them, even though they often behaved like thugs, inflicting physical violence as retribution, intimidation, or just as a joke. And they were (and are) still adored.

Sex as Recognition

There's an even more obvious way Led Zeppelin can illuminate the concept of recognition. Gratification offered as an expression of recognition includes sexual gratification, and the name "Led Zeppelin" is nearly synonymous with groupies. And having sex is as direct a way of "associating" with someone as there is. ("I'm With the Band," as Des Barres titled her book.) Curiously, neither Hegel nor his latter-day followers in recognition theory have considered the case of groupies. Titillating as the subject may be, important philosophical issues are missed when one ignores groupies.

Considering sex as both association and gratification, it initially seems that groupies are entirely on the giving end of recognition, as if, to return to Hegel's master-slave dialectic, an individual was hastening to take the slave position. But this is to miss the fact that being a groupie is itself a struggle for recognition. The girls and young women who wished to be "with" Led Zeppelin were competing against each other for some recognition (in the form of association, if nothing else) from members of the band. Furthermore, attaining this recognition from a member of the band achieved recognition from the other groupies, which manifested itself in the form of envy or jealousy, which is best analyzed under the heading of "emulation." In the introduction of her book on groupies, Pamela des Barres notes that many aspiring groupies have sought her advice over the years on how to score with rock stars.

Second, by making the connection between groupies and recognition, we can get some insight into problems that arise in feminist theory. Since the 1950s, feminist theory has produced a profusion of brilliant, interesting, and insightful philosophical theories and analyses. However, these theories, and feminism itself, have hit a wall, and this barrier seems to be a disagreement about the answer to one question: is it legitimate for women to strive to appeal to men's sexual desire? Is this a legitimate form of empowerment, of gratifying one's own desires, or is it self-objectification, a result of false consciousness? Since the type of recognition which groupies received from the band derives from sexual appeal, a look at groupies raises the issue in a very striking way.

The Empowerment of Groupies

On one side would be the claims of Des Barres and other groupies that they are doing what they want to do, and thus should be seen as empowered, not subordinate. In support of Des Barres's claims, Susan Fast connects female pursuit of Led Zeppelin with earlier rock'n'roll examples:

> . . . in the wake of a growing disenchantment with the prospect of marriage and life in the suburbs, young white girls saw in the Beatles or, previously, Elvis several things. Elvis "stood for a dangerous principle of masculinity," a "hood" who was "visibly lower class and symbolically black (as the bearer of black music to white youth)"; the Beatles "while not exactly effeminate, [were] at least not easily classifiable in the rigid gender distinctions of middle-class American life." Further, these were not men with whom the girls would marry and "settle down"; the "romance would never end in the tedium of marriage. . . . Adulation of the male star was a way to express sexual yearnings that would normally be pressed into the service of popularity or simply repressed. The star could be loved . . . with complete abandon." In other words, the Beatles and Elvis offered both alternative constructions of gender to these young women and a safe way to explore their own sexuality. Idolizing these performers was an empowering act. (*In the Houses of the Holy: Led Zeppelin and the Power of Rock Music*, p. 161).

This passage could be taken to show that groupies are even more empowered than fans, who are only empowered in fantasy. This idea, that being a successful groupie is empowering, is expressed in Des Barres's story of meeting Patti Boyd in a restroom. According to Miss Pamela, Patti said "George and I think you're the star of *this* show."[4] It's also expressed in books like the *Rough*

---

[4] Pamela des Barres, *I'm With the Band* (Chicago Review Press, 2005), p. 254.

Guide to Led Zeppelin and Danny Goldberg's *Bumping into Geniuses*, where Page and other famous rock stars are listed as "conquests" of Des Barres and Bebe Buell.

It's not clear whether Fast herself sees it this way, since although she does note that Des Barres's activities as a groupie involved attaining power, she dismisses Des Barres as an example because, according to Fast, "her mode of engagement is exceptional and has little to do with the music" (p. 161). According to Des Barres and other groupies, being a groupie has everything to do with the music. This is especially clear in Des Barres's later book of interviews with other groupies, where they make a sharp distinction between themselves, who are after musicians because of the music, and those who are after them because they are celebrities. This point is also made explicitly and rather pointedly in the movie *Almost Famous*.

Fast, in her own analysis of Zeppelin fandom and gender, turns away from groupies to focus on regular fans. She argues that being a Zeppelin fan can be empowering for a woman in spite of the fact that she agrees with the view that hard rock cultures, including Zeppelin's music, are "sometimes overt and crude celebrations of machismo . . . perpetuating patriarchal values" (p. 168). Fast's view is that the female fan can, in fantasy, take on the position of Plant or Page, imagining themselves as the leader of the band. Some of these fans might even take that position in actuality, by taking up the guitar or singing and forming a band. (I won't consider the GTOs here: check them out on YouTube.) In terms of the elements of recognition noted above, Fast is exclusively on the side of emulation, while groupies devote themselves to association and gratification.

Many feminists would object to both Fast's and Des Barres's claims that Zeppelin fandom and groupiedom can be empowering for women. Some would note that sexual and romantic attractiveness arises from characteristics which are not equally distributed, hindering solidarity among women. However, no matter how far one wishes to distance oneself—and others—from taking physical beauty as the object of one's desire, whichever characteristics one says that people should find attractive, it needs to be demonstrated that such characteristics are not also unequally distributed. The fact is, sexual and romantic interaction is unavoidably a struggle for recognition. This critique of groupies runs aground in the same way as Hegel's political concept of recognition; both try in vain to impose an egalitarian conception on a competitive, hierarchical endeavor.

Other feminists would note that actions take place in a social and historical context and that any argument that ignores this context is an irrelevant abstraction. Groupies, they would argue, are striving to objectify themselves; thus they are actively trying to take up the subordinate position in a gender hierarchy. It may be conceptually possible that one could feel empowered by fandom of "cock rock" or being a groupie, but social relations take place in the context of stereotypes, and as a practical matter, groupies reinforce stereotypes which work to the disadvantage of all women, including themselves. There is no logical reason why a woman couldn't be both an object of physical desire and a thinking, creative being, but the mutual exclusivity of these two roles is built into gender stereotypes.

For her part, Des Barres does distinguish between being "accomplished," which is creative and intellectual, and being romantically and sexually desired (pp. 149, 163). Not surprisingly, she wants to be both: "It was my twenty-first birthday, and what I wanted was an exciting lengthy resume or an engagement ring from Jimmy Page." Although in her memoir these goals don't seem to conflict, in her book of interviews with other groupies she identifies a conflict between being a groupie and pursuing her own creativity (*Let's Spend the Night Together*, p. 174). However, this is not because of social pressure from stereotypes but because it's difficult to find the time necessary to pursue both activities.

The position of groupies neatly illustrates the dilemma faced by contemporary feminism. On the one hand, the liberation of women's desire is claimed to be a triumph of feminism. Feminists on this side would be satisfied with the references by rock writers to Jimmy Page and other rock stars as the conquests of Pamela des Barres. On the other hand, it is claimed to reinforce gender hierarchy in a way which disadvantages women. The issues are complex, involving hierarchy, stereotypes, and sex. I'll leave it for feminists to find the solution.

Led Zeppelin and Art

"Can rock'n'roll be art?" "Isn't Led Zeppelin's music art?" Some variant of these questions is the start of many dorm room discussions, or used to be. (I imagine now the question involves rap and Jay-Z.) These questions, and the distinction between art and popular culture they imply, involve claims of recognition. Fans of popular culture seek to attain for their own favorites, and thus also for themselves, the prestige they see accorded to high art. Nor is it only fans who do this. Plant called Page the "Mahler of the Telecaster" and said, "What we talk about is creating something as notable as Beethoven's Fifth. Not just something that will still be remembered in fifty years, but something so mammoth that it would last . . . forever."[5] Such remarks situate Zeppelin in relation to high art as part of a struggle for recognition.

In this struggle the positions are radically contested. On the one side, the advocates of art claim that there is a sharp divide between art and mass culture, in which art is clearly superior. Art is said to be beautiful, or sublime, or transcendent, or timeless, or all of the above, and mass culture is said to be mere enjoyment, entertainment, escapism. On the other hand, advocates of mass culture see the art position as mere snobbism, a pretentious and unjustified claim to superiority when all culture is merely a matter of likes and dislikes, and the likings of anyone are just as good as those of anyone else. Any foray into these subjects will inevitably hurt some feelings. No doubt it would hurt the feelings of Bay City Rollers fans to know I used them as the miserable example in my argument in the previous section.

This split is so sharp there isn't even a neutral set of words to use to describe it. The word "art" itself carries an aura of prestige which introduces bias. Moreover, the terms preferred by the high-art position tend to be pejorative: high culture vs. low, art vs. entertainment. On the other hand, the pop culture position denies the very existence of a hierarchical split in culture, rejecting distinctions of high and low.

In this dispute, two arguments suggest the high culture position is correct. First, the mass culture position demands claims to equal recognition which we've already found untenable. Second, boundaries of high and low can't be crossed at will. It might be thought that Led Zeppelin has a claim to high-art status because they incorporated improvisation, an element of jazz, into its music. Jazz has been considered high culture for quite some time, and improvisation is antithetical to the norms of mass culture, which prefers the expected, the formulaic. However, the question is one of how something is done, not what is done. Led Zeppelin successfully

---

[5] Quoted in Shadwick, *Led Zeppelin*, p. 211.

incorporated a high-art element in order to make a fresher, more compelling version of pop culture, rather than lifting their music into the art tradition, or accomplishing the rare feat of attaining both mass and artistic success.

A helpful example is Yes. A lot is made of the fact that the members of Led Zeppelin were superb musicians, and this is undeniable. But what exactly is this supposed to prove? The members of Yes were superb musicians as well, and instrument for instrument, they were probably a match for Led Zeppelin. Yes's career can also be seen according to the struggle for recognition: they were trying to incorporate values from classical music (symphonic structure, complexity) into rock. Ultimately it didn't work. Meanwhile, Zeppelin was striving to realize their fresh vision for better rock music. Page didn't try to compete with Yes in a "high art" contest, though he attended art school. This decision served him well, as any comparison of Zep to their progrock contemporaries shows.

Claims to high art status on behalf of Led Zeppelin take place in the context of a struggle for recognition, and such claims can go wrong. Consider Case's biography of Jimmy Page. Throughout the book, Case shows admirable restraint, refraining from making high art claims on behalf of his protagonist. But he does slip at one point, claiming that Stairway to Heaven "may stand as one of the landmark artistic achievements of the twentieth century."[6] But Case's terms of comparison are all wrong. He spends ten pages establishing Page's superiority to the likes of Tony Iommi, Ritchie Blackmore, Angus Young, Eddie van Halen and others of that ilk, but makes no attempt to place Page's work in the broader context of art music (pp. 180–190). Similarly, Case argues Zep's music is more important than punk because punk's success was short-lived and Led Zeppelin were far more popular (p. 192). If one wishes to claim art status for Zeppelin, such claims are an embarrassment; where art is concerned, popular scorn is a better recommendation than success. More importantly, the members of Led Zeppelin recognized punk and its importance. Robert Plant said that punk reminded him of early Zeppelin, and John Paul Jones said that "Punk had severely embarrassed us" (*Rough Guide*, pp. 161, 138). Page was so taken with punk that when it was released, the

---

[6] George Case, *Jimmy Page: Magus, Musician, Man* (Hal Leonard, 2007), p. 114.

Damned's debut album was his favorite record (*Led Zeppelin*, p. 211).

Susan Fast does a better job in trying to make a claim for Led Zeppelin's artistic merits, by appealing to Page's improvisations, his use of the violin bow and theremin:

> These sound experiments coincide with those that have been made in "experimental," "avant-garde," and electronic music in the art music tradition. Unfortunately, for reasons that probably have more to do with the pigeonholing of Led Zeppelin negatively as the progenitors of heavy metal, Page's experimentations were taken less seriously than similar attempts made by others—John Cale's in the Velvet Underground, for example. (p. 29)

Fast's claims are made in the appropriate terms, but again, it isn't the elements that are used but their uses that matter. One can use high art elements to make a better (or worse) version of popular culture, just as one could use popular elements to make a new version of art. The comparison between Zeppelin and the Velvet Underground bears further consideration. The Velvet Underground had their own version of "light and shade," with the light being a lot lighter and the shade being a lot darker than Zeppelin's. Some of the Velvet Underground's songs go far beyond the limits of a pop song, and many of the rest have far darker lyrical subject matter. To the extent that Led Zeppelin has been eclipsed in the history of rock, this is as much due to the delayed influence of the Velvet Underground as to the immediate effect of punk.

If we look back at the comment by Plant referring to Beethoven, we can say that if he meant that they wanted to make music that people revered, and would listen to for a long time to come, then such a comment (and ambition) is unexceptionable. But art music has a tradition no less than pop music. And art must be original, so taking musical values from Beethoven and ignoring everything that has happened since will fail to put one in the running for recognition as an artist. Musical values from the great art musicians of the mid-twentieth century are more to the point, such as John Cage, Morton Feldman, and Pierre Boulez. (When asked on "Fresh Air" if he was ever inspired by popular music, Boulez replied, "Of course not.") If a case is to be made for the artistic relevance of Led Zeppelin, I think it would have to be done by comparing the repetition within the songs on *Physical Graffiti* with the early minimalism of Philip Glass and Steve Reich, slightly earlier than but nearly contemporaneous with Led Zeppelin's oeuvre.

So when the old topic "Can Zeppelin's music be art?" is raised and the argument starts to get heated, take a break and listen to Christopher Rouse's orchestral percussion composition, "Bonham." (You can find it on YouTube.) Note the way it's an homage to Bonham and also transforms Zeppelin's music. Read what the critics said about symphony performances of the piece.[7] Has Zeppelin won another struggle for recognition?[8]

[7] For example, Thomas Goss, "Heart, Body and Soul, All on Percussion", *San Francisco Classical Voice* (March 17th, 2000), and Allan Kozinn, "A Temple of Classics Has Room for Rock," *New York Times* (August 10th, 1992),

[8] Thanks to Andrew Baird, Charles Siegel, and Carla Stine for helpful discussions on this chapter. And many, many thanks to Scott Calef for the patient care and thoughtfulness of his comments and suggestions, which have vastly improved this chapter. Thanks especially to Scott for his invitation to participate in this project, which led to many joyous hours of air guitar while I re-connected with the music of Led Zeppelin.

15
Reliving the Concert Experience?

PHILLIP S. SENG

I grew up after Led Zeppelin had already broken up, so I never had the chance to see the band perform live. I've seen the remaining band members together on-stage in the intervening years, though never in person. I saw them perform at Live Aid, at Atlantic Records' anniversary bash, and maybe one or two other big events from the safe and inexpensive distance television allows, but I was never in a position to shell out the hefty sums of cash needed to see them in person.

I did, however, see Robert Plant on his *Now and Zen* tour, and I saw Jimmy Page on his *Outrider* tour. I even saw John Paul Jones when he toured with singer and songwriter Diamanda Galas—that was a really interesting show. But I've never seen the remaining band members on-stage together in person. And for not having a chance to see the original group perform live I'll always feel like I missed something special.

The concert movie is a way of seeing something I'll never be able to see. Since I came to Led Zeppelin's music after the band had dissolved, I'd never be able to see the original band in concert. The movie, and other recordings of their performances since released, was the only way I'd ever get a sense of what they were like live in concert. But with *The Song Remains the Same*, and even with other concert footage like the newer *Led Zeppelin* DVD (2003), I still really don't understand what they were like in concert because there's a huge difference between watching it at home on my TV and being there in person amidst all the smoke, sweat, and screams, and the *really* loud music. What I lack is what some philosophers call the ritual or aura of the concert event.

Waiting in Line

As every concert-goer knows, there's a ritual that comes with attending a concert. Susan Fast describes her own experiences of going to see Led Zeppelin in this way:

> The experience of going to concerts was (and still is) similarly ritualistic and transformative for me. Hearing the announcement that musicians important in my life will tour, buying the tickets, getting to the concert, and, finally, seeing the performance can, depending on how much I admire the artists, serve as important frames in my life. (*In the Houses of the Holy: Led Zeppelin and the Power of Rock Music*)

Lovers of music mark their lives in terms of who they saw perform in any given year. "Oh yeah," they'll say in remembering a certain event, "that was around the time I saw so-and-so in Kansas City. They opened with that really good local band." Concerts become a way of marking time on the calendar.

But even more than standing out in our memories as important past events, concerts also get us to plan our future actions. If I were seriously invested in seeing one of my favorite bands perform in concert I would have to undertake some planning. Of course there's the process of getting tickets—you have to set aside time to call just when tickets go on sale so that you can have your pick of seats and venues. In his novel, *Suzy, Led Zeppelin, and Me*, Martin Millar recounts his experiences as a young lad in Glasgow, anticipating an upcoming Zeppelin show:

> It was almost time to go and queue for Led Zeppelin tickets. Even the thought of queuing for a ticket to see the band had Greg and me shaking with excitement. "Look," I said, holding up my hand, "I'm shaking with excitement." (Soft Skull Press, 2008, p. 62)

Millar's entire book takes readers through the familiar emotions and activities of going to a concert, from buying records, memorizing lyrics, following news reports of the band, to buying tickets and arranging rides and post-concert revelries. *The Song Remains the Same* movie builds the anticipation of the Madison Square Concert gigs with the scenario from Peter Grant's imagination, and then with the arrival of the band in New York.

Once you purchase tickets you have to wait for the concert date to arrive. Waiting for a concert is a feeling of hope. Anyone who has anticipated seeing a favorite musician for weeks or months knows that at some point their daily lives become charged with the expectancy of things to come, of seeing the concert. With this antic- ipation, daily tasks become troublesome, as Millar explains from his own story:

> Next day my picture was on the cover of a Glasgow newspaper, hap- pily clutching my ticket. One of our teachers showed it to the class, with disapproval. However I didn't get into trouble about it. I wouldn't have cared if I did. After all, with a Led Zeppelin ticket in my pocket, what would I have cared about some trouble at school? "To hell with you all," I would have said. (p. 67)

You get the point. The nearer you get to the concert date the more the concert becomes the focal point of your life. The experience becomes what Susan Fast calls it: a ritual.

Performing the Concert Ritual

Perhaps the most recognizable aspect of concerts is the shout-out performers give to whatever city they happen to be in. "Hello St. Louis," the lead singer yells after the opening set of songs. In *The Song Remains the Same* the band powers through "Rock'n'Roll" and "Black Dog" before Robert Plant says "Hello" and "Good evening" to the crowd. The movie then has Plant describe a little bit about the tradition of blues before they play "Since I've Been Loving You."

The playing of a couple songs or more before greeting the audi- ence is not unique to Zeppelin, nor is it even unique to rock con- certs in general. It follows a pattern of making people feel an intimate connection with performers who have traveled long dis- tances to play in their presence. It is as classic as the epic poems of Homer, especially his *Iliad*, which depicts the last days of the Trojan War.

As the rhapsode—what the ancient Greeks called a person who performed poems—comes to the list of warriors in the massing armies in Homer's *Iliad* he would naturally want to make his audi- ence feel special. We know how it feels when musicians call out our home towns between songs. It feels special, we get goose- bumps and we feel like there is a real connection between us and them, between ourselves and the musicians. The Greek rhapsodes were no different, and in performing the *Iliad* they endeared themselves to their audiences by placing in the list of warriors one or two local heroes of past renown. This recognition would make the audience feel a connection not only to the performer, and not only to the poem being recited, but also to the tradition of which the poem is a part. Millar recounts a similar experience in his book when Robert Plant dedicated a song to a local hotel. "It's good to have Led Zeppelin mentioning a building in our city," he writes. "We feel honoured" (p. 146).

In the movie *The Song Remains the Same* Robert Plant does not mention any specific city. We know he's in New York City, since the concert footage was taken from three evenings of shows at Madison Square Garden. But the fact that the editors omit the bands' specific identification of the place of the performance is significant. I think they're trying very hard to make the movie, the recorded concert, appeal to everyone rather than just New Yorkers. In calling out no particular city at all Plant ends up welcoming all of us who watch the movie in any city at all. If there were explicit mention of New York then I would have felt a bit less special when I watched it for the first time back home in Nebraska.

Concert rituals create a certain, unique connection in time and place with the performers and the music. A ritual's a special thing, and can't really be generalized to appeal to everyone everywhere. The movie of the concerts, though, is trying to appeal to all people no matter when or where they watch it. It's trying to have a mass appeal, and thus has to avoid being too much of a ritual.

Remaining the Same

The activity of going to see a concert—the feeling of being in the presence of a band like Led Zeppelin and of feeling the music emanating from the speakers and losing your hearing for a few hours— is an activity that is not so easily reproduced in its entirety.

And yet the very idea of a concert movie is an attempt to reproduce the experience of seeing the band in concert. Since records have been made and concerts have been recorded, there's been a market for bootleg albums. Fans scour the markets for recordings from the shows they've been to, or try to get recordings from the shows they weren't able to see live. Fast suggests that making sure of the playlist is an important activity for fans, since incremental changes—the substitution of one song for another, for example—take on incredible significance, changing the shape and nature of the ritual for that particular audience (hence one feels privileged, singled out, especially blessed). (p. 54)

In other words, simply putting the concert you've seen into the tradition of the other concerts on the current tour is a process of becoming a part of the ritual of the band's performances. In fact, much of Zeppelin's (and other bands') rituals depended on a certain amount of stability in their tour set list. Fast explains the importance of consistency for the experience of rituals:

I would suggest that the centrally important notion of re-enactment in this definition of myth was manifested in Led Zeppelin's performances in two ways. First, fans came to expect certain elements to be part of every performance (the bow solo, the use of the double-neck, and so forth). Second and this is critical not only to Led Zeppelin performances but also to much stadium rock—the stability the set list on a specific tour makes the entire concert a ritual act that is repeated again and again. (p. 54)

Now, the ritualistic aspect of concerts is something experienced by both fans and band members alike. So, while the band certainly had certain behaviors and activities that made their performances ritualistic for themselves, I am discussing here how fans' experiences of the concerts are like rituals, and how these experiences are carried over to the concert DVD.

Fans of Zeppelin come to expect a certain order of songs from certain concert recordings. While the band may have tried to maintain a consistent set list during the course of a tour—thus performing in some sense the same concert for fans throughout the tour—each night's show would have its own composition, improvisations, and unique circumstances.

Millar describes the experience of Page's solo during "Dazed and Confused" as "a different reality" in which "Page plays some weird improvised noise and as he does so he actually walks off the stage and says to me, 'Hello. I'm playing this bit just for you.' Then he walks back over the heads of the crowd and keeps on playing, all without missing a note. It's awesome" (p. 161). Anyone who has heard a Page solo in concert may have had a similar feeling, and understands how each performance is unique yet a part of a repetitive ritual, performed in every show.

Just a few moments ago I was suggesting that there's something very unoriginal about the concert movie, since it can be watched by anyone in any location. And now I'm suggesting the concerts were intended to be as similar as possible so that anyone anywhere would get the same experience. Have I written myself into a contradiction? I don't think so, but to get clear I need to rely on another perspective about the uniqueness of the actual performance.

Losing the "Battle of Evermore"

What we need to understand about concerts is something anyone who has been to a concert understands: they are unique experiences that no DVD or CD recording can ever really hope to duplicate. Nothing can be substituted for the actual experience of seeing a band in person. We can be reminded of seeing a band live, but it's not the same as actually seeing them in person. Nothing can ever be substituted for standing on my chair for two hours while watching Jimmy Page. Concert experiences are incapable of exact duplication and reproduction.

Walter Benjamin suggested that these kinds of experiences had something to do with what he called the "aura" of the artwork. Benjamin was thinking more of painting, but we can think of seeing a Zeppelin concert in the same way. Benjamin wrote that all artworks have a certain history and tradition.

> Even the most perfect reproduction of a work of art is lacking in one element: its presence in time and space, its unique existence at the place where it happens to be. This unique existence of the work of art determined the history to which it was subject throughout the time of its existence. This includes the changes which it may have suffered in physical condition over the years as well as the various changes in its ownership. (*Illuminations: Essays and Reflections*, Schocken, 1968, p. 220)

In terms of a Zeppelin concert we can understand that even the most perfect shows, when the band was really *on*, are still understood in context of a tour, in relation to a certain album, certain events in fans' lives, and so on. Concerts are a part of history. The important point Benjamin makes about the aura of art is that original works of art have a certain kind of "authenticity" that copies do not possess (p. 221). With the case of concerts I think this point is even more clear and easy to illustrate.

Concerts occur at specific times and places. They occur once and then they are finished. There are extended concert tours, but each show is a separate performance. Seeing one concert cannot be substituted for another night of the tour, even if there are consecutive nights in the same city, as Zeppelin often performed. So, we can say that each concert has its own aura since each concert is a unique performance. We know that these shows are all unique simply because of the "sloppiness" of Jimmy Page's playing or the fluctuations in Plant's voice or the improvisational segments worked into certain songs (*In the Houses of the Holy*, p. 149). These traits actually give *more* authenticity to a concert—they make the show unique and special, different from all the rest. Fast describes one way in which improvisations are important:

> Experiencing the lengthy improvisational sections at Led Zeppelin shows, or now via bootleg recordings of those shows, is like experiencing someone in transition, in a liminal state: the potential for transformation comes through these improvisational moments. Hence they have a ritualistic importance that cannot be underestimated. (p. 79)

We learn more about the band through witnessing their improvisations, through their interpretations of other songs. And being in the presence of their creativity creates a unique experience for us, if we are at their shows.

When we watch *The Song Remains the Same* we see the band perform, but we are detached from the experience of the performance. We don't really know what it was like to be in Madison Square Garden and listening to Zeppelin perform, not from watching the DVD at least. We can see and hear the band, and that's important—it helps bring us closer to the band and their music more than simply listening to their albums—but we aren't actually there as participants in the concert.

Remaining the Same, But in a Less Unique Way

Our contemporary media—DVDs, CDs, MP3s, and others—are based on the premise that everything is reproducible. One DVD is just as good as any other copy, barring scratches, and one CD or MP3 is just as good as any other recording of the same song or songs. If you couldn't catch last week's performance, or the Grammys or any other little show, you can probably watch it online. In other words, the way we create our performances today is based on the presumption that they are recordable. We organize our events with an eye towards reproducing them technologically, without any consideration of the importance of the original event.

Benjamin thought the development of photography and movies was a really big turning point for us and the way we live our lives. He thought that until the development of photographic techniques in the 1800s we still acted as though art and performances had an aura—we treated our experiences of things as irreplaceable. But, with the development of technology that allows mass duplication of images and sounds—photos, musical recordings, movies, and now with webcasts and other technologies in this century—we have given up our concern for the uniqueness of events. He explains it this way:

> Unmistakably, reproduction as offered by picture magazines and newsreels differs from the image seen by the unarmed eye. Uniqueness and permanence are as closely linked in the latter as are transitoriness and reproducibility in the former. To pry an object from its shell, to destroy its aura, is the mark of a perception whose "sense of the universal equality of things" has increased to such a degree that it extracts it even from a unique object by means of reproduction. Thus is manifested in the field of perception what in the theoretical sphere is noticeable in the increasing importance of statistics. The adjustment of reality to the masses and of the masses to reality is a process of unlimited scope, as much for thinking as for perception. (p. 223)

Let me explain a few points about this long quote, because it's not always clear what Benjamin intends to say. He writes that when we experience things personally we get a sense of the "uniqueness and permanence" of them. He means that when we see a band perform right in front of our eyes we get a sense of the timeless quality of the ritual they are enacting, and we feel as though we're a permanent part of that ritual because we are there too.

When Benjamin writes that newsreels and magazines (or movies and photography) are related to "transitoriness and reproducibility" he means that the technologies of mass reproduction—audio recording, photography, cinema and webcasts—have an effect on how we experience the very events that are recorded. By recording a concert we have decided that there is a part of the experience that we can transmit to others without their being at the concert. When we treat the concert as an event that can be recorded and shared with millions of other people we treat it differently than when we value the ritual of concert-going. According to Benjamin technologies of mass reproduction make fans forget the ritualistic aspect of seeing our favorite band in concert. Instead, we just want the latest release in the cheapest format possible.

"Prying an object from its shell" is Benjamin's way of saying that cameras and microphones take the Zeppelin concert out of fans' personal experiences. Even though a fan might have gone through the ritual process of planning and traveling to the show and enjoyed the event in person, putting the performance on DVD or CD makes the event available for everyone in the same way. Very few people will have had an experience like the fan's—just those people in attendance had this experience—but the fact that the event is available in a recorded format makes the in-person experience less unique, and therefore less valuable.

When Benjamin suggests that the mass audience attains a new "sense of the universal equality of things" he means that all of the different experiences of the performance become equally valuable. In other words, Benjamin argues that producing and watching the *The Song Remains the Same* on DVD can make audiences feel like they've seen the band in concert, like our experience of Led Zeppelin rivals the experiences of the fans who were actually there in person in 1973. I think most everyone would agree that the DVD is a poor substitute for being at the show, and Benjamin would stand in line with us.

Sneaking In through the Back Door

In *The Song Remains the Same* there's a wonderful scene of two security guards letting a couple of fans sneak into the backstage area. We all wish we could have been those two lucky souls—they got to see the show live, go backstage, and then see the concert movie and later buy the recordings. They got to experience what Benjamin calls the "aura" of the concert, and then also to relive that experience through the recordings on LP, CD, and DVD.

But, consider this point: A fan who was in the far recesses of Madison Square Garden for one of Zeppelin's shows might get a new take on their concert experience by watching the concert movie. The different camera angles, the better sound quality and the lack of annoying neighbors might all make for a new and better experience than the in-person experience. The concert movie *might* be worthwhile and open up new avenues for appreciating the show. Obviously, I'd have rather been to the concert than watch it on DVD, but while sitting on my sofa I can hear the music clearly, pause or rewind the show and see the band from a number of different angles that would be unavailable to anyone at the concert.

We behave as though it's more impressive to go to the stadium than to watch a game or concert on TV. The very fact that ticket prices are ridiculously high should be proof that we value the live experience more than the recorded experience, right? There really is no comparison between watching the concert in person and seeing it on DVD. They are completely different kinds of experiences in Benjamin's understanding.

The price of the tickets for Led Zepplin's one-off performance at London's O_2 Arena was £125.00, or about $250.00 back when the show took place. That's a hefty value, but the price tag for me to see the show when they (inevitably) get around to releasing the remastered version of it on DVD will be little in comparison to that price. And I'll be just as avid to have the DVD as someone who could afford the trip to England was avid to see them live. In fact, I'll have pretty good seats and camera views that most of the audience could only dream of having. But I'll have none of the anticipation, expectancy, camaraderie, or elation of being with a mass of like-minded people. In short, I'll miss out on the ritual of it all.

The mass production, as Benjamin suggests, levels out the uniqueness of experiences of things, in this case concerts. In making the movie or the DVD or buying or renting it, we have assumed that we can get something of value out of the concert. In effect, we've already decided that the value of the concert *is not necessarily seeing the band perform live*. The value is simply in seeing and hearing the band perform, and knowing that the performance was live at one time.

Now, I know this will sound like I'm just playing games with words, but there really is a difference. I used to attend record conventions and sift through racks and racks of albums looking for the one great Zeppelin bootleg to round out my (small) collection. I once found a bootleg of a concert that took place on my birthday, and I thought that was pretty special. After a while I came to accept that the recording wasn't all that great—pretty scratchy and not from the sound board but from somewhere in the audience—so it wasn't something I had to have to make my life complete. For some reason I thought there was some cosmic importance in owning a mediocre recording of a concert I never saw. Well, I was thinking about something other than the ritual of the concert.

There's a distinct difference between listening to the music and seeing the music performed. And beyond that distinction, there is another distinction characterized by seeing the music performed live and in-person as opposed to watching it on a DVD or some other recording. Fast explains her own experience with Led Zeppelin:

> The way in which rock musicians use their bodies in performance is critically important to an understanding of the music. I first came to know Led Zeppelin's music through the studio recordings, and when I eventually saw them in performance I came not only to a richer understanding of the music, generally speaking, but also to a decidedly different understanding of it and of the people making it. (p. 114)

There's something visceral and sensual about being at a concert. Anyone who has been to a concert will know what I'm talking about. And there are even differences between seeing concerts in different venues. A local bar provides a much different experience than a stadium show, and a better view too.

Benjamin used the word "unarmed" to describe the eye that sees things personally. Seeing things for ourselves is dangerous, it involves going out into the world and being witness to events. It also involves ascribing value to original and unique things. But for Benjamin this attitude was passing away with the rise of mass production of objects. The eye that watches things on screen or from a removed distance or time is thus "armed." It is protected against original things, it is sheltered in some way. The armed eye also has the ability to judge and assign value built into it. But it doesn't weigh values in terms of ritual importance, in terms of how meaningful the experience will be in one's life, but rather in terms of price, for example, what is this DVD worth? Is the quality of this bootleg good enough to merit the price?

Benjamin's way of understanding the different kinds of human experience can be a little bit depressing. His ideas basically make us realize that the way in which we value things no longer has anything to do with the ritual service a thing provides for us. It's not necessary to actually attend a concert, or lecture, or art exhibit or anything like that to get the gist of the experience. I'm *not* saying that it's not valuable to do all these things, but Benjamin is trying to point out that *we do not act* like these activities have any inherent value.

We can digest the important parts of a book from a guy named Cliff, or hear the book read to us as we drive on our morning commutes, or read someone's blog or Twittering about the show last night. Reading or living for ourselves thus becomes devalued due to our busy schedules and the availability of new technologies. We don't have to do a lot of things for ourselves anymore—we can simply research the internet and find what other people have to say. Thus, we can substitute the experiences of other people for actually having these experiences ourselves. That seems to be the point of the concert movie in general.

Benjamin thought that the new technologies of media put us, the audiences, in a very difficult position. He put it this way:

> The film makes the cult value recede into the background not only by putting the public in the position of the critic, but also by the fact that at the movies this position requires no attention. The public is an examiner, but an absent-minded one. (pp. 240–41)

The "cult value" he mentions in this passage is the value of an object or event when it figures into a ritual or some other activity requiring our presence. You have to have been there to see the show, not just hear about it or see it on DVD. Film, photos, and other more recent media strip away the need for this kind of interaction with things. In effect, as Benjamin claims, these technologies of mass reproduction put us in the position of critic. We're the ones determining the value of events simply because we're now able to witness them from afar. In a movie theater or at home on our sofas we are in the position to judge the quality of a movie and the value of scenes recorded for our viewing. We are the "examiners," as Benjamin claims, but this new job-description requires absolutely no training and no experience. So, I go about my duties without reflecting on the fact that I probably am not the best judge of what a Led Zeppelin concert was like since I never saw them perform in person. I've only seen the DVD. Does that make me a good judge of their performances? Hardly.

But, I'm really only trying to talk about the movie, right? How is *The Song Remains the Same* as a concert movie? It's got great music. I don't know what Zeppelin was like in person, so it's the best I can ever get. As Millar closes his novel:

I'm not a music journalist. I don't have any desire to persuade anyone that Led Zeppelin were any good. You can think whatever you like. You either feel it or you don't. The same as any music. The same as any art. You feel it or you don't. The same as being in love. You can't be persuaded. You either feel it or you don't. I'm not going to try and change anyone's mind. Led Zeppelin. Greatest rock band in the world, oh yes. (p. 212)

16

A Bootleg in Your Hedgerow

MARK D. WHITE

The brilliance of Led Zeppelin's studio output is well-known, and to a large extent unquestioned. Reasonable people can disagree over which is better: the rawness of *Led Zeppelin I* versus the refined elegance of *Presence*, the electric bombast of *Led Zeppelin II* versus the acoustic serenity of *Led Zeppelin III* versus the perfect combination of both on *ZOSO*. But let's face it—it's all incredible. Page, Plant, Jones and Bonham left a truly unique recorded legacy that changed the face of rock music, and will surely stand among the best of twentieth-century music for generations to come.

But their live shows are a different story. Now, before you raise the hammer of the gods, let me explain! Certainly, those that were lucky enough to witness live Zep in its prime are unequivocal in their judgment—the band was transcendent, treating the studio recordings as mere blueprints, inspiring improvisational flurries that left the audience shell-shocked. What Zep may have lacked in precision they more than made up for in spirit, drive, beauty, and rage. But for those of us who were not so lucky—or perhaps may not have been born when Zep tread the boards the first time around—how were we to know? Despite rumblings to the contrary, as of this writing they've refused to put on a full-fledged tour, so there was no real chance to see them live. And aside from the pseudo-concert film *The Song Remains the Same* (and its soundtrack), Zep would not release a proper live album until 2003's *How the West Was Won* (featuring material from 1972).

What was a Zep-obsessed fan to do in the meantime? Today, of course, you'd just go to an internet site and download a show, but let's turn the clock back a bit, at least to the first couple years of the twenty-first century (and earlier). If you were lucky, and you had access to a small, independent, off-the-beaten path record store—in other words, probably not in a mall, though I've been to a few cool mall record stores—you might have seen some Led Zeppelin CDs (or LPs) in the rack that didn't seem familiar, with titles like *Live on Blueberry Hill* or *Destroyer*.[1] They sure looked like live albums, but you hadn't heard of any live albums being released by Atlantic Records, Zep's longtime record label. They had shoddy artwork, some of the song titles were misspelled, the jewel cases fell apart, but who cared—if these CDs contained what they promised, this was the Unholy Grail, live Zep! We'd finally be able to hear what our older brothers and sisters, or maybe even our parents, had being telling us about.

But hold on—why don't you see these records or CDs in your local Wal-Mart, Tower, or Camelot? Everyone's going to want to buy these! Is there—is there something *wrong* with them? Could they be—gasp—illegal? Why do you start hearing the *Law and Order* theme—is that Sam Waterston over there? What's the deal? You don't want to go to jail, you're too pretty . . .

As some readers will no doubt know, those CDs are commonly referred to as *bootlegs*, and they are unauthorized live recordings (or unreleased studio material).[2] (Bootlegs are not to be confused with pirated recordings, which are copies of officially released CDs, DVDs, and so on.) It certainly won't surprise any readers of this book that Led Zeppelin is one of the most heavily bootlegged artists in the history of rock. In 1999, the British Phonographic Industry listed Zep as *the* most bootlegged rock artist, surpassing the Beatles, the Rolling Stones, and Bob Dylan.[3] And it's not hard to understand why: Given the short supply of official live material, and the heavy demand on the part of fans to hear their classic live performances, it's clear that if bootlegs hadn't existed before Led

---

[1] See Luis Rey, *Led Zeppelin Live: An Illustrated Exploration of Underground Tapes* (Hot Wacks Press, 1993), for the most extensive description of Zep bootlegs in print; there are also numerous websites with similar content.

[2] I'm only considering live recordings here. Unauthorized release of studio recordings is examined more in James C. Klagge, "*Great White Wonder*: The Morality of Bootlegging Bob," in Peter Vernezze and Carl J. Potter, eds., *Bob Dylan and Philosophy: It's Alright, Ma (I'm Only Thinking)*.

[3] "Led Zeppelin Rock Bootleg Chart," BBC News (August 17th, 1999), http://news.bbc.co.uk/2/hi/entertainment/422948.stm, accessed March 7th, 2009.

Zep, they would have been invented just for them! And the band took notice. Zep's manager Peter Grant famously went into record stores and personally "trampled underfoot" any bootlegs he found. Grant also assaulted a sociology student at a Vancouver Led Zeppelin concert, thinking he was recording it for a bootleg release, while he was actually trying to measure the volume!

So what kind of "property" is a live performance? Is it "property" at all? Who does a live performance "belong" to? Is a recording of a live performance different from the performance itself? Does the addition of packaging and distribution change the nature of the live recording as "property"? What can the owner of this "property" do with it? Are property rights unlimited or not? And can (or *should*) considerations of happiness and utility be more important than matters of rights when it comes to property?

What's That Confounded Term, "Property"?

The classic view of property and ownership comes to us from John Locke (1632–1704), who wrote that, most basically, we own ourselves (our bodies), and based on that, we own whatever we produce with our bodies from what we find in the land (trees, rocks, or whatever):

> Though the Earth . . . be common to all Men, yet every Man has a Property in his own Person. This no Body has any Right to but himself. The Labour of his Body, and the Work of his Hands, we may say, are properly his. Whatsoever then he removes out of the State that Nature hath provided, and left it in, he hath mixed his Labour with, and joyned to it something that is his own, and thereby makes it his Property. It being by him removed from the common state Nature placed it in, it hath by this labour something annexed to it, that excludes the common right of other Men.[4]

It then follows that if we own what we make ourselves, we can trade it for something made by someone else, and then we'll own that too. Of course, we can trade our property for money, which we'll also own, and can use to buy other goods, or invest it and possibly own a part of a business. You can see why Locke's concept of property is essential to the operation of a market economy,

---

[4] John Locke, *Two Treatises of Government* (1689), II, paragraph 27.

and is very popular with philosophers, political scientists, and economists alike.

But here we already see ourselves getting away from the simple "stuff" concept of property. If I own stock in Atlantic Records, that doesn't mean there's a brick, stapler, or case of Led Zeppelin swag at the company's headquarters that has my name on it, and that I'm entitled to go take whenever I want. But I do "own" a piece of that company, in that I have a voice (however small) in how it's run, and I share in the profits (whether distributed or not).

The idea is similar when we talk about what are known as *intellectual property rights*, including books, movies, and music (as well as patents and other non-artistic "things"). Sure, we can touch a book, a DVD, or a CD, but you don't buy these things for the paper or plastic—you buy them for the "content."[5] The problem is that once this "content" is created and sold, it can become very hard to control it—content can be duplicated much more easily than physical goods. (The same problem applies to patents.) Copyright law exists to prevent making copies of books, movies, and recorded music without the creators' or owners' permission.

But music is a little different—what if I don't make an illegal copy of Led Zeppelin's recording of "Good Times Bad Times," but instead I simply sing it to a friend? Or with my band at a birthday party, or at a show? The song—the composition itself—is protected by a different area of law than the recording itself, and no band— not even Led Zeppelin—is making an exact copy of the recording when they perform it in a club somewhere. But we're not talking about my lame-ass band doing "Good Times Bad Times"—the bagpipes work, dammit, just give them a chance—we're talking about the mighty Zep performing it, and then other people recording the shows for their enjoyment, for others' enjoyment, and perhaps for profit. Since we're not dealing with exact copies anymore, copyright law isn't much help. So who "owns" a live performance?

Most artists would say the live performance is theirs—after all, they created it in the original Lockean sense, from their fingers and hands against strings, wood, and rubber, and they intended it to be enjoyed by those in attendance (the "audients," to use King Crimson founder—and virulent bootleg-hater—Robert Fripp's

---

[5] That is, unless it's a collector's item, such as the first pressing of *Led Zeppelin III* with the Aleister Crowley quotations on the runoff groove—you don't *want* to play that!

term), and nobody else. Furthermore, they may argue that each live performance is a unique, once-in-a-lifetime event, to be experienced in the moment and not afterwards. While this may not be true for precisely arranged and choreographed arena pop shows, it certainly was true for 1970s hard rock bands like Led Zeppelin, Deep Purple, and Uriah Heep, for whom improvisation was central to the live performance. (Of course, this goes double for bands like the Grateful Dead and Phish, whose ethic was even closer to that of jazz, where improvisation is the primary goal—and who have adopted very liberal policies regarding live recording, as we'll see later.) Since it's unique, each live show is special, something for the audients to remember and hold in their minds as their own, not to be shared with anyone else. (Unless, of course, the band or label deigns to release a live album—*then* it's okay!)

But obviously many fans would disagree—after all, the band performed for them, and they may feel they have the right (morally, if not legally) to record the performance for their later enjoyment. In this sense, they have mixed their "labor" with the band's performance, and therefore made something of their own. (Ironically, this point becomes even stronger if we consider the bootleggers' activities of producing and packaging the CDs.) And if they didn't record it themselves, they feel they should be free to seek out a recording from someone who did—either through a trade with another collector, or buying a bootleg from the recorder or from a store. And, in fact, law has reflected this—in some countries, you do have the right to buy and own (not sell) a recording of a show you attended.[6]

But what about sharing or selling the recording? Things get complicated here, and of course this directly affects not only bootleggers, but traders as well. Even if you, the fan, have the (legal) right to own a copy of the show you attended, simply by virtue of having attended the show yourself (according to the laws mentioned above—I didn't write the laws!), this right would not extend to others you might share the show with (whether for money or other shows), unless they were also at that show. So . . . could you give away your only copy of the show? You could give away your copy of an official release with no difficulties, but that's more like

---

[6] See Clinton Heylin, *Bootleg: The Secret History of the Other Recording Industry* (St. Martin's Griffin, 1996), for in-depth coverage of the legal history of bootlegs.

ordinary property—you own it because you paid for it (we'll assume!), and you're free to give it away or sell it as you choose. But if you have a right to a live show only because you saw the show yourself, does that mean you must destroy the recording if you don't want it anymore? Does the reason you have the right to the recording in the first place really dictate what you are allowed to do with it when you're done with it?

A Bundle in Your Hedgerow

Actually, this corresponds fairly well to the legal understanding of property rights, which are usually understood to be *bundles* of rights specifying what the rights-holder can do with her property. Such rights typically—but not always—include the right of exclusion (allowing you to keep others from using or taking your property), the right of use (allowing you to use the property as you see fit), the right of sale (duh), and the right of disposal (allowing you to get rid of your property in any way). Think of your property right in your car: all four of these rights are included, but they are also limited. You can keep most people from using your car, but not a police officer who needs to commandeer it to pursue a suspect. You can use your car for your own purposes, but only according to traffic laws. You can sell the car, but you have to follow your state's and country's transfer-of-title laws. And you can scrap your car, but you can't leave it on the side of the highway or in your neighbor's driveway.

But, of course, none of this depends on how and why you got the car in the first place (assuming you got it by legitimate means), so why should this matter in the case of live recordings? The difference is due to the nature of the "thing" we're talking about: a car is an ordinary physical object, while as we've seen, a recording of a live performance is much different. Here's an example: Imagine your friend gives you a copy of *The Hammer of the Gods*, but in a very particular way. She gives you the book, but she wants you to keep it, to read it, to treasure it. She would be very hurt if you gave it away, sold it, or threw it in the trash; if you wanted to do any of those things, she would rather you give the book back to her. Furthermore, let's assume your friend is a lawyer, and writes all of this into a contract or title. You would have property rights in the book, but your rights of disposal and sale would be very limited.

The property right you have in your live recording is quite like this hypothetical "contract" with your friend. As we saw, in many places you are entitled to own a recording of a show which you attended, as if it were a gift from the band to the folks in attendance that night. The gift is for you (and the rest of the audients) and as such you are not allowed to give (or sell) the recording to anyone else—the law grants you rights of use, exclusion, and disposal, but not sale. This is just one step above official recordings, which you can certainly give away or sell, but not make copies of to give to other people—your property right in an official recording is limited as well, although slightly less.

Whole Lotta Utility

We've been focusing on rights, specifically property rights, so far, but there are other approaches to looking at these issues. For instance, we haven't looked at the effect of bootlegs or their prohibition on the well-being or happiness of the various persons involved. We have ignored this point until now; you could say we were implicitly assuming that rights were more important, as some philosophers would have it. But others—namely, *utilitarians*—would argue that rights are only useful insofar as they promote the general happiness of all.

To a utilitarian, an action is justified if doing it will increase the total utility (or happiness, or satisfaction) of all persons affected. More specifically, *rule utilitarians* focus on rules and institutions, rather than individual acts, and decide if following an institution (like property rights) would increase total happiness. Most rule utilitarians would endorse a basic system of private property rights like Locke's (enforced by law), since it offers the peace of mind that people need to live their lives, buy and sell things, and basically live long and prosper.[7] Strong property rights are absolutely essential to the operation of markets, and if you believe the market economy increases total happiness, property rights as an institution are justified by utilitarian logic.

As with our discussion of property above, this is pretty simple when it comes to property rights in physical, tangible stuff, but things might get more complicated when it comes to intellectual property rights, which are literally ideas (or expressions of ideas).

---

[7] Wrong book—sorry!

While you and I can't both drive the same car at the same time, we can read the same piece of literature, watch the same movie, and listen to the same song (or show) at the same time—these things are *nonrival*, in that my use of them does not block your use.[8] The right of exclusion to using my car is valuable to me, and contributes to my happiness, and there is no similar notion when it comes to stories, movies, or music. All else the same, if more people can enjoy a movie, song, or book, there will be more happiness in the world.

So does that mean we shouldn't have intellectual property rights, especially in artistic creations? Actually, it provides a strong argument for them—property rights provide the incentive for the producers of such content to create and distribute it very widely, since they stand to benefit from selling or licensing it. Artists, writers, and musicians may not need this incentive to create their art, but they, or their agents, publishers, and record labels, need it to distribute it to the fans who will enjoy it. The fans are happy, the artists are happy, the middlemen are happy—it's win-win-win, right?

This all makes sense when it comes to officially released content, such as studio and live albums, but what about live performances, the focus of this chapter? Does the prohibition of live recordings— or at least their distribution—increase total happiness? Maybe yes and maybe no. (How's that for commitment?) What I mean is that it makes some parties in the situation happy, but others very unhappy. First off, it makes the fans happy—those who enjoy hearing unauthorized live recordings are better off, and those who don't are no worse off. Second, it makes bootleggers happy—if they continue to do it, they must be doing it for some reason, for either money or the love of the music. But obviously it does not make the bands happy, at least those bands that do not allow live taping and trading (unlike the Grateful Dead and their musical progeny).[9] And it does not make the record companies happy, since they often try to prohibit live taping even when the band is open to it.

The fans' support of taping, trading, and (to a lesser extent) bootlegging is understandable, but why are the artists and record companies so against it? The most obvious reason has to do with money, especially for the record companies (and Peter Grant!),

---

[8] Except, of course, when rude bastards stand up or talk non-stop at shows— but this is a chapter about property, not the nature of radical evil!

[9] Many (but not all) such bands have their live shows freely available for download at the Live Music Archive (http://www.archive.org/details/etree).

who are concerned that the availability of bootlegs will cut into the sales of official CDs. But the impact of bootlegs and traded live recordings is uncertain—most people who trade in such items are diehard fans of the band, who probably already own all of the official releases. And with Led Zeppelin in particular, we already talked about the egregious shortage of official live material from the band—if there were more of it, surely the fans would buy it! But there isn't, and the record companies aren't losing any sales if they're not selling any live albums to begin with. And live recordings are hardly a threat to sales of the studio recordings, especially with bands like Led Zeppelin whose live performances are so different from the studio versions.

The Music Remains the Point?

As far as the artists are concerned, it may also be a matter of quality control—they may want to tightly control the material that is available to fans. This applies most obviously to bootlegs of studios demos or album outtakes, material which the artists decided was not good enough to release on their albums, or they're holding onto in hopes of working on it more later, or they're saving them for bonus tracks or compilations (like *Coda*). But this concern can certainly extend to live performances, especially ones like Zep's that were so experimental, skirting the edge of brilliance every night, and—sorry to say this—sometimes missing it. If the boys had a bad night, it's understandable that they'd rather not have the world listening to it over and over again.[10] Of course, a bad night in the eyes (or ears) of the band, perhaps one that involved wild experimentation and risks, may be regarded as a terrific night from the viewpoint of the fans—who's to judge? Many fans of live recordings, especially the tapers themselves, consider it their responsibility to archive the live history of their favorite band, and that means good times and bad times—every band's had its share!

But many people argue that making live recordings more widely available—explicitly endorsing them, as in the jamband

---

[10] In 1993, Deep Purple released a three-CD set named *Live in Japan*, containing all three shows that made up their classic *Made in Japan* album from 1973. Fans who hadn't heard bootlegs of the three nights were shocked to learn that guitarist Ritchie Blackmore messed up the classic riff to "Smoke on the Water" on two nights, leaving only one version good enough for the original release.

community, or at least tacitly allowing them, as many rock artists do—helps promote the bands' official releases. I've heard from many people, personally and online, that became interested in a band after hearing a bootleg or fan recording, and then went on to buy all the band's official releases, DVDs, merchandise, and more. (This argument has also been used to support piracy of official releases, but it has less merit in that case, since it is the official releases themselves that are being pirated.)

So, based on this logic, a bootlegger or taper could argue, "the recordings I make, distribute, or sell are helping promote the band's catalog, so it's helping the band and the label—what I'm doing is actually for everyone's benefit, whether they realize it or not, so it's justified." Like it or not, this is valid, if overly simplistic, utilitarian logic. And therein lies a central flaw with that way of thinking—it allows you (anybody, really) to make decisions about the well-being and interests of other people, and to do things that affect them, without their input or consent.

If we do regard this input or consent to be important, this brings us back to the issue of property rights—do, or should, artists have a property right in their live performances and the recordings of them? In other words, so what if *you* think live recordings benefit the artists—isn't it more important what *they* think? If you agree, then perhaps artists should have property rights in their performances. You may think I would be happier if I quit my job, but that doesn't mean you should tell my boss that I quit! Ultimately, it's my decision, good or bad—it's my right. By the same token, it doesn't matter what you think is good for the band or the record company—they have the right to look after their own interests, which may imply a property right in their live performances. If you agree that they do have such property rights, then they can exercise that right however they choose, whether you think it's smart or not. That's the nature of a right: in the view of legal philosopher Ronald Dworkin, rights—at least the most important ones—"trump" utility.[11] Rights give the rightholder the prerogative to do things that may not be in the interests of total utility—or even the rightholder's utility. So even though fans may think it's in Led Zep's interest to allow unauthorized live recordings to circulate, the band may still have the right not to—the decision is theirs, for good or bad.

---

[11] Ronald Dworkin, *Taking Rights Seriously* (Harvard University Press, 1977).

What Is Sold and What Should Never Be Sold

Let's introduce one more example of this. If you spend enough time in the live music trading community, you will come upon the term "liberated bootleg," which refers to a commercially manufactured bootleg CD which is "ripped" to a computer by a fan and then distributed freely online (or between traders on CDRs). This is a term of pride among traders, who consider the sale of unofficial recordings of their favorite bands' live performances to be heresy, but the free (in every sense) distribution of them among fans is no problem. Even Jimmy Page seems to agree: "The legitimate part is where fans trade music, but once you start packaging it up and you do not know what you are getting, you are breaking the rules legally and morally."[12] (After which he threw a TV out the window . . . Just kidding! But seriously, when did rock stars become so sanctimonious? I blame Bono.)

But from the viewpoint we discussed before, this is still very problematic. If the live performance is the property of the band, then unauthorized distribution of it, no matter how, is wrong. The band may actually prefer that the bootleg be sold, as the high price (along with limited availability and substandard sound quality) would dissuade many casual buyers from purchasing them. (Typically, in the US, before the advent of CD burners and downloading, bootleg CDs would cost about $25 per CD. Many of Zep's shows took three CDs—you do the math!) But the interests of the fans and the band are obviously not the same: the fans want to spread the music as widely as possible, while the band wants to restrict it to official releases only. The fans feel that the bands and labels shouldn't mind, but whose opinion really matters? Should the fans make the decisions for the band? Or should the band be free to make decision regardless of the fans' wishes?

Coda

So what do we do about the issue of unauthorized live recordings? Should fans feel justified in having, trading, or buying bootlegs because Led Zeppelin has released so little official live material, and has performed live so seldom since the late 1970s? Or should

---

[12] Quoted in "Star Page witness in bootleg case," BBC News (July 26th, 2007), http://news.bbc.co.uk/2/hi/uk_news/scotland/glasgow_and_west/6917449.stm, accessed January 28th, 2009.

they respect the band's decisions and be happy with what they and the label have released? Maybe the question is WWRFD (What Would Real Fans Do)?[13] Whatever your answer is, you're revealing a little bit of how you feel about property rights, which in turn reveals a little bit of how you feel about ethics, politics, and law. You may not put these feelings or opinions in the same terms philosophers use, but that's what philosophers are here for. So when you argue with your friends about bootlegs—or admittedly bigger moral issues, like the effects of stadium lights bouncing off Jason Bonham's big shiny head—you're doing a little philosophy yourself. And that's the way it oughta be . . .

---

[13] For more on the duties and loyalties that bands and fans owe each other, see my chapter "Metallica Drops a *Load*: What Do Bands and Fans Owe Each Other?" in *Metallica and Philosophy: A Crash Course in Brain Surgery*, edited by William Irwin (Blackwell, 2007), pp. 199–209.

17

Why We Listen to Led Zeppelin, Really

JERE O'NEILL SURBER

> Many is a word that only leaves you guessing,
> Guessing 'bout a thing you really ought to know.

If you go searching Led Zeppelin's lyrics for signs of profound insight into the order of the universe or deep philosophical reflection on the human condition, let's face it: this is about as far as you're going to get.

Maybe there are things "you really ought to know," but LZ isn't about to try telling you what they are. Instead, their songs really do remain pretty much the same, at least thematically. A lot of them, often addressed to the ubiquitous "babe," are about love (or, maybe more accurately, lust) pursued, fulfilled, or blocked. There are a fair number of odes to "ramblin' on." And once in a while you'll find some fragmentary and cryptic invocations of Nordic or Middle-Earth mythology. But overall, if you just look at the lyrics, you'd have to conclude that one of their contemporaries, Edie Brickell, captured their own stance toward philosophical reflection pretty well:

> I'm not aware of too many things,
> I know what I know if you know what I mean.
> Philosophy is the talk on a cereal box.

Of course, as any LZ fan will tell you, *that's* not why you listen to them! If you want flights of intricate philosophical fancy, put on some of the Beatles' later albums or the conceptual outings of the Moody Blues. If you want to grapple with the depths of the human

265

condition, try Pink Floyd or the early Dylan. But, if you want hardcore, blues-based, balls-out, high-decibel, guitar and rhythm driven rock'n'roll, then you can't do better than Led Zep.

So, if the lyrics don't offer us much to go on and the main point lies in just experiencing the raw power and technical fireworks of the performance itself, what more philosophically is there to say about Led Zeppelin (and, in fact, a lot of 'mainstream' rock'n'roll)? As it turns out, this itself poses a philosophical question that goes back at least to Kant, that provoked Nietzsche to publish his first major work, and that may not have found any very productive answer until quite recently in the post-structuralist thought of Gilles Deleuze.

Music and the Limits of Philosophy

During the last two decades of the eighteenth century, the German philosopher Immanuel Kant (1724–1804) proposed what was then a radical idea: that human reason and its most profound product, philosophy, had definite and determinable limits. Before Kant, being a philosopher was thought to entitle one to speak with knowledge and authority on practically any topic whatever. After all, since Plato and Aristotle, the subject matter of philosophy was taken to be 'being', and, since anything that exists must share in 'being,' then anything whatever was fair game for the philosopher. Kant, however, suggested that what we take to be or exist is a matter of what we, as human beings, are capable of experiencing and knowing. Since philosophy was a form of human knowledge, then any limitations upon human knowledge would also circumscribe the range of topics appropriate for philosophy. In other words, there were just some things about which philosophy had little or nothing important to say.

Kant mapped these new contours of human reason using a twofold strategy. On the one hand, he tried to demonstrate that anything that we could possibly know must first be capable of appearing to us in the space and time of our own experience. On the other, he attempted to show that actually knowing such an appearance involved characterizing it in terms of fundamental concepts which allowed us to make verbal statements about it. Without experience, there was nothing to talk about; without concepts, there was nothing meaningful to say.

Originally Kant had been concerned with the status of scientific knowledge about natural objects and felt confident that his view confirmed its procedures and results as well as outlined its limits. However, when, in his third major work, *The Critique of Judgment* (1790), he turned his attention to humanly produced works of art, he discovered another sort of limit to philosophy. He found that, while philosophy could make some headway in clarifying in very general terms the sort of experiences and ideas that define an object as an artwork, it had little or nothing to say about the particular and unique meaning of any individual artwork or artistic style.

In a move which was adopted by most of his successors among the Romantics and German Idealists with respect to artworks, he outlined a sort of 'compromise position' by claiming that there was a hierarchy of 'artforms', based on the degree of 'conceptual content' that a given artform possessed. At the top was poetry, since it employed language and its conceptual determinations could thus (at its best, in his view) express philosophical ideas. By contrast, at the very bottom of the hierarchy was music, which he characterized as a "mere play of sound sensations." Following Kant's view, music became, for most philosophers immediately after him, a sort of absolute limit or 'zero point' for philosophical reflection and interest, a place where philosophy encountered its own limits and could only remain silent.

This at least helps us better understand the philosophical problem posed by Led Zeppelin. For a philosopher influenced by Kant (which so many have been and still are), music which lacks any very sophisticated lyrics or verbal content and is mainly driven by sound and rhythm represents a limit for philosophy. Lacking the conceptual content which is an absolute requisite of philosophy on this view, there is, for the philosopher, indeed nothing further to say. To slightly pervert a phrase of Frank Zappa, "I'll shut up; you can play yer guitar."

Nietzsche's Re-evaluation of Music

In the time separating Kant from Nietzsche, both philosophy and music changed dramatically, moving along trajectories that ultimately crossed in the figure of the composer Richard Wagner (1813–1883), whose works provoked Nietzsche's first major publication, *The Birth of Tragedy from the Spirit of Music* (1872). Wagner's eccentric megalomania drove him to style himself as the premier philosopher as well as the foremost composer of his age. In his own self-styled philosophical publications, he claimed to have succeeded in doing precisely what, to Kant, was the impossible: to have made music thoroughly philosophical and to have expressed philosophy in the form of music. He promoted his 'music dramas' (most of us would call them operas) as what he called 'total works of art', productions which mustered all other artforms—including music, painting, architecture, acting, and poetry—into what he regarded as a total and final philosophical view of the universe. In this respect, he probably anticipated certain types of modern epic filmmaking as well as such conceptual rock performances as The Who's *Tommy* and Pink Floyd's *The Wall*.

While the young Nietzsche had no desire to return to Kant's rationalistic 'limits of philosophy' in the face of music, he also came to think that something important about both music and philosophy had been perverted by Wagner's grandiose visions. However, unlike Kant, who championed conceptual philosophy against the "mere play" of music, Nietzsche took the side of music against the abstract conceptual idiom of philosophy as well as Wagner's attempt at a forced wedding between them.

Nietzsche's *Birth of Tragedy* is most famous for introducing the distinction between the 'Apollonian' and 'Dionysian'. The namesake of the first was the Greek sun-god Apollo, the symbol of heavenly luminosity, clarity, individuality, self-control, intellect, reason, and civilization. That of the second was Dionysus, the subterranean god of intoxication, violence, excess, irrationality, and the 'darker forces' within human beings and brute nature. Ultimately, Nietzsche developed this opposition into a conflictual cosmic vision which manifests itself in every register of human experience, social life, and history.

However, it was the realm of art that first provided Nietzsche access to this vision and that has remained its most fertile ground for application. Specifically, Nietzsche came to view music, understood in its most elemental sense as rhythm, perhaps chanting, and dance, as the most fundamental and 'Dionysian' of the artforms and that from which, early in the Greek world, others emerged under the 'rationalizing' and 'civilizing' influence of the 'Apollonian'. The view of art developed in *The Birth of Tragedy* then became an attempt to recover the importance of music and its 'Dionysian' powers from the 'civilized' and, to Nietzsche's mind, decadent forms that art had assumed in the history of European culture since the Greeks.

One crucial aspect of Nietzsche's discussion was that philosophy itself, as inaugurated by Socrates and Plato, was a wholly 'Apollonian' countermeasure directed against the psychic and political chaos associated with the spirit of essentially 'Dionysian' music, something that helps explain Plato's negative attitude toward art as well as later critics' moral outrage at the 'immorality' and excesses of such rock bands as Led Zeppelin. Still, Nietzsche insisted that the Greek tragedies were born from the 'spirit of music' and that philosophy (initially in the form of the Platonic dialogues) in turn emerged from them as an assertion of Apollonian authority directed against the violence and chaos enacted in the Greek tragedies.

Nietzsche, then, is important for our discussion of Led Zeppelin for two reasons. First, he completely reversed Kant's view of the relation between philosophy and music. Where, for Kant, the 'defect' of music was its lack of any 'conceptual content', positioning it as the least philosophically accessible and significant of the artforms, for Nietzsche music became just the opposite, that art which not only lay at the basis of philosophy but from which philosophy stood to learn the most about its own subterranean origins, motivations, and nature. On a Nietzschean view, it is exactly the fact that the music of Led Zeppelin is so viscerally 'Dionysian' and so lacking in 'Apollonian' verbal or philosophical content that makes it interesting and important to the philosopher.

Second, in suggesting that there was a subterranean connection between music and philosophy, Nietzsche opened the possibility for the philosopher to speak meaningfully and productively about music, something that Kant had entirely disallowed. Nietzsche, then, would encourage us to leave the self-affirming security of more traditional philosophical problems and concepts in approaching Led Zeppelin and risk creating a new language in which to describe and reflect upon the visceral and mostly unconscious effects that draw us to their music in the first place.

Still, there's a danger lurking in Nietzsche's view of the Apollonian-Dionysian contrast when applied to music like that of LZ. It is that, so long as we continue to proceed as traditional Apollonian philosophers, when we confront and try to describe something essentially Dionysian, we will tend to convert the Dionysian into another, if somewhat different, version of our own still Apollonian view. Nietzsche is often claimed to be, among other things, a forerunner of psychoanalysis and existentialism and, read in this way, there is a tendency to try to find some sort of 'deeper' philosophical meaning expressed in the music. While this 'depth approach' may be helpful in thinking about bands like Pink Floyd, whose lyrics and music lend themselves to psychoanalytic or existential analyses, we're still inclined to say, in the case of Led Zeppelin, "*That's* also not why you listen to their music; you're still not getting it." So what to do?

Music and Deleuze's Philosophy of Surfaces

In the eighteenth chapter of *The Logic of Sense* (1969), the French post-structuralist philosopher Gilles Deleuze (1925–1995) presents what he calls "three images of philosophers." He characterizes the first image as that concerned with 'height'. He associates it most closely with Plato and says that "the philosopher's work is always determined as an ascent and a conversion," such as Plato describes in his famous 'Cave' image. More generally, the 'philosopher of height' emphasizes the mind and works with and thinks in terms of ideas, concepts, and linguistic meanings, those universals that transcend the world of ordinary experience. Beyond Plato, this image could also describe all approaches to philosophy that emphasize logical reasoning, verbal meaning, and the analysis of propositions and texts. The philosopher of height clearly corresponds to what Nietzsche called the "Apollonian."

The second image is that of 'depth'. The 'philosopher of depth' focuses upon all those subterranean desires, passions, and forces that we most immediately associate with the unconscious mind and the existential anxieties that it provokes. Rather than ascending to universal concepts, 'depth philosophy' descends, digs down into the tensions and conflicts underlying life, language, thought, and philosophy. Deleuze cites the pre-Socratic philosophers (as interpreted by Nietzsche) as the original 'depth philosophers,' but comes to include such modern projects as psychoanalysis and existentialism among them. Again, there's a strong parallel with Nietzsche's idea of the Dionysian.

The third image is that of the philosopher concerned primarily with what Deleuze calls 'surfaces'. The history of philosophy as yet offers only few examples and Deleuze regards this stance as "a re-orientation of all thought and of what it means to think: *there is no longer depth or height.*" For Deleuze, the philosopher of surfaces neither tries to ascend to rational, transcendent ideas nor attempts to unearth the hidden forces and unconscious processes that underlie human life and experience. Rather, he or she holds firmly to the conviction that all is 'pure immanence', a flow of lived bodily experience, and refuses to grant philosophical standing or significance either to supersensible ideas or subterranean mechanisms or structures. A philosopher of surfaces doesn't deny that there have historically been other images of philosophers, but he or she insists that ideas and unconscious structures are mere 'secondary' or 'illusory effects' of the ongoing flow of our immediate lived bodily experience, effects that can always be reduced to its own operations.

The 'surface', then, is exactly where we live our lives, as embodied beings, on a minute-by-minute, day-by-day basis. As Deleuze describes the human being at the beginning of his most famous work, *Anti-Oedipus*: "It breathes, it heats, it eats. It shits and fucks." This is the fundamental stratum of existence that makes up our lives from moment to moment and it wouldn't be possible to think about abstract philosophical questions or probe the 'deeper meaning' of our existence' without it. Neither thought nor feeling, it is the immanent and original flow on the basis of which we produce the dual illusions of 'higher truths' or 'underlying meanings'.

When he turns to art, Deleuze, like Nietzsche, gives music a privileged place, but for different reasons. Rather than being a human activity that stands in contrast to the Apollonian and discloses some 'deeper meaning' about the hidden Dionysiac element of human existence to us, music is that art most able to 'sync us up' with the flow that is our surface life. Here, finally, we've gotten closer to saying something philosophical about Led Zeppelin: We listen to Led Zeppelin, not because of the conceptual heights to which the lyrics may lead us or because it sets off speculation about the 'deeper meanings' of things; rather, we listen mainly because the music affects us in a very physical, bodily way. The surface flow of our moment-to-moment bodily experience is kicked into another gear and rides along with the rhythm and sound qualities of the music in a way that makes us aware . . . of what? That, for a moment, we are intensely alive and, yes, rockin'. *That's* why we listen to Led Zeppelin.

I Got My Flow(er), I Got My Power

But Deleuze doesn't leave it at this; it turns out that a 'surface philosopher' can have a good deal more to say about the music of Led Zeppelin without quoting lyrics or a lot of soul-searching. In fact, much of Deleuze's philosophy is devoted to developing a new vocabulary with which to describe and analyze 'surface flows.'

To begin with, a surface is basically a physical or bodily flow of forces. As a flow, it has varying speeds or velocities, just as sometimes, when we're bored or tired, we say "I'm moving pretty slow today" and on others, when we're excited or nervous, we say, "I've been screaming along all day." This, of course, has nothing to do with 'clock-time' or 'map distance' but with the overall flow of our bodily experience. In listening to LZ, though we don't always think about it, our bodies directly register the differences in tempo between their hard rockin' numbers and their slower pieces as well the changes of rhythmic flow within a piece. Think, for example, of how "Stairway to Heaven" builds from a slow, ballad-like beginning to the searing conclusion. This, at least as much as its cryptic lyrics, make it one of the classic anthems of rock.

As forces, surface flows also have intensities, exactly as when we describe an experience or musical performance as 'intense' or 'blah'. Led Zeppelin's music is distinctive and immediately distinguishable from all imitators because it involves an interplay among several distinct intensities: a killer rhythm section; Robert Plant's signature voice, which often strays from almost a whisper into probably the most intense falsetto scream of any vocalist; and the brilliantly modulated guitar work of Jimmy Page. Such an interplay of intensities can't be taught and has probably never been equaled.

Surface flows also experience blockages. We're all familiar with this when we're cruising down the ski slope and suddenly catch an edge and fall, or when we're feeling great and we get a phone call from a bill collector or an angry partner. Interesting things, however, sometimes happen around blockages, since they often create open spaces for altering our 'trajectories' (another favorite Deleuzian word) and establishing alternate flows. Led Zeppelin were masters of this device, especially in their live performances, where, in segues between songs or within their trademark marathon improvisations, they would seem to allow the energy to grind briefly to a halt, only to re-establish another and different flow going in new sonic directions. For a great example of this, check out the twenty-five-minute version of "Dazed and Confused" on their 1972 live recording, *How the West was Won*, which contains, besides the title song, segues into "The Crunge" and "Walter's Walk," together with a lot of other 'flow-blockage-new flow' patterns.

There are several discussions of musical flows in Deleuze's *A Thousand Plateaus*, where a central theme that we might call "the same (only different)" appears. According to Deleuze, the very heart of musical flow consists in the repetition of beats, themes, choruses, instrumentation, and so on. Illustrated very simply, one beat is meaningless noise, two establish a rhythm, the beginning of a musical flow. The key to music as art (and one important thing that makes it different from machine noise like the ticking of a clock) is that every repetition (which involves 'the same') is also different, due to many factors such as its place in the overall song or performance and slight variations in such things as tempo, volume, and instrumentation. For Deleuze, artistic creativity in general is a matter of exactly this: repetitions of 'the same', each of which is also 'slightly different'. Both within individual songs, where verses often alternate with choruses, and in live performances, where every concert goer knows that they often play the same songs but never the same way twice, the music of Led Zeppelin is never monotonous or boring. We always know that, however often we've heard a refrain or song, there is always the excitement, too, of anticipating something different that the band will bring to it on every repetition.

Finally, Deleuze also discusses the issue of verbal meaning and lyrics in music. He writes (*A Thousand Plateaus*, p. 96), "We are not suggesting any correspondence [between music and language]. We keep asking that the issue be left open, that any presupposed distinction be rejected." His discussion, in fact, seems to suggest that, in the context of music, lyrics must first be fitted to the music's basic flow and thus serve a role subordinate to the surface flow of the sound itself. Lyrics that are too complicated, poetic, or philosophical (!) can thus distract us from that which is most fundamental about music—it's surface flows and blockages. Maybe the very fact that LZ's lyrics don't overly call attention to themselves is part of exactly what makes their music so popular as rock'n'roll. It's revealing that sometimes, especially in live performances, Robert Plant simply drops the lyrics, using his amazing voice simply as another instrument (which, to a great extent, it usually is anyway).

Is Led Zeppelin, after All, the Most Philosophical of Rock Bands?

After considering Deleuze, we might be led adopt a new perspective. If we're still committed to being 'height philosophers' like

Plato and Kant, we'll probably say that there's not much of philosophical interest for us in Led Zeppelin, that their lyrics don't have much 'philosophical content' and that their music isn't sufficiently 'experimental' to draw us into novel aesthetic reflections. If we remain 'depth philosophers' like Nietzsche and the existentialists, we'll probably miss the Angst-driven soul-searching and psychic trauma in the music and lyrics of a band like *Pink Floyd*. But . . . if Deleuze has convinced us to become 'surface philosophers', then we're likely to say that, after all, Led Zeppelin is one of the most philosophical of all rock bands.

It's not that Led Zeppelin itself addresses old philosophical questions or articulates new truths, nor that it compels us to probe the 'deeper meaning' of our existence. Rather, what they do is enact, amplify, and put us in direct touch with that which is most fundamental in our experience and lives: the bodily 'surface flow' in which we exist from moment to moment, in other words, 'being' as it is lived and 'repeated with differences', not just talked about or analyzed.

That's why we listen to Led Zeppelin! And, don't forget, Deleuze has taught us that, if we're willing think in some new terms, there's still a lot to say about this. But no conceptual analysis or existential soul-searching needed . . . you have to start by just rockin' on with the band!

Many Times I've Wondered: 77 Zep Facts, Anecdotes, and Trivia

1. The schoolgirl on the back cover of *Presence* is Samantha Gates, one of two child models used in the shoot for the *Houses of the Holy* cover. The other model on *Houses* is her brother, Stefan, who has gone on to present BBC2's *Cooking in the Danger Zone*.

2. If you hold the mountain inside the gatefold of *Led Zeppelin IV* to a mirror, you can see a great beast (or is it a black dog?) in the rocks.

3. The hermit on the summit of the mountain on the inner gatefold of *IV* appears to have a horn coming out of the side of his head.

4. The guitar symphony at the beginning of "In the Evening" is from Page's abortive soundtrack to Kenneth Anger's *Lucifer Rising* film. Kenneth Anger, by the way, claims "Sympathy for the Devil" was inspired by conversations he had with Mick Jagger.

5. Zep have arguably sold more official releases (not counting compilations) than any other band in history.

6. When in Vegas with Miss Pamela of the GTOs, Jimmy Page received an invitation to meet with Elvis. He declined. The band later met the King in LA while in town for their West Coast Swan Song inauguration party in 1974.

7. The original cover concept for *Led Zeppelin III* was based on crop rotation charts.

8. The drum solo in "Moby Dick" on *II* is a composite of a number of different solos.

9. One of the original cover concepts for *Presence* was to be an aerial photo of the ZOSO sign over the Nazca lines in Peru.

10. "Stairway to Heaven" has been played on American radio more than five million times, despite never being released as a single. It was first performed live at the Ulster Hall in Belfast on March 5th, 1971.

11. Jimmy Page's first child, Scarlet Lilith Eleida Page, was conceived with Charlotte Martin while Page and Plant were at Bron-Yr-Aur, the cottage in Wales where much of *Led Zeppelin III* was composed. The name "Scarlet" is taken from Aleister Crowley's Scarlet Woman; "Lilith" was the name of one of Crowley's own children.

12. The first ever vinyl Zep bootleg was of a Vancouver concert given on March 21st, 1970. It was called "Pb", the chemical abbreviation for lead.

13. When *Led Zeppelin II* went to number one in the US, the album it knocked out of first place? The Beatles' *Abbey Road*. Not bad, boys!

14. *Led Zeppelin IV*, despite being the fourth best selling album in history, never made it to Number One in the US. It was kept out of the top position by Carole King's *Tapestry*. It did, however, spend three years in the US Top Forty.

15. Led Zeppelin were invited to play at the Woodstock festival in 1969, and declined the offer.

16. Prior to their February 28th, 1970, gig in Copenhagen, Led Zeppelin were threatened with a lawsuit by Countess Eva Von Zeppelin, a direct descendant of the famous airship designer. The Countess indignantly refused to allow such a scruffy-looking lot of "shrieking monkeys" to sully her cherished family name. The band nearly charmed her into relenting, but then she saw the cover of LZ *I* in the group's dressing room and her outrage returned, now more intense than ever. The boys ended up doing the concert billed as "The Nobs".

17. Robert Plant's son Karac was named after Caractacus, a famous Welsh general.

18. During live performances in 1973, Plant noticeably lowered his voice an octave when singing parts of "Stairway to Heaven" and "Over the Hills and Far Away". Sometime after the end of the 1973 US tour (culminating in their filmed shows at Madison Square Garden in late July) Plant underwent surgery to his vocal chords. According to Dave Lewis, the operation probably occurred at the end of 1973 or early 1974. The band didn't perform together live again until their January 11th, 1975, concert in Rotterdam, a concert hiatus of almost eighteen months.

19. Some have suggested that Jimmy Page's symbol, *ZoSo*, is to be given a Luciferian interpretation. The "Z" is a stylized lightening bolt, signifying the fall from heaven of Lucifer, the shining one. Concerning "oso", the two circles each have a dot in their center. They thus represent Saturn, the ringed planet. The "S" also stands for Saturn, being the planet's initial. We have, then, three sygils representing Saturn, the sixth planet in the solar system; thus, "666", the number of the Beast in the apocalyptic Book of Revelation.

20. In alchemy Saturn rules the element Lead. Jimmy Page's symbol probably represents Saturn, which is appropriate since Page leads, and hence "rules", Le(a)d Zeppelin.

21. An alternate account of *ZoSo* has been offered based on the clue "Thursday" that Page once gave. (If the Saturn theory were correct, we would expect the clue "Saturday".) Thursday is Thor's day. Thor, the Norse counterpart to the Greeks' Zeus, was a hammer-wielding storm god. As before, we have the stylized lightning bolt expected in connection with a god of thunder, but the upright appendage to the "tail" of the Z is Thor's hammer of the gods. And of course, lightning is electricity, the power source for Page's heavily amplified guitar army.

22. The original idea for the *Houses of the Holy* cover art put forward by Storm Thorgersen of Hipgnosis involved a picture of a tennis racket on an electric green tennis court. Page rejected the concept for its insinuation that Zep's music was a racket.

23. The printed lyrics to "D'yer Mak'er" conclude with the parenthetical question "Whatever happened to Rosie and the Originals?" The Rosie in question is Rosie Hamlin, a one-hit wonder with the 1960 song "Angel Baby." At the time *Houses of the Holy* was released in 1973 she was a member of the Blossoms singing backup for Elvis Presley.

24. One of the boulders near the bottom of the *Houses of the Holy* cover is shaped like a heart.

25. Page's solo on "Stairway to Heaven" is played on a Fender Telecaster that was given to him by Jeff Beck.

26. The song "Black Dog" is named after a black Labrador Retriever that wandered around the Headley Grange mansion, where the band was recording *Zeppelin IV*. In various tales and legends, including Goethe's *Faust*, demons (and sometimes the devil himself) were wont to appear in the form of a black dog. Since most of the band's

members found Headley Grange a rather damp and dismal place, it's interesting that Winston Churchill famously talked about his bouts of depression as visits from the "black dog."

27. The song "Four Sticks" is named after the trick Bonzo used to get the massive drum sound on that track: he played the part using four drumsticks—two in each hand.

28. A Zep joke went awry in 1974 when there was a big dinner party to celebrate the founding of Swan Song Records. Some groupies convinced the guys to go in drag and spent hours dressing them up and doing their hair and makeup. When the Zep boys were led to their table later that evening, they were a bit shocked to find out that Stevie Wonder was sitting with them. Because Wonder is blind, the boys worried that he would be offended and think the whole thing was a joke at his expense. Whether Wonder was amused is unclear. Pictures from the evening of the four guys in drag can be found in some of the cutout windows on the *Physical Graffiti* album cover.

29. The classic 1975 film, *Monty Python and the Holy Grail* was financed in part by Led Zeppelin.

30. Two parts of the movie, *Spinal Tap*, were directly inspired by Led Zeppelin. The first is lead guitarist Nigel Tufnel's solo tour de farce, where he plays the guitar using a violin (rather than a violin bow)— an obvious nod to Page's legendary live performances of "Dazed and Confused". The second is Spinal Tap's infamous Stonehenge stage set. During their 1977 tour, Zeppelin used a Stonehenge stage set, that included the same pi-shaped piece that Spinal Tap used on stage during the ill-fated dwarves' dance—except in Zeppelin's case it was actually eighteen feet tall, not eighteen inches.

31. Many years after Zeppelin's breakup, Jimmy Page ran into one of the stewardesses that used to work on the "Starship" and "Caesar's Chariot," the planes they leased for US tours. (Starship was used on the '73 and '75 tours and the Chariot on the '77 tour.) She told him that the stewardesses would eagerly wait until the band and its entourage passed out and then they'd go through the cabin snatching up all of the rolled up $100 bills that had been used to snort cocaine.

32. The Starship rented by Zeppelin—a Boeing 720B that seated forty— was owned by teen-idol Bobby Sherman, one of the co-creators of the Monkees.

33. Plant's swordfight sequence in *The Song Remains the Same* was filmed at Raglan Castle, a fifteenth-century ruin located between Abergavenny and Monmouth in South Wales.

34. Peter Grant and Richard Cole's fantasy sequence was filmed in Sussex at the Hammerwood Park Estate, a site the band once contemplated buying for a rehearsal and recording space.

35. The mountain Page is climbing during his fantasy sequence in the movie is Meall Fuarvounie, near Boleskine House. Aleister Crowley also climbed the mountain. (By 1901 all of the world's mountaineering records except one were held by either Aleister Crowley or Oscar Eckenstein.)

36. Mick Wall notes that when, near the conclusion of Page's fantasy sequence in *The Song Remains the Same*, the Hermit slowly sweeps his wand in an overhead arc, it turns eleven colors. Eleven, for Crowley, is the "general number of magick."

37. "Swan Song" was originally the title of a Page instrumental. The twenty-minute piece had evolved out of his Yardbirds' guitar showcase, "White Summer," but was never released. Some suspect parts of "Swan Song" found their way into "Ten Years Gone" on *Physical Graffiti*. According to Chris Welch, Page overdubbed fourteen guitar tracks on the cut.

38. When "Ten Years Gone" was performed live, John Paul Jones played a unique triple-necked instrument combining six-string and twelve-string guitars and a mandolin. He plays an eight-string Alembic bass on "Achilles' Last Stand."

39. Among the first bands signed to Zep's Swan Song label were the Pretty Things. Their pre-Swan Song album *Parachute* (1970) was *Rolling Stone*'s album of the year. It was the only album ever so recognized by the magazine which didn't go gold in the US.

40. At the Swan Song launch party in New York, the "swans" hired by the band turned out to be geese. Several were killed by rush hour traffic after being chased outdoors by—who else?—Bonzo and Cole. Among the dignitaries at the Swan Song launch party in Los Angeles was none other than Groucho Marx.

41. The UK launch of Swan Song wasn't to be held for another six months—on Halloween night, 1974. The date was set to coincide with the Swan Song release of the Pretty Things' *Silk Torpedo*. Among other wonders, the event featured strippers costumed as topless nuns.

42. The first group signed to the fledgling Swan Song label was Bad Company. Their first single, as well as their debut LP, both went to Number One in the US. The album was recorded at Headley Grange—where much of *Led Zeppelin IV* was also recorded.

43. When Page bought Tower House in London's Holland Park—one of his several residences—he was bid against by David Bowie.

44. "Custard Pie" on *Physical Graffiti* has as source material Blind Boy Fuller's "I Want Some of Your Pie" (1939), Sonny Terry and Brownie McGhee's "Custard Pie Blues" (a 1947 reworking of the Fuller tune), and Sleepy John Estes's "Drop Down Mama" (1935).

45. Plant allegedly intersperses his cries of "Oh, my Jesus!" on "In My Time of Dying" with "Oh, Georgina!"—a shout-out to a conquest from the road.

46. "Boogie with Stu" (named after Ian Stewart, long-time Rolling Stones collaborator) is an adaptation of Richie Valens' "Ooh My Head," which itself is an adaptation of Little Richard's "Ooh My Soul."

47. The line "One day soon you're gonna reach sixteen" on "Sick Again" is a likely reference to Lori Maddox, Jimmy Page's underage girl-friend.

48. According to rumor, Jimmy Page was under consideration to replace the recently departed Mick Taylor on the Rolling Stones' 1975 US tour. Ronnie Wood took over instead. Page was again considered as a replacement for Keith Richards in 1978 when the latter faced a possible seven year sentence for a drug bust in Toronto.

49. The album cover concept for *Physical Graffiti* was lifted from Jose Feliciano's *Compartments* (1973), which featured a similar brown-stone, complete with windows through which the building's occupants could be seen. The buildings photographed for *Physical Graffiti* are from 96 and 98 St. Mark's Place, New York. The Rolling Stones filmed a music video—"Waiting for a Friend"—in front of these same buildings.

50. David Bowie invited Jimmy Page to visit his home on 20th Street in New York as they both shared an interest in the occult and Bowie was curious about Jimmy's work on the Kenneth Anger film. When Page did come, his presence—his aura—so unnerved Bowie that the latter rudely asked him to leave—by means of the window! Afterwards, Bowie had the house exorcised because he thought it had become overrun with demons conjured by Crowley disciples.

51. Lynn "Squeaky" Fromme, a member of the Manson family who was eventually arrested for an assassination attempt on then-President Gerald Ford, attempted repeatedly to see Jimmy Page in LA to "warn" him of dangers to his life that she had seen in "visions."

52. During the 1976 presidential campaign, Susan Ford, daughter of incumbent Gerald Ford, announced on the Dick Cavett show that her

favorite group was Led Zeppelin. Not to be outdone, Ford's challenger, democratic nominee Jimmy Carter, claimed for his part that he listened to Led Zeppelin records while working late nights as governor of Georgia.

53. Page voted Tory in the 1979 general election that would bring Margaret Thatcher to power. This was a very un-punk thing to do.

54. Neither Peter Grant, John Paul Jones, nor Jimmy Page attended the funeral for Robert Plant's son Karac. Many feel this insensitivity is what Plant is referring to when, on "Hots on for Nowhere," he sings "I've got friends who will give me fuck all." Page is especially singled out on the later "Carouselambra" lyric "Where was your helping / where was your bow?"

55. There were six different album covers for *In Through the Out Door*. The inner bag holding the record featured two black and white drawings which became colored if water was brushed over them.

56. The members of Def Leppard, from Sheffield, saw Zeppelin headline at Knebworth, drove home, and the next day signed their first record deal with Phonogram.

57. Led Zeppelin's road manager, Richard Cole, previously worked for The Who. Danny Goldberg, who handled US public relations for the band during 1973–75 later went on to run Geffen records and manage Nirvana. One time Zep publicist B.P. Fallon also worked for Marc Bolan.

58. Where were Led Zeppelin presented with their first gold records, for their debut album? Eugene, Oregon. (Go Ducks!) Atlantic executive vice president Jerry Wexler did the honors on July 31st, 1969.

59. Led Zeppelin were under consideration to appear in the Rolling Stones' Rock and Roll Circus TV special. However, Mick Jagger, after hearing their tapes, thought their sound too guitar-heavy and opted to invite Jethro Tull instead.

60. The idea of playing the electric guitar with a violin bow was suggested to Jimmy Page by a fellow session musician, who additionally was the father of David McCallum of *Man From UNCLE* fame. Besides Page, Eddie Phillips of The Creation also used to bow his guitar. Page used the technique pre-Zeppelin on the Yardbirds' "Tinker, Tailor, Soldier, Sailor" and "Glimpses", both on *Little Games*.

61. The 1980 tour of Europe was the only Zep tour where Jimmy didn't incorporate a violin bow solo into the band's live act.

62. According to Peter Grant, the first time Pagey used a Gibson Les Paul onstage with Zeppelin was at San Francisco's Fillmore West on

January 9th, 1969. Before that, he had played a Fender onstage. One of Page's first Les Pauls was a 1958 model that he bought from Joe Walsh, then of the James Gang.

63. Zep's last ever TV appearance was recorded in Paris for *Tous en Scène* on June 19th, 1969. The performance was broadcast on French TV on September 5th of the same year. You can see the performance as one of the extras to Disc One of the Zep DVD.

64. In 1969 and 1970, Led Zeppelin contemplated adding a fifth member. Anthony "Top" Topham, who played guitar in the Yardbirds until Eric Clapton took over his spot, was one candidate. Others included Chris Squire of Yes and Keith Emerson, later of Emerson, Lake and Palmer.

65. According to Keith Shadwick, Plant's "banshee howl" on "Immigrant Song," so evocative of Valhalla and Viking hordes storming the keep, actually derives from a more placid and sunny setting. The cry mirrors the opening measures of "Bali Ha'i," as featured in the Rogers and Hammerstein musical *South Pacific*.

66. By some estimates, between 1963 and 1965 Jimmy Page did session work on between fifty and ninety percent of all records produced in England.

67. Although John Paul Jones's symbol on the fourth album is usually taken to stand for skill, precision, and competence, according to Rudolph Koch's *Book of Signs*, from which it was taken, it is used to exorcise black magic. Hmmmm. . . .

68. Because of gaps in the film coverage of the Madison Square Garden concerts which were to be the basis for *The Song Remains the Same* film project, the group had to gather in a sound stage months after the fact to perform the numbers again. Because he had cut his hair during the interim, John Paul Jones was forced to wear a wig for the shooting!

69. One very probable source of inspiration for *The Song Remains the Same* film project was Marc Bolan's 1972 film *Born to Boogie*, directed by Ringo Starr. The Bolan film also intermixed concert footage with "fantasy" sequences. *Born to Boogie* mentions Zep explicitly when, during the Mad Hatter's Tea Party, Bolan's butler reads a poem called "Union Hall" inviting Zep and other bands to "keep on rockin'." Unlike the Bolan sequences, however, the Zep fantasy vignettes were almost entirely devoid of humor. (At least, intentional humor!)

70. Following their 1973 US tour, John Paul Jones informed Peter Grant that he was considering leaving the band to become the choirmaster

at Winchester Cathedral. Jones later admitted the choirmaster bit had been a joke, blown out of proportion by an over-zealous journalist.

71. After forming Swan Song, Page and Plant briefly considered buying the Sun Records and Chess labels, which were for sale at the time. Peter Grant and the other band members nixed the idea, however.

72. Keith Shadwick notices that the opening fanfare chords for *Houses of the Holy*'s "The Song Remains the Same" are the same as those used in the Yardbirds' 1967 "Tinker Tailor Soldier Sailor" Check it out. You'll recognize the chords instantly.

73. Though Led Zeppelin's *Song Remains the Same* double-LP soundtrack went to number one in Britain in November 1976, it was kept from the top spot in the US by Stevie Wonder's *Songs in the Key of Life*, peaking instead at Number Two.

74. "We're Gonna Groove", which surfaced on *Coda*, was originally recorded for inclusion on *Led Zeppelin II*.

75. The song "Hey Hey What Can I Do", originally the B-side to the Zep's 1970 "Immigrant Song" single in the US, is available on a re-released two track "Immigrant Song" / "Hey Hey What Can I Do" CD single.

76. Page's solos on "For Your Life" and "Hots on for Nowhere" from *Presence* were his first recordings with the 1962 Lake Placid blue Fender Stratocaster he obtained from one-time Byrd Gene Parsons. The guitar can be seen in the Knebworth footage of the Zep DVD.

77. Page's favorite album during Zep's 1977 tour of the States was *Damned Damned Damned*, the debut by . . . The Damned! When in London in late '76, all four members of Led Zeppelin attended a concert by the Damned at the Roxy. On a separate occasion Plant attended a Sex Pistols show, also at the Roxy in London. He was mocked from the stage by Johnny Rotten during the show.

Top Eleven Contributor Top Ten Lists

Some of the contributors to *Led Zeppelin and Philosophy* thought it would be fun to offer their sometimes serious, sometimes whimsical opinions on a variety of Zep-related topics. Enjoy! You can post your own lists, read others', and enhance your knowledge of philosophy and LZ on the *Led Zep and Philosophy* Facebook page!

Calef's Top Ten Led Zeppelin Resources

10. RollingStone.com CD review archives. This isn't as much fun or useful as it once was, since *Rolling Stone* evidently has succumbed to long-overdue embarrassment and replaced some of their more excoriating original reviews (such as John Mendelsohn's rant against LZ's debut or the original attack on *Houses of the Holy*) with others written in the last few years, but you can still get a fair sense of why Zep didn't dig the media, straight from the horse's mouth.

9. The Tight But Loose web site: http://www.tightbutloose.co.uk. Probably the most up-to-date place to go for any and all Zep-related news. Hats off to Dave Lewis!

8. Led Zep's official site: http://www.ledzeppelin.com/ Of greatest interest are the discussion forums and LOTS of videos.

7. *Suzy, Led Zeppelin, and Me* by Martin Miller (Soft Skull Press, 2008). This is by no means a gratuitous choice. This book describes in *perfect* detail what it was like to be, well, *me*! If you ever wanted to know what you missed 'cuz you weren't around at the time, or, if you were but just never got to see Zep, here it is, in all it's heart-rending, charming, adolescent beauty and absurdity. Plus, it's freaking hilarious!

287

6. *Hammer of the Gods* by Stephen Davis (1985, 1997). What can I say? I've got a penchant for the classics. Chapter Three: "The Year of the Shark." Say no more.

5. *Led Zeppelin's Led Zeppelin IV*, Volume 17 in Continuum Books' 33⅓ series, by Erik Davis (Continuum, 2007). With all due respect to Susan Fast?s *In the Houses of the Holy*, this is the closest thing to a philosophy book on Led Zeppelin next to this one. Smart-alecky, clever, and opinionated, a nice work for intellectually curious fans.

4. *Led Zeppelin: The Story of the Band and Their Music 1968–1980* by Keith Shadwick (Backbeat, 2005). An intelligent if biased account of the band and, most particularly, its music by someone who knows music well. Plus, oodles of gob-smacking photos. Probably the best single source on the band not written by a Zep insider or someone just out to cash in on the band's well-known tour antics. It has a disappointingly scanty index, however.

3. *Led Zeppelin: The Concert File* by Dave Lewis and Simon Pallett (Omnibus, 2005). The closest thing we have to a Led Zeppelin encyclopedia. Comprehensive, smart, and filled with fascinating anecdotes, photos, and memorabilia. Much more than just the set list from every show Zep ever played.

2. For the meaning of Jimmy Page's notorious symbol from the fourth album, you can't do better than this: http://www.inthelight.co.nz/ledzep/zososymbol.htm. This awesome website has much additional information, including not only discussion of the other symbols, but detailed maps and descriptions of how to get to such places of Zep pilgrimage as Headley Grange, Bron-Yr-Aur, Page's Tower House residence in London, and others. (On the meanings of the symbols, much of webpage creator Duncan's work has been incorporated into Robert Godwin's *The Making of Led Zeppelin "Four Symbols."*)

1. The Garden Tapes: http://www.thegardentapes.co.uk/index.html. Billed by Eddie Edwards as "the complete guide to the construction of Led Zeppelin's film and album *The Song Remains The Same* from the three concerts at Madison Square Garden, New York on the 27th, 28th, and 29th of July 1973" it is all that and much, much more. An extraordinarily thorough accounting of every edit on all officially released live Zep recordings, whether on CD or DVD. A phenomenal and eye-opening achievement.

Dick's Ten Track Led Zeppelin-Schopenhauer Mix

These songs embody the "Arthur Schopenhauer mood," at least as evidenced by his essay, "On Women." I do love my Zeppelin, but fathers, if your daughter's boyfriend gives her anything close to this mix to woo her, nail the windows shut and man the shotgun.

10. "That's The Way." And here you have it, this is what happens when you let your daughters date rock'n'rollers—they most often end up alone.

9. "Immigrant Song." All the talk of Valhalla is clearly about conquest of a sweaty sort.

8. "Whole Lotta Love." I've never heard of love being measured in inches.

7. "The Girl I love She Got Long Black Wavy Hair." Plant sings in this one, "Her mother and father, lordy, they sure don't allow me there." Any father in his right mind wouldn't.

6. "Trampled Under Foot." Google the lyrics on this one. All of the car talk in this one can get you ASE certified—or pregnant.

5. "Hey Hey What Can I Do." This one seems to be a testament to the difference between Schopenhauer and Zeppelin. See, Schopenhauer would be out looking for his woman that "won't be true," but she would be in the bars listening to Zeppelin, even though they'll leave her and head on to the next town.

4. "The Wanton Song." Zeppelin's "fire needs a brand new flame, so the wheels roll on . . ." The title alone tells you where the mood of this one is going—somewhere lascivious.

3. "Heartbreaker." Annie calls her lovers by other names. Schopenhauer probably also believes this is typical behavior for women, but I'll bet rock'n'rollers do the same thing.

2. "Living Loving Maid." One needn't delve too deeply into this song to see why Art would dig it: "Livin', lovin', it's just a woman." Women apparently aren't even good enough for personal pronouns.

1. "Black Dog." Don't let the lyrical story fool you. Any man who says "Tell you what, you do me now" with any kind of seriousness is going to be the one who wrecks the relationship.

Stone-Mediatore's Top Ten Sublime Led Zeppelin Songs

10. "Achilles' Last Stand." Coupled with Bonham's explosive drumming, Page's murky arpeggiated intro and inspired progressive riffing are sublime *par excellence.*

9. "Kashmir." Page's suspenseful, chromatic guitar riff and the grandeur of Jones's keyboards and orchestration capture the stark, sublime beauty of the mountainous region from which the song takes its name.

8. "The Song Remains the Same." The sublimity of the song lies not in its lyrics or vocals, but in Page's stunning, high-energy guitar work. Longinus would have approved.

7. "When the Levee Breaks." This song's raw and massive groove moves with the unstoppable force of the Mississippi. Once again, we see how simplicity and understatement can generate great sublimity.

6. "No Quarter."John Paul Jones's gloomy keyboard introduction sets the stage for this sublime song of war, and its themes of difficulty, pain and death. As in Page's signature guitar riffs in "Whole Lotta Love" and "Immigrant Song," the song's main riff illustrates how a simple music pattern can be sublime in effect.

5. "Immigrant Song." The theme of Viking warfare, Plant's dissonant cries, and the churning dynamo of sound that accompanies them illustrate many aspects of Burke's and Longinus's theories. The song also features some of the most sublime verses Plant ever wrote.

4. "Whole Lotta Love." Page's signature riff is undoubtedly sublime in its primal power, but it's the song's middle section that lands it a high place on this list, with its disorienting dissonance, bestial vocals, psychedelic panning techniques, and searing guitar solo.

3. "Battle of Evermore." Forgoing Bonham's powerful drums and Page's electric guitar, this acoustic composition achieves great sublimity through its lyrics and musical structure. The all-pervasive darkness of the song and its themes of warfare, pain, and death powerfully illustrate Edmund Burke's theory of the sublime.

2. "Dazed and Confused." From its murky chromatic introduction to its ending, this song epitomizes the sublime characteristics of gloom, despair, confusion and power. The eerie, other-worldly sounds that Page conjures from his Tele with a violin bow during the solo contribute no small part to the song's sublimity.

1. "Stairway to Heaven." There are good reasons why this song is repeatedly voted the greatest rock song ever recorded: one is arguably its supreme sublimity. The essential aspects of Burke's, Kant's, and Longinus's theories of the sublime can all be found right here. Yet the song also manages to counterpoise its awe-inspiring power with the timeless, gentle beauty of its madrigal-like opening.

Macan's Top Ten Most Progressive Led Zeppelin Tracks

10. "Carouselambra." As with "In the Evening," the remainder of the song doesn't quite match the intensity of the opening, and structurally it doesn't hang together quite as well as some of the band's other epics. But there's still a great deal of energy here (including arguably John Paul Jones's finest bass performance), and it's interesting to hear Zep in an ELP mode.

9. "In the Evening." The body of the song doesn't quite live up to the inspired opening riff, although Page's kinetic guitar solo almost makes up for it. But what truly makes the song distinctive is its chilling droning prelude, which gives us some sense of what was lost when Page was unable to complete the *Lucifer Rising* soundtrack.

8. "No Quarter." Murkily atmospheric and intense, Zeppelin's lone (yet highly successful) foray into Pink Floyd-like musical territory.

7. "The Song Remains the Same." Scintillating and virtuosic, possibly Page's finest moment with some amazing arpeggiated parts. If Page and Plant had teamed up with Chris Squire and Alan White of Yes after Zeppelin's demise, I would like to think it would have sounded something like this.

6. "Battle of Evermore." Only a musician of Page's invention could have imagined the mandolin in this context, and the duet between Plant and Sandy Denny remains as impassioned as ever. The song has lost none of its incantational power.

5. "Achilles' Last Stand." A cornerstone of later prog-metal, and John Bonham's finest moment.

4. "Dazed and Confused." One of the founding texts of what later became known as "heavy metal," the shadowy, menacing sound collage in the middle of the song shows what a subtle and inventive band Zeppelin were even in their earliest days.

3. "In the Light." Zeppelin's invention was such that they could craft two East-meets-West epics on the same album, and brand each with

a distinctive individuality. "In the Light" captures something of "Stairway"'s sense of inevitable growth, but in a completely different context.

2. "Kashmir." East-meets-West had been done before in a rock context, but never with this sense of monumentality and inevitability.

1. "Stairway to Heaven." Arguably the most influential rock song of the 1970s; a whole body of songs, several of which were very fine in their own right ("Freebird," "Don't Fear the Reaper," "More than a Feeling," "Heaven and Hell") grew out of this. But the seamless, inevitable progression from quasi-Elizabethan acoustic to screaming proto-metal remains inimitable.

Wilson and Rees's Top Ten Led Zeppelin Oral Fixations

I know we've taken a few liberties, but hell, so did Percy:

10. You might not expect the boys to have a sweet tooth:
    Tutti-frutti (ice-cream) and lollipops ("Boogie with Stu")
    Chocolate ("Candy Store Rock")
    Sugar ("Candy Store Rock" / "Royal Orleans")

9. They also like a Custard Pie ("Custard Pie")

8. And, it appears, a surprisingly wide range of fruit in general ("Carouselambra"), and more specifically:
    - Cherries ("Sick Again")
    - Apples ("I'm Gonna Crawl" / "Battle of Evermore")
    - Tangerines ("Tangerine"), and
    - Plums ("Travelling Riverside Blues")

7. The old favorite, the Hot Dog ("Hot Dog")

6. Someone else's Tongue! ("Dazed and Confused" and "Kashmir")

5. A nice piece of Fish! ("Down by the Seaside" and "That's the Way")

4. And what do you squeeze on your fish? A bit of Lemon, of course! ("For Your Life" / "Travelling Riverside Blues" / "Lemon Song")

3. Chill your drink with some Ice ("Immigrant Song")

2. Any band featuring Bonzo naturally has a good range of alcohol:
    - Booze (generally) in "Dancing Days"
    - Beer ("Black Country Woman")

- Wine ("Going to California"), and
- Bourbon ("Royal Orleans")

1. Since we're English, it has to be:
   - Toast ("All My Love") with
   - Honey ("Black Dog" / "Candy Store Rock" / "Ozone Baby")
   - or Jam* ("Good Times Bad Times"),
   - and most importantly of all, Tea ("Misty Mountain Hop" / "Tea For One")!!

* that's jelly, for the American of understanding!

Gracyk's Ten Most Notable Led Zeppelin Appearances as Sidemen

10. Robert Plant, duet with Tori Amos on "Down by the Seaside" (1995)

9. John Paul Jones, bass, guitar, and arrangements on Diamanda Galas's *The Sporting Life* (1994)

8. John Paul Jones, string arranging on R.E.M.'s *Automatic for the People* (1992)

7. John Bonham (via sampling), drums on Dr. Dre's "The Chronic" (1992)

6. John Bonham (via sampling), drums on The Beastie Boys' *Paul's Boutique* (1989)

5. Led Zeppelin (via sampling) on Robert Plant's "Tall Cool One" (1988)

4. Jimmy Page, guitar solo on Roy Harper's "The Same Old Rock" (1971)

3. Jimmy Page, guitar and production on Screaming Lord Sutch's *Lord Sutch and Heavy Friends* (1970)

2. John Paul Jones, bass and (possibly) Jimmy Page, guitar on Donovan's "Hurdy Gurdy Man" (1968)

1. Jimmy Page and John Paul Jones, guitar and bass on Jeff Beck's "Beck's Bolero" (1967)

Flynn's Top Ten Dionysian Zeppelin Songs

According to Nietzsche, although our existence as individuals appears real, we're just temporary and excruciating manifestations of overwhelming natural forces. Nietzsche thinks this "Dionysian wisdom" is expressed in all art. Good Dionysian songs redeem this lamentable fate by celebrating our struggle against, and ultimate release into, the very forces that undo us.

10. "Heartbreaker." A reminder that love's irresistible power is our undoing; for its wicked sake some people cry and some people die.

9. "Communication Breakdown." The sense and intelligibility of the world eventually breaks down, as the music here manically attests.

8. "Dazed and Confused." The ways of love are not only wicked, but also disorienting. When satisfaction is this destructive, we're left to conclude that the soul of the woman was created below, with Lucifer, arch-transgressor.

7. "I'm Gonna Crawl." The traveling blues considered from the other side; at home in love, crawling is immanent.

6. "Traveling Riverside Blues." The classic traveling blues expresses the fact that we are will, driven down the road, pursuing love, on the run from love.

5. "The Lemon Song." Sexual longing is relentless and futile. One way or another, we're gonna have to leave all our love down on this killing floor.

4. "In My Time of Dying." A death moan in which the singer's words bleed into the music. The Christian invocations notwithstanding, this song is nature yearning to take its body home.

3. "Kashmir." The road song to transcend all road songs, standing in majestically for the fact that we're homeless, bound to be consumed by the sands of a storm that turns all things to brown.

2. "Whole Lotta Love." To hell with opening the doors of perception. This song shakes them off their hinges and steps over the threshold. Are you sure you wanna whole lotta love?

1. "When the Levee Breaks." This is the motherlode. "When the Levee Breaks" laments the inevitable destruction of the self by excessive forces of nature. Yet it celebrates nature's power, and in celebrating it redeems the doomed life.

Bicknell's Top Ten Non-hard-rock Cover Versions of Led Zeppelin Songs

What do I mean by "non-hard-rock"? Basically I just want to avoid the kind of Zeppelin imitators that Plant refers to collectively as "Deep Sabbath." The list is not in any particular order.

10. John Cowan with The Waybacks doing "Ramble On."

9. "D'yer Mak'er" by Sly and Robbie. There's something very satisfying in the straightforward reggae treatment of this reggae-inspired song.

8. Blues singer Charles Thomas King's take on "Hey, Hey What Can I Do?"

7. Another great country version of "Stairway to Heaven" by Iron Horse.

6. Dolly Parton, "Stairway to Heaven." The interplay between the fiddle and the acoustic guitar is gorgeous.

5. "Fool in the Rain" interpreted by Mo'Fone—a jazz/funk trio of two sax players and a percussionist.

4. Collective Consciousness Society (CCS) instrumental funk "Whole Lotta Love." You can see it on YouTube: http://www.youtube.com/watch?v=sjRqKVI9j5c.

3. Jazz crooner John Alcorn's spookily laid-back version of "Whole Lotta Love."

2. Tina Turner's very sultry take on "Whole Lotta Love."

1. Alison Krause and Robert Plant doing "When the Levee Breaks." They play this live sometimes in their concerts. I particularly like the version recorded at the New Orleans Jazz Fest, 2008. Available on YouTube: www.youtube.com/watch?v=I_fkcgdaO9E.

Calef's Top Ten Songs Not Listed on the Rock and Roll Hall of Fame List

On Led Zeppelin's induction page the Rock and Roll Hall of Fame provides a list of ten essential Led Zeppelin songs. They are: "Stairway to Heaven," "Whole Lotta Love," "Kashmir," "Rock and Roll," "Dazed and Confused," "Black Dog," "The Song Remains the Same," "When the Levee Breaks," "Immigrant Song," and "Communication Breakdown." It's a great list, but my list is of songs *not* on their list. Although every aspect of Led Zeppelin's awesome music gives me chills, their greatest appeal of all, for me, has always been Jimmy Page's guitar work and production. My selections are largely, but not entirely, determined by that.

10. "Travelling Riverside Blues." The jangly sound and slide guitar make this pure joy. The band sounds like they're having such a good time it's infectious. And the solo, though brief, is classic Page in it's distinctive, I'd-recognize-that-sound-anywhere phrasing. Pay attention, kids!

9. "In My Time of Dying." This is the one that, without fail, would blow the fuses on my Pioneer amp. I especially like the version on the Zep DVD. Page is lightning fast, though the song is perhaps a trifle long.

8. "Out on the Tiles." Great riffs, and filled with those weird, characteristically-Zep stop-start time changes so effectual on songs like "Black Dog." An amazing groove from start to finish.

7. "Sick Again." Great, powerful, bludgeoning riffs and trademark Zeppelin fuzz. *Graffiti*'s "Communication Breakdown." Plus, I dig the flash "Levee"-style ending.

6. "Good Times Bad Times." The mightiest first track from a debut album ever recorded. From the first two notes, which punch like a boxer with a freight train at his back, Zep are throwing down the gauntlet. This is why they were the last band of the Sixties and first band of the Seventies. Loud, brash, sloppy and audacious, Zep announced the beginning of a new musical world order. To be played at maximum volume.

5. "Heartbreaker." Exhibit A for all those claims that Page has "sloppy" technique. The song makes a good case. And, it works perfectly! But where it really cooks is after Page's a capella solo when the rest of the band kicks in with the new riff. At that point, the solo and the song are launched into an entirely different, utterly mind-blowingly phenomenal realm. No wonder it opens side two as the counterpoint to side one's "Whole Lotta Love." Pure bliss, no matter how many times you've heard it.

4. "Achilles Last Stand." The opening arpeggios are a perfect illustration of why Page was one of rock's greatest producers. The *sound* is unlike anything you've ever heard from any other band. Page considered his solos on "Achilles" every bit the equal of "Stairway's" and he's right. Plus, the song has my favorite Led Zeppelin lyrics and Jones and Bonham have never been better.

3. "The Rover." In my controversial opinion, the best track on *Physical Graffiti*, and that's saying something. This dates back to 1970 and has the *feel* of early Zep, which is great, since by 1975 Plant's voice had lost a little of its youthful range. Zep chronicler Dave Lewis correctly notes that "Page strings together one of his most perfectly constructed solos." Melodic, concise and powerful. A neglected and unfortunately underrated gem.

2. "Since I've Been Loving You." The only song from *III* besides "Immigrant Song" that has attained the status of a Zep classic. The finest studio example of a Jimmy Page blues, and a track that single-

handedly refutes any and all criticism that Zep were inauthentic and that their blues lacked feeling. Plant and Page's performances continue to induce shivers after hundreds of listens.

1. "The Lemon Song." My all-time favorite guitar song and probably my most-played Zeppelin song. All I can do is bow in the presence of greatness and repeat "I'm not worthy!" Fantastic bass fills and chock full of the little flourishes that show what an uncommonly attentive perfectionist Page was in the studio. Genius.

Gimbel's Top Ten Ways You Know Your Fascination with Led Zeppelin Is Unhealthy

10. Your only pet is a black dog.

9. You broke up with a girlfriend by leaving "What Is and What Should Never Be" on her answering machine.

8. You insist on using a double necked fly swatter.

7. You think the live version of "Moby Dick" is romantic mood setting music.

6. All of your plants are named Robert.

5. You find yourself at baseball games cheering the defense by yelling "That's a whole lotta glove."

4. You still dress with button down shirts only buttoned up to your navel.

3. Your signature includes runes.

2. You've been thrown out of multiple restaurants for your response to being asked by waitresses if you'd like some lemon in your tea.

1. You go on the John Bonham Diet.

Lewis's Top Ten Zep Gigs Attended

I was lucky enough to see Led Zeppelin perform live on fifteen occasions. This is a list of the ten most memorable Zeppelin shows I witnessed, in descending order of when they took place.

10. Empire Pool, Wembley, 21st November, 1971

Pure rock'n'roll wonderment on a perishing cold English night. After watching Led Zeppelin perform "Immigrant Song" live right in front of my eyes—seeing was believing. Life was never going to be the same for this particular teenager.

9. Alexandra Palace, London, 23rd December, 1972

   Christmas came early in the confines of the famous Ally Pally. Watching them road testing future tracks from *Houses of The Holy* was immensely exciting.

8. Earls Court Arena, London, 23rd May, 1975

   Commencing a weekend that for me encompassed over ten hours of live Zep. These were indeed the days of our lives . . . and theirs too.

7. Earls Court Arena, London, 24th May, 1975

   Perhaps the greatest night of all—three and a half hours, "Tangerine," the acoustic set, over thirty minutes of "Dazed," and a "Stairway" to die for. All viewed from the second row.

6. Earls Court Arena, London, 25th May, 1975

   The final acclaim of the peak years – the encores of "Heartbreaker" and "Communication Breakdown" saw them in a world of their own. Simply astonishing.

5. Knebworth Park, Stevenage, 4th August, 1979

   After all the lay offs, they had a lot to lose but they pulled it off—the last half hour was as good as it gets. Pure Zeppelin theater.

4. Knebworth Park, Stevenage, 11th August, 1979

   I was proud to be at this final UK swan song that culminated in another killer encore of "Communication Breakdown." Then as it was . . . it would not be again.

3. Sporthalle, Cologne, 18th June, 1980

   From the moment Page stepped on the wah wah to blast out "Train Kept a-Rollin'," this was an utter rejuvenation.

2. Olympiahalle, Munich, 5th July, 1980

   Their penultimate gig including guest drummer Simon Kirke jamming on "Whole Lotta Love." America beckoned again, but it was not to be.

1. 02 Arena, London, 10th December, 2007

   The magic returned for one night only . . . and at last the story had a happy ending.

Elders of the Gentle Race

RANDALL AUXIER got his first Led Zeppelin album for his thirteenth birthday in 1974. It was the Runes album, but being barely a child past twelve, he had never *seen* the cover and did not recognize or understand what he had so generously received (Thanks, Mom and Dad, *really*). Randy's parents had asked a best friend what to get, and the friend had rightly guessed at the *best* present, but Randy said, and I quote, "What is *this*? I don't want *this*!" and, I swear to God, he tossed aside the old man with the sticks to get on to "better" presents. All things correct themselves in time. These days he teaches philosophy at Southern Illinois University in Carbondale—at least, that's what he does when he isn't playing too damn loud with a garage band in the local bars, or writing silly chapters in pop culture books.

JEANETTE BICKNELL grew up in rural south-western Ontario, where "Stairway to Heaven" was always the last song played at the end of high school and community dances. She's the author of *Why Music Moves Us* (2009) and enjoys perplexing her students by playing "When the Levee Breaks" before class starts, without explanation.

SCOTT CALEF is Professor and Chair of the Philosophy Department at Ohio Wesleyan University. Besides publishing in Socratic studies, the philosophy of religion, political philosophy and applied ethics, he has contributed chapters to volumes on the Beatles, Bruce Springsteen, Pink Floyd, and Metallica. In the best summer of his life he met his wife and experienced the California sunlight, sweet Calcutta rain, and Honolulu starbright. Scott thinks the soundtrack version of "Dazed and Confused" one of Jimmy's finest moments and constantly asks the kids, "Where's the confounded remote control?"

LUKE DICK resides in Nashville, where he writes songs, essays, poetry, and teaches at Nashville State. While not occupying himself with such leisurely occupations, he does his best to keep the black dogs away from his mind and his daughter Emily's window. He's convinced the Led should be let out under the right circumstances.

ERIN FLYNN is Associate Professor of Philosophy at Ohio Wesleyan University. Though his main gig is teaching and writing about nineteenth-century German philosophy, he still fronts bands from time to time. He came to Zeppelin relatively late, while working in a record (actual vinyl) store and chain-reading Tolkien.

STEVE GIMBEL is a philosophy professor at Gettysburg College in Pennsylvania. Author and editor of several books including *Defending Einstein* and *Methods and Models: A Historical Introduction to the Philosophy of Science*, his primary research focuses on the philosophical ramifications of the theory of relativity. He recently taught a course in the philosophy of cosmology because stars fill his dreams; he is a scholar of both time and space.

THEODORE GRACYK teaches philosophy in Minnesota. But he'd rather be in his home state, where the mountains and the canyons tremble and shake. His most recent book is *Listening to Popular Music: Or, How I Learned to Stop Worrying and Love Led Zeppelin*. Yes, you read that right. He didn't always love them. But in the end, their sense of humor won him over.

DAVE LEWIS first heard the music of Led Zeppelin in 1969 at the age of thirteen. The effect has been a lasting one. He's now acknowledged and respected throughout the world as a leading chronicler of the group. He is editor of the long running Led Zeppelin fan magazine *Tight But Loose*. His books include *Led Zeppelin: The Final Acclaim, Led Zeppelin: A Celebration, Led Zeppelin Celebration 2: The Tight But Loose Files*, and *Led Zeppelin: The Concert File*. His work has also appeared in *Record Collector, Q, Mojo*, and *Classic Rock*. Dave continues to chronicle the work of Led Zeppelin and the solo projects of the ex-members via the *Tight But Loose* website (www.tblweb.com) and magazine. His latest book, *Then As It Was: Led Zeppelin at Knebworth 1979—30 Years Gone*, is a much-acclaimed monumental account of Led Zeppelin's final UK gigs. To get hold of a copy, email davelewis.tbl1@ntlworld.com. Dave lives in Bedford, England, with his wife Janet, son Adam, and daughter Samantha.

EDWARD MACAN is Professor of Music at College of the Redwoods, Eureka, California. He is the author of *Rocking the Classics: English Progressive Rock and the Counterculture* (1996), *Endless Enigma: A Musical Biography of*

Emerson, Lake and Palmer (2006), and a contributor to *Pink Floyd and Philosophy*. He's still awaiting that elusive Led Zeppelin reunion album so he can find out exactly what happened at the May Queen's Spring Clean.

EMMA L.E. REES is Senior Lecturer in English Literature at the University of Chester in the U.K. A specialist in Renaissance studies, she has more recently published in the field of gender and representation. Although she grew up in the English Midlands, not far from where Led Zeppelin came from, it wasn't until the summer of 1988 in a student house in Norwich that she first listened properly to the band. Prior to that she had believed music began with Motörhead and ended with Metallica. Pierced in twelve places, tattooed in three, and with bright red hair, she's old enough to know better and young enough not to care. Her favourite drink is tea. Proper tea. As Proudhon once said: "Proper tea is theft." The opening bars of "Kashmir" never fail to give her goosebumps.

THEODORE SCHICK, JR. is a Professor of Philosophy at Muhlenberg College and Director of the Muhlenberg Scholars Program. He has contributed to a number of volumes in the Popular Culture and Philosophy series including *Seinfeld and Philosophy, The Matrix and Philosophy, More Matrix and Philosophy, Lord of the Rings and Philosophy*, and *Star Trek and Philosophy*. When he's not trying to contact his Holy Guardian Angel, he is trying to raise the dead with his guitar playing in his band, The Doctors of Rock.

PHILLIP SENG teaches philosophy at the University of Maryland, Baltimore County, where he tries to understand how students can listen to music on their iPods while also listening to class discussions. He has written for several Popular Culture and Philosophy books, and co-edited *The Wizard of Oz and Philosophy*. Since spending so much time listening to bands in small venues and Led Zeppelin through headphones he fears he might have damaged his ears, but he can easily hear his chi-gong ring tone for his cell phone from over the hills and far away.

RALPH SHAIN teaches philosophy at Missouri State University. He has published scholarly articles on recognition, the split between high and low cultures, and the philosophers Derrida and Wittgenstein. When he is publishing academic papers, he feels as if he's dropping them in the ocean, and he can hear the ocean snore. It really makes him wonder: Has the ocean lost its way?

JOHN STONE-MEDIATORE is a Ph.D. candidate in the Department of Comparative Literature at the University of Chicago. He also teaches in the Philosophy and Humanities-Classics Departments at Ohio Wesleyan University. His dissertation, which he's currently completing, is a study of postmodernist fiction and schizophrenia. In his parallel life, he has performed extensively around Ohio as lead guitarist in various rock bands. While he can convincingly play many of Jimmy Page's riffs and solos, he has come to accept that he will never, ever look as cool.

JERE O'NEILL SURBER may not have attended the School of Rock but he paid his way through TCU and Penn State playing roadhouse rock. After that, he studied philosophy at the Rheinische-Universität, Bonn, where he wrote his dissertation on language in German Idealism. Since those days, he's been a regular professor at the University of Denver with visiting gigs as such places as Katholieke Universiteit, Leuven, Oxford University, and the Johannes Gutenberg Universität, Mainz. He's a veteran author in the 'rock' area of this series and publishes on such topics as German Idealism, ethics and aesthetics, comparative philosophy, and various themes in the 'modernism-postmodernism' debate. Was he a Led Zeppelin fan? Well, could Jimmy Page play the guitar?

MARK D. WHITE is an associate professor in the Department of Political Science, Economics, and Philosophy at the College of Staten Island/CUNY, where he teaches courses combining economics, philosophy, and law. His edited books include *Watchmen and Philosophy* (2009), *Theoretical Foundations of Law and Economics* (2009), *Batman and Philosophy* (with Robert Arp, 2008), and *Economics and the Mind* (with Barbara Montero, 2007). He has also written dozens of scholarly articles and book chapters, plus philosophical essays on Metallica, *South Park*, *Family Guy*, *The Office*, and the X-Men. Finally, he's not afraid to admit that the *Coverdale-Page* album still shakes his tree.

RICHARD E. WILSON is Academic Director of a company in the UK which runs English Language courses for non-native speakers. He teaches academic writing and study skills and is also a dyslexia support tutor. People think this makes him a terrible pedant. He disagrees: he's a very good one. He discovered 'proper' music when he heard Gillan's *Mr Universe* at the age of fifteen. His record collection numbers almost five thousand items, many of which are 45s from around the world. He has previously contributed to an encyclopedia of Heavy Metal but this is his first full-length article. Standing 6'7" tall he can confirm that, having met Bruce Dickinson, Lars Ulrich, and even Ian Gillan, rock stars are in fact disappointingly short. Led Zeppelin's range continues to enthrall him, from the mellowness of "Gallows Pole" to the energy of "Communication Breakdown."

With a Word She Can Get What She Came For